Leadership Organizations in the House of Representatives

In recent Congresses, roughly half of the members of the U.S. House of Representatives served in whip organizations and on party committees. Rank-and-file representatives who use party service to advance their own careers benefit from this growing rate of participation in the party hierarchy, as do the party leaders who use participation in order to advance the party's agenda through coordination, communication, and persuasion.

According to Scott R. Meinke, however, rising electoral competition and polarization over the past 40 years have altered the nature of party participation. In the 1970s and 1980s, as extensive archival evidence proves, the participation of a wide range of members was crucial to building consensus. Since then, in the partisan battle for control of the chamber, organizations responsible for coordination in the party have become dominated by those who follow the party line. At the same time, key leaders in the House use participatory organizations less as forums for internal deliberations over policy and strategy than as channels for exchanging information with supporters outside Congress and broadcasting sharply partisan campaign messages to the public.

This transformation of leadership organizations generally serves a party's collective goals in an era of close electoral competition and ideological polarization. Yet it also hinders a party's ability to reach a strategic consensus over divisive issues and to develop its own policy alternatives even as polarization makes the parties the vital centers of House policy making.

**Scott R. Meinke** is Professor of Political Science at Bucknell University.

LEGISLATIVE POLITICS & POLICY MAKING

*Series Editors*

Janet M. Box-Steffensmeier, Vernal Riffe Professor of Political Science,
The Ohio State University

David Canon, Professor of Political Science, University of Wisconsin, Madison

RECENT TITLES IN THE SERIES:

*The Committee: A Study of Policy, Power, Politics, and Obama's Historic
Legislative Agenda on Capitol Hill*
BRYAN W. MARSHALL AND BRUCE C. WOLPE

*The Whips: Building Party Coalitions in Congress*
C. LAWRENCE EVANS

*Indecision in American Legislatures*
JEFFREY J. HARDEN AND JUSTIN H. KIRKLAND

*Electoral Incentives in Congress*
JAMIE L. CARSON AND JOEL SIEVERT

*Gendered Vulnerability: How Women Work Harder to Stay in Office*
JEFFREY LAZARUS AND AMY STEIGERWALT

*Politics over Process: Partisan Conflict and Post-Passage Processes
in the U.S. Congress*
HONG MIN PARK, STEVEN S. SMITH, AND RYAN J. VANDER WIELEN

*On Parliamentary War: Partisan Conflict and Procedural Change
in the U.S. Senate*
JAMES I. WALLNER

*The Rise of the Representative: Lawmakers and Constituents in Colonial America*
PEVERILL SQUIRE

*Implementing Term Limits: The Case of the Michigan Legislature*
MARJORIE SARBAUGH-THOMPSON AND LYKE THOMPSON

*The Modern Legislative Veto: Macropolitical Conflict and the Legacy of* Chadha
MICHAEL J. BERRY

*Leadership Organizations in the House of Representatives: Party Participation
and Partisan Politics*
SCOTT R. MEINKE

*Minority Parties in U.S. Legislatures: Conditions of Influence*
JENNIFER HAYES CLARK

For a complete list of titles in this series, please see www.press.umich.edu.

# LEADERSHIP ORGANIZATIONS IN THE HOUSE OF REPRESENTATIVES

*Party Participation and Partisan Politics*

Scott R. Meinke

University of Michigan Press
Ann Arbor

First paperback edition 2019
Copyright © 2016 by Scott R. Meinke
All rights reserved

Published in the United States of America by the
University of Michigan Press
**Printed and bound by CPI Group (UK) Ltd, Croydon, CR0 4YY**
First published in paperback February 2019

A CIP catalog record for this book is available from the British Library.

Library of Congress Cataloging-in-Publication Data

Names: Meinke, Scott R., author.
Title: Leadership organizations in the House of Representatives : party participation and
    partisan politics / Scott R. Meinke.
Description: Ann Arbor : University of Michigan Press, 2016. | Series: Legislative politics
    & policy making | Includes bibliographical references and index.
Identifiers: LCCN 2015037512| ISBN 9780472119790 (hardback : acid-free
    paper) | ISBN 9780472121779 (ebook)
Subjects: LCSH: United States. Congress. House—Leadership. | United States. Congress.
    House—Committees. | United States. Congress. House—Caucuses. | Political
    leadership—United States. | Political parties—United States. | United States—Politics
    and government—1989– | BISAC: POLITICAL SCIENCE / Government / Legislative
    Branch. | POLITICAL SCIENCE / Political Process / Political Parties.
Classification: LCC JK1410 .M45  2016 | DDC 328.73/0762—dc23
LC record available at http://lccn.loc.gov/2015037512

ISBN 978-0-472-03734-6 (pbk.)

*For Lynda*

# Contents

*Preface and Acknowledgments*   ix

ONE  Party Leadership Organizations at Work: Four Examples   1

TWO  Participation in the Party: A Framework for Understanding
Leadership Organizations   17

THREE  Leadership and Membership Perspectives on
Party Participation   38

FOUR  Coordination in Party Leadership Organizations   88

FIVE  External Communication and Party Leadership Organizations   114

SIX  The Process of Persuasion in Party Leadership Organizations   135

SEVEN  Conclusion   167

*Appendixes*   179

*Notes*   183

*References*   207

*Index*   223

# Preface and Acknowledgments

About ten years ago, I was teaching my Bucknell undergraduate course on Congress, and the class was discussing congressional party leadership. I had mentioned the party whips and the fact that dozens of members worked as whips for each party in the House. A student asked: "what do they all *do*?" (or something to that effect). I offered the student a brief, not-too-detailed answer. Later, since I wished I had a better answer, I did a little reading and found there wasn't all that much more to say about the whips or about the members who participated in other party organizations like the Republican Policy Committee and the Democratic Steering and Policy Committee.

My resulting curiosity about House party organizations and their members led me to do some preliminary research of my own, focusing on the whip systems. But my initial findings left me with many unanswered questions about the whips and other participants in the life of the House party. Why are they there? What *do* they do—and for whose benefit? How does this broad system of party participation benefit the members themselves? How does it benefit each party and the leaders at the top? And, maybe most importantly, how have the dramatic changes in House partisanship since the 1970s affected the parties' organizations?

To answer these questions, I found that I needed *process* evidence to show what the parties' participatory organizations do. To address the question about change over time, in particular, I needed evidence of their membership and actions across the decades since the House reforms of the 1970s. So I spent time in the archives of former party leaders in the House—Speakers, majority and minority leaders, and majority and minority whips, as well as a few members who had served as leaders of party committees. From these far-flung archives, I learned a great deal about what members of the whip organizations, policy committees, and steering committees have done and how they have done it, and I observed how the parties' top leadership employed these organizational tools differently over time. The archives also provided new sources of data for quantitative analysis of party organization membership.

This archival work allowed me to peer into the "black box" of the congressional party, to see how the party operates internally through extensive participation by its members. As I show in this book, participation in the House parties directly serves the collective interests of the party (and its top leaders), but it also advances the goals of individual party members. On the individual level, service to leadership organizations enables representatives to advocate within the party for constituency interests while providing opportunities for advancing their own political careers. On the party level, by widening access to positions of influence, top elected leaders—including the Speaker and the minority leader—more effectively pursue collective electoral and policy objectives. They use the participatory organizations to pursue *coordination* within the party caucus, to *persuade* members to support the party in the long run and in the short term, and to facilitate two-way *communication* on priorities with the White House, other party leaders, and important groups in the party's electoral constituency.

Although these individual and collective benefits of a participatory party have been in place across the past four decades, rising polarization and electoral competition has changed the nature of party participation. In the heterogeneous parties of the 1970s and 1980s, participation by a wide range of members was crucial to building consensus within increasingly powerful parties. Since then, as the parties have polarized and battled for control of the chamber, the roles of participatory party organizations have changed in important ways. First, organizations responsible for persuasion and coordination have become less representative of the full range of views held by party members, and they are now dominated by members who vote loyally with the leadership. Second, top leaders now use broadly participatory organizations less frequently as forums for open deliberation on policy and strategy, and they treat them more often as channels for sharing information with party supporters outside Congress and broadcasting sharply partisan campaign messages to the public. The loyalist-dominated organizations continue their work to increase party support from House members, but this process is now under more centralized leadership control. These changes generally serve the party's collective goals in an environment of close electoral competition and ideologically polarized congressional parties. But these developments leave the parties in the House with less capacity to work toward policy or strategic consensus when intra-party divisions do emerge, as they have in the Republican Conference since 2010. In the end, the new archival evidence and quantitative analysis in this book offer an internal, participatory view of the parties in the House, both in the majority and in the minority, and the evidence sheds new light on power, party leadership, and member careers across a period of growing partisanship.

I could not have completed the research for this book without the support and assistance of a great many people. I am especially grateful to the Dirksen Congressional Center, which financially supported the majority of the archival research for the book with a Congressional Research Award. Librarians and archivists have generously helped me to navigate members' archived papers, both in person and from afar—I thank Frank Mackaman (Dirksen Center), Cheryl Gunselman (Manuscripts, Archives and Special Collections, Holland and Terrell Libraries, Washington State University), Justine Sundaram (Burns Library, Boston College), Carolyn Hanneman (Carl Albert Center, University of Oklahoma), Molly Kodner (Missouri History Museum), William LeFevre (Walter P. Reuther Library, Wayne State University), Leslie Conrad (Pasquerilla Library, Saint Francis University), Susan Swain (Texas Christian University), and Randy Marcum (West Virginia Archives and History Library). Representative David Bonior kindly allowed me to access very helpful material in his archived papers. William F. Connelly, Jr. shared his invaluable interview-based research on the Republican Policy Committee and Democratic Steering and Policy Committee in the 1980s. Paul Wilkinson provided important perspectives on the Republican Policy Committee and directed me to useful documents. And several excellent Bucknell students, including Clark Bogle, Alexandra Campbell-Ferrari, Andrew Clarke, Carl Marchioli, and Emily Miller, have helped me with data collection and background research and provided me with helpful insights and ideas. I consider myself very fortunate to teach at a university where smart and talented undergraduates like them are eager to participate in faculty research.

A number of people have provided important feedback and comments on portions of this work at various stages. Bucknell colleagues John Enyeart and Robin Jacobson helped me to broaden my thinking about the project as I began to work, and Eric Heberlig, Kevin Scott, and Susan Tabrizi offered helpful comments on an early paper. I presented some arguments and very early findings from this project at the 2006, 2007, 2008, and 2010 Midwest Political Science Association meetings and at the 2006 American Political Science Association meetings, where I received useful critiques from Christian Grose, Greg Robinson, Steve Smith, and Sean Theriault. I am especially grateful to Sean Kelly and an anonymous reviewer for the University of Michigan Press, who each read two drafts of the book manuscript and offered incisive and constructive comments that shaped a necessary rethinking of the book's approach. Although the shortcomings that remain are mine alone, it is a better book for the revision that they helped to guide.

I also must acknowledge two significant intellectual debts behind this project. The first is to a group of scholars who wrote about the internal structures of the two House parties in earlier periods—Barbara Sinclair and David Rohde on the 1970s–1980s Democrats and Charles Jones on the 1950s–1960s Republicans. Readers will find those authors' names cited frequently on these pages; my archival research has supported their claims about the time periods they studied, and I have built directly on their insights in developing my argument about the roles of the House party organizations over time. The second is to the scholarly duo of Scott Frisch and Sean Kelly, who have been effective evangelists for archival research in American politics in general and congressional research in particular. Just as I was beginning to think about the questions behind this project and how to study them, I happened to attend an APSA short course on archival research that Frisch and Kelly organized. Their short course helped me to envision the use of archival evidence for quantitative and qualitative analysis of the party organizations, and their own published work continues to provide a model of what is possible with this kind of research.

In the process of revising and publishing the book, I have been very fortunate to work with Melody Herr at the University of Michigan Press. Melody has been supportive and honest and an unfailingly patient guide through the entire review and publication process, and I thank her, as well as Allison Peters, for their advice and direction. Series editors Jan Box-Steffensmeier and David Canon also provided support and guidance in the revision process for which I am very grateful. I also thank three generous colleagues—Lauren Bell, Michael James, and Margie Williams—who helped this former "article person" with important advice about how to propose and publish a book.

A small portion of the ideas and evidence presented in the book have appeared in some form in my earlier articles. Some ideas from chapter 2 and a preliminary version of the whip system analysis in chapter 3 appeared in "Who Whips? Party Government and the House Extended Whip Networks" (*American Politics Research* 61:445–57). A few examples discussed in the last section of chapter 3 were used in "Presentation of Partisanship: Constituency Connections and Partisan Congressional Activity" (*Social Science Quarterly* 90:854–67). And some portions of chapters 3, 4, and 5 that deal with the Republican Policy Committee are revised from "The Changing Roles of House Party Leadership Organizations: The House Republican Policy Committee." (*Congress and the Presidency* 41:190–222). I gratefully acknowledge those journals' permission to reuse the earlier work here.

Finally, I am happy to dedicate this book to my wife Lynda, who has been a constant source of support and help through the long process of researching and writing this book. My travel to do the archival research for the book was very time consuming at a point when our careers and our young family left little time for such a new adventure to consume. I could not have done this work without Lynda's selfless support during the research and her confidence and encouragement during the writing and revision. And Lynda—along with Grace, Aaron, and Madeline—have also done the important work of reminding me when it was time to put aside my reading, number-crunching, and writing to have some fun.

# ONE

# Party Leadership Organizations at Work

*Four Examples*

Beneath the familiar top layer of elected House party leaders—the Speaker, the majority leader, and the minority leader—is a set of majority and minority party organizations with broad member involvement and a range of important roles in the modern congressional party. The Democratic caucus in recent Congresses has maintained a whip system involving as many as 100 members and a staff payroll of almost 30, and a Steering and Policy Committee with about 50 members and a staff of about 10, in addition to the Democratic Congressional Campaign Committee (DCCC). On the Republican side, the modern Republican Conference has a whip organization that has involved more than 70 members and two dozen staffers, a Policy Committee of about 40, and a separate, slightly smaller Steering Committee (about 30), along with the National Republican Congressional Committee (NRCC).[1]

These organizations compose the modern extended party leadership systems in the House. As basic features of the congressional party institutions, they are not recent innovations. The Republican and Democratic whips, which the parties had established around the turn of the 20th century, had small networks of assistants by the time of the New Deal (Herring 1934, 66–70; Ripley 1964, 565–66), and the direct ancestors of the modern party policy committees emerged in the late 1940s (Connelly 1991). The two congressional campaign committees (DCCC and NRCC) have their origins much earlier in American history, in the electoral struggles of the Civil War-era party system (Kolodny 1998, 22–36).

Despite their long-standing status on Capitol Hill, the current parameters and roles of the partisan organizations did not begin to take shape until the reform era of the 1970s. Between the 94th Congress (1975–77) and the 110th Congress (2007–9), both Democrats and Republicans reformed and greatly enlarged their extended leadership organizations, creating a system of broad-based member participation in the regular tasks of the congressional party. The two parties have followed somewhat different paths in developing expansive extended leadership organizations. The Democrats began to expand their leadership ranks in the mid-1970s, growing the system gradually through the early 1980s and then sharply by the late 1980s. About a third of the Democratic caucus was involved in either the whip organization or the Democratic Steering and Policy Committee by the 99th Congress (1985–87); nearly half of the caucus was involved a decade later. Republicans, by contrast, maintained a set of leadership organizations in the 1970s and 1980s that was fairly constant in structure. After taking majority control in 1995, Republicans expanded and revised their leadership system—the Republican whip organization, for instance, grew from fewer than 30 members in 1987 to more than 60 members in 1997. As both parties made significant changes in the parameters of their extended leadership organizations, they also altered both the character of the membership and, in many cases, the roles of the organizations.

Despite their long history and growing scope within the two House parties, these participatory leadership organizations are not especially familiar. Their activities are often, but not always, behind the scenes, and attention from the press and even congressional scholars has been limited. This relative obscurity belies their importance for linking the top leadership and the rank-and-file in pursuit of policy and electoral objectives, allowing the party to carry out its regular tasks more efficiently and effectively. Four examples—one from the 1970s, one from the 1980s, and two from a recent Congress (the 112th)—begin to illustrate the varied roles these organizations and their participants have played in achieving the parties' core policy and electoral goals in the House.

### Party Leadership Organizations at Work: Four Examples of Participation in the Collective Action of the Party

#### 1978: Full-Employment Policy

In the midst of economic troubles in the late 1970s, Democrats in Congress and the White House began to take seriously a long-standing legislative proposal from Representative Augustus Hawkins (D-CA) and Senator Hubert Humphrey (D-MN) to address unemployment. Humphrey-Hawkins attempted to set federal policy on a course toward low unemployment targets—4 percent by 1983—with provisions for government jobs to reach the goal in the absence of private sector jobs. The controversial legislation had passed out of the Education and Labor Committee in 1976, but it never reached the floor in the 94th Congress. Democrats eventually saw the bill through the House in March 1978 (257–152), but only after difficult committee and floor consideration that featured several attempts to weaken or redirect the bill through amendments. House Democrats in the end produced only a small portion of what the bill's sponsors had originally sought to achieve, and the bill (HR 50) was further weakened in the Senate (*Congress and the Nation* 1981b). Still, the bill was an important symbolic victory for many in the Democratic caucus: the Humphrey-Hawkins legislation had long been a key goal for labor and minority constituencies of the Democratic Party.

Getting to that victory required an extensive effort among House Democrats to build core support within the caucus, to prevent Republicans from sinking the bill through floor strategies, and to coordinate with a Democratic administration that offered only late and tepid support for the bill. Democrats in the House used member participation through party leadership organizations—the Democratic Steering and Policy Committee (DSPC) and the recently expanded Democratic whip organization—as well as organization staff resources in various ways to accomplish these goals. At the committee stage, DSPC staff were "deeply involved" in negotiating between the Education and Labor Committee, the Administration, and labor interests.[2] During these early stages, the DSPC's membership met with outside interests to hear concerns and update on progress.[3] As the legislation progressed toward the floor, the Democratic leadership initiated both a full whip count, involving appointed and elected whip system members, and a 20-member Speaker's task force, headed by DSPC member Charlie Rose (D-NC), to gather information and rally support. The leadership used outside labor groups to lobby members:[4] targeted members were linked to persuasive outside interests as well as to personally assigned members of the task force or the leadership.[5] Staff for the DSPC coordinated the simultaneous efforts of the whip system, task force members, and outside groups.[6]

The DSPC conducted a meeting with the Education and Labor Committee chair (Hawkins) and the chair of the president's Council of Economic Advisors, with both defending the legislation and discussing Republican amendments and political implications for members.[7] In the DSPC forum, Democratic members from different types of constituencies presented the leadership with electoral concerns about constituent perceptions of the bill and discussed the need for a substitute for an electorally attractive GOP amendment.[8] Near the end of the fight for Humphrey-Hawkins, the DSPC met with top labor leaders, including George Meany and Lane Kirkland, to convey the party's efforts to pass a strong bill and defeat weakening amendments.[9] The DSPC's members issued a formal endorsement of the bill, and the DSPC endorsement was used by the top leadership and the task force to signal to the rank-and-file the importance of the vote. As the legislation worked its way toward final passage, staffers for the DSPC collaborated with standing committee staff to craft explanations and party position documents on the amendments that threatened the bill on the floor.[10]

The leadership achieved a difficult and limited victory on the Full Employment and Balanced Growth Act of 1978 "only by taking extraordinary steps in legislative management" (Peters 1997, 223), steps that used the whip system, a very effective ad hoc task force, and the DSPC to link the leadership, the membership, the White House, and outside interests. In the end, the party's efforts at coordination and persuasion grew an initial whip count[11] of 160 Democratic yes or leaning yes votes to a final total of 233 Democratic yes votes.

Meanwhile, Republicans faced major disadvantages in their effort to defeat the Democratic bill. Republicans held no institutional veto points in Washington in 1978, and their share of the House of Representatives was at one of its lowest points since the New Deal. In the face of these obstacles, Republicans used the organizational structure of their Conference to press against the bill overall and to advocate alternatives and amendments. Republicans recognized that the 1978 model of the Humphrey-Hawkins legislation was greatly downsized and made little substantive policy change, but the overall priorities and direction remained objectionable: Humphrey-Hawkins was in part a statement in opposition to the supply-side economics then ascendant among Republicans.[12] In the Republican Policy Committee, members issued a strong statement against the bill and in support of a Republican-crafted alternative, refuting the "central economic planning thesis" of the Democratic bill and focusing instead on the economic effects of inflation and taxes and on the narrower issue of youth unemployment.[13] Simultaneous with the Policy Committee's deliberations and statement, the Republican whip organization conducted a full whip count on the bill, with regional whip members providing the leadership with information about member positions a little over a week before the final floor fight. The GOP whip system yielded very accurate intelligence on HR 50, incorrectly predicting only 5 Republican votes and splitting the 20 recorded undecideds nearly evenly.[14] Republicans used their well-established system of internal party organizations to facilitate a coordinated battle against the key Democratic bill, forcing the large majority into several very close votes on alternatives and presenting a nearly united front on final passage.

## 1989: The GOP and Campaign Finance Reform

Campaign finance reform was a perennial issue in the congresses of the late 1980s and early 1990s. House Republicans, a bipartisan House task force, both Senate caucuses, and the Bush White House offered a variety of proposals during this time period, and in the House, the issue drew out divisions not only between the congressional parties but also within them.[15] As is typically the case with the politics of campaign money, the controversy focused not only on principles of competitive elections and free speech but also on the electoral interests of the congressional parties (e.g., Moscardelli and Haspel 2007). Within the House Republican Conference, Minority Leader Bob Michel (R-IL) initiated a debate in early 1989 by proposing a set of campaign finance reforms in an attempt to kick-start the issue after reform failed in the Senate during the 100th Congress. The issue had the effect of dividing more senior Republicans and the activist junior members of the Conference who, as *Congressional Quarterly* put it, "sought to overthrow a system they consider[ed] the bulwark of the House's Democratic majority" (Alston 1989).

To work for a party position on the complex and internally divisive issue, House Republicans used the participatory leadership system to sort through the competing views of members and arrive at a Conference position on existing proposals. Starting in July 1989, the House Republican Policy Committee held a series of meetings to discuss the controversial components of campaign reform that were then on the table. First, the GOP co-chair of the bipartisan campaign finance task force (Guy Vander Jagt, R-MI) presented the Policy Committee with the existing task force proposals, including those on which the bipartisan leadership had been unable to reach agreement.[16] Over the next several weeks, the Policy Committee met at least seven times to deliberate over the campaign finance issue. A large number of House Republicans—more than half of the Conference—attended these open Policy Committee meetings, with members both supporting elements of reform and expressing intense opposition. House Republicans in opposition told the Policy Committee, among other things, that "reform sucks" and "the party wants to destroy itself."[17] As a result of these meetings, the Policy Committee marked up a list of proposals—including restrictions on PAC activity, new tax incentives for individual donations, and relaxed limits on party contributions—and rejected others, including spending limits on House races and a proposal to limit use of franked mail.[18] The Policy Committee then presented the significantly changed package of reforms to the full Conference, and the Conference supported a very similar version.[19]

The end result of the extended leadership's activity was a proposal that could command broader support in the Conference relative to the proposals by the Republican House leader and the Republican president. The Republican Policy Committee provided a legitimate context in which the minority leadership could work out a broad compromise on campaign finance. The procedure was not a bottom-up process of independent policy development by the committee; rather, the top elected leadership began with a framework and used the Policy Committee as a location for testing its viability, gathering views, venting intraparty conflict, and revising the proposal accordingly to arrive at a more unified position. The membership gained the opportunity to hold the leadership accountable for the actions it was taking and to direct its course. Within the more intensely partisan political environment of the late 1980s, the committee allowed the leadership to coordinate and coalesce the rank-and-file and to satisfy the conflicting demands of groups within the Conference. The open nature of the process afforded legitimacy to the result within the party and provided a coherent public position for Republicans.

### 2011: Minority Party Position-Taking

After four years in the House majority, Democrats lost the House in the devastating 2010 midterm elections; Republicans took back all of the Democratic gains from 2006 and 2008 and then some, arriving at a larger majority than they had held during the 1995–2007 period. With Republicans driving the House agenda and the Obama administration as the focal point for Washington Democrats in policy debates, the House Democratic leadership in the 112th Congress looked ahead to the 2012 congressional elections and adapted to a new role articulating opposition to the energetic and conservative House Republicans. Early in 2011, Minority Leader Nancy Pelosi (D-CA) began holding public meetings of the Democratic Steering and Policy Committee in order to call attention both to Democratic priorities and to possible consequences of Republican legislation and procedural choices (Hunter 2011b). The public hearings involved members of the DSPC itself as well as key standing committee members and invited outside guests. In January, a DSPC hearing focused on the most popular elements of the Affordable Care Act, which were threatened by the GOP effort to repeal the Act. A press release from Nancy Pelosi cast the event as "the only hearing where parents of young children and young adults, Americans with pre-existing medical conditions, small business owners and seniors will have the opportunity to testify about the real-life effects of undoing critical patient protections."[20] In another public 2011 hearing, the DSPC heard from a range of high-profile experts on the debt ceiling issue that gripped the House in summer 2011.[21] Other hearings in the 112th focused on gas prices and pay equality.[22]

As a tactic for the House's party leadership organizations, the DSPC's communications activity in the 112th Congress was nothing particularly new.[23] But the "mock hearings," as *Roll Call* called them, helped to call press attention to Democrats' positions and to unpopular Republican actions. In the best-known example, Democrats held a DSPC hearing in February 2012 to hear testimony on insurance coverage for contraception.[24] Republicans on the Oversight and Government Reform Committee had held hearings a few days earlier on the issue of religious freedom and required contraception coverage under Obama administration rules implementing the Affordable Care Act. Committee chair Darrell Issa (R-CA) did not permit committee Democrats to call a sympathetic witness, Georgetown law student Sandra Fluke, to testify on the importance of contraceptive coverage (Kliff 2012). Democrats responded with the DSPC hearing featuring Fluke and successfully generated media attention to the incident and the issue (helped along by Rush Limbaugh's ad hominem attacks on Fluke) (Milbank 2012; Stetler 2012). The extended party leadership organization provided, in these instances, a center for the Democratic caucus to gain public attention for its positions and its electoral case against Republicans, despite the lack of institutional resources associated with House minority party status.

### 2011: Coordinating a Factious GOP Majority

When the Republican Party took control in the 2010 elections, the new House majority was ideologically conservative—and relatively cohesive in its conservatism—but the new GOP leadership faced strong internal divisions over the party's strategy for lawmaking with the Democratic president and Senate. Many Conference conservatives, particularly junior members motivated by Tea Party fervor from 2010, demanded uncompromising positions on the budget and the federal debt ceiling, and they expected sharp confrontation with President Obama and the Democrats. This new majority posed a challenge for the Republican leadership, including Majority Whip Kevin McCarthy (R-CA). Adopting an open approach that embraced "chaos," the majority whip organization was sometimes ineffective in the first years after the 2010 election, and some of its failures in gathering information and persuading members on floor votes were embarrassing for the new majority (Draper 2012, 77–78, 131–32). But some of the whip organization's efforts in the 112th Congress demonstrate the value of coordination in a participatory party organization for a divided caucus.

McCarthy and the rest of the leadership faced their first big test early in the 112th Congress with the battle over the continuing resolution (CR) to fund the rest of FY2011. Although Republican leaders initially planned for legislation that would make moderate cuts in the CR, they eventually shifted course and passed an initial bill that cut an annualized $100 billion from the 2011 budget and included several controversial conservative policy riders, setting up a months-long episode of brinkmanship with the White House. The House GOP's shift followed from McCarthy's early use of Republican whip "listening sessions," in which leaders of the whip system and committee figures offered policy lessons to junior Republicans and heard from those rank-and-file members about their preferences on the central issue of budgets. The top leadership moved abruptly toward the more conservative and confrontational strategy as a result of the coordination activity in these two-way "listening sessions" (Austin 2012; Stanton 2011).

This mode of intraconference coordination became a central tool in the GOP leadership's effort to manage an ideologically coherent but politically factious majority in the 112th Congress. McCarthy's whip organization involved a diverse array of members in party coordination and persuasion (Drucker 2013; Draper 2012). As the CR prelude gave way to the Republican effort to frame the debate through its 2012 budget proposal, whip leaders and Budget Committee Chair Paul Ryan (R-WI) used the listening sessions to communicate policy information and to "get buy-in from Members" by involving them in the policy process before the budget plan was finalized (Palmer and Hunter 2011). These sessions took the form of small-group meetings, allowing the whips to build support on the multifaceted and politically fraught "Ryan budget." This low-key whip effort went beyond member-to-member information exchange and persuasion, however. Employing a tool that both Democratic and Republican whips had used in earlier decades, the whips held "sidebar listening sessions" with members and outside conservative players (Draper 2012, 140), reassuring members who may have been concerned about the broader political consequences of their positions on the budget. The Republican effort on the Ryan budget involved coordination among the membership, informal efforts at persuasion, and communication between the House party and the expanded Republican political network.

A third round of budget battles and listening sessions came in the summer when House Republicans used the threat of government default as leverage to achieve additional cuts. This confrontation—which ended with a last-minute agreement on a debt ceiling increase, budget cuts, and the "supercommittee" and sequestration plans in the Budget Control Act (Austin 2012)—was marked by serious difficulties for Republican leaders. Many members were opposed to a debt limit increase under any circumstances, and McCarthy used whip listening sessions again to educate members on the debt (including field trips to the Bureau of the Public Debt) and to gather intelligence for the leadership on what policies conservatives would seek in return for supporting an increase in the debt ceiling (Draper 2012, 224–27). In the end, a large number of House Republicans (66) would oppose the final bipartisan compromise, and the Budget Control Act passed the House only with substantial Democratic support. However, the whips' efforts to gradually educate and persuade Republicans helped to make the uneasy compromise outcome possible.

As the 112th Congress drew to a close and the 113th Congress brought renewed conflict in the Republican Conference, McCarthy's approach received criticism, especially from mainstream GOP figures, for emphasizing consensus-building over aggressive persuasion (Drucker 2013).[25] Despite the criticism, McCarthy's use of the extended leadership system as an "idea factory" (Wyler 2013) for participatory policy and strategy development had strong parallels with earlier House party leaders who faced a caucus split over issue positions, political approaches, or both.

## Participation in the Party

These four examples—two from an earlier period with the House under a Democratic majority and two from a more recent Congress with a Republican majority—illustrate the importance of partisan organizations to majority and minority parties in the House. In the Humphrey-Hawkins case, we see the party's top leadership and committee chairs making use of the members in the whip system, the Steering and Policy Committee, and an ad hoc task force to coordinate party strategy, to facilitate communication both within the party and with outside groups and the White House, and to persuade members to support the party on key floor votes. Minority Republicans in the 1980s used the Republican Policy Committee to encourage broad participation in deliberations over a potentially divisive party position, and the committee's activity served the interests of both leaders and regular members of the Conference by allowing coordination of positions and a check on the direction of the leadership. In the case of Democrats in the 112th Congress, the party's collective electoral goals motivated use of publicly oriented DSPC hearings to communicate public priorities in service of the party's electoral objectives and to replace lost institutional resources for Democratic member participation. The Republican whips' listening sessions in the 112th Congress illustrate coordination activity as well as efforts at informal persuasion as the leadership. As whip, Kevin McCarthy sought to share information with rank-and-file members about party priorities, to collect information about the positions those members would have the party take and how they should be pursued, and to use the connections he built to persuade uncertain Republicans to follow leadership positions.

The four examples together illustrate the ways in which party leadership organizations facilitate the regular functioning of both House political parties through participation by the membership. Political scientists have built a sophisticated understanding of how congressional parties develop and use control over the legislative process to advance a majority party agenda and thwart minority efforts to derail that agenda. However, if the House majority and minority parties are understood as pursuing both policy and electoral goals—and assisting their own membership in pursuing individual goals—then it becomes necessary to consider how the parties organize internally to do more than affect the floor agenda. There are several key questions about party organizations that are not yet well-answered in the extensive literature on the House. *How do broadly participatory leadership organizations serve the collective objectives of the party caucuses? What does the elected leadership gain through these complex organizations? For the many members who participate in the parties through these organizations, how does participation serve varying individual objectives? Finally, how has participation in party leadership changed as the parties have polarized and leaders have enjoyed more delegated authority with strengthening party government conditions?*

As chapter 2 discusses in more detail, the role of participatory party organizations can be best understood as a part of the delegation process that creates party leadership authority. In the familiar principal-agent view of congressional parties, House members cede some authority to the party leaders to pursue the long-term policy and electoral goals of the coalition. As the leadership gains power, though, the membership's interest in being involved in party activity increases. Rank-and-file party members remain, in a sense, active principals who have incentives to participate in leadership activity both to hold the empowered party leaders accountable and to take advantage of the resources in the leadership. For the leadership, in turn, participatory party leadership organizations facilitate the regular tasks of the party leadership by filling several interrelated roles. First, the party's organizational structures formalize the party's *coordination* function, forging connections on both policy positions and political strategy between the top leadership and the regular membership. Second, the institutionalized political party structures a participatory process for *persuading* members to support leadership positions to advance collective party goals both in the short term and in the long run. The party's organizations also engage in *communication* beyond the legislative branch, both to connect members of the House party with the larger network of the party and to communicate the House party's positions with opinion leaders and voters. And *participation* in party organizations itself serves individual electoral, policy, and career goals of rank-and-file members and gives legitimacy and accountability to the authority exercised by top leaders; it also provides leaders with a selective benefit to offer. Because the party leadership must pursue both electoral and policy goals and because the difficulty of the leadership's tasks changes based on party government conditions, the balance of these activities and the nature of member participation should vary in predictable ways over time.

## Analytical Focus and Methods

The central objective of this book, then, is to set out a theoretically grounded account of the Republican and Democratic party organizations in the House, demonstrating with a range of evidence how these participatory organizations have become important to the modern caucuses[26] and explaining in depth how and why they have changed. My analysis of the Republican and Democratic leadership organizations centers on a three-decade time frame beginning with the mid-1970s (94th Congress), when the Democratic-led House underwent major reforms, through the 110th Congress (2007–9). This time frame covers significant changes to congressional politics and to both parties, and it allows me to view the operation of the party organizations during a period of weaker party government followed by the strong polarization and cohesion of the last two decades. It also includes multiple reversals of House and White House party control, such that all configurations of Republican and Democratic control of the presidency and House are included.

The substantive focus of the research is on two Democratic organizations and three Republican organizations. The *Democratic Steering and Policy Committee* (DSPC) makes decisions about membership and leadership on standing committees for the caucus under the direction of the Democratic minority leader or Speaker, and the DSPC has had, at different times, important roles in coordinating and communicating strategy and policy for the caucus. The DSPC includes top party leaders and committee chairs/ranking members as well as many other members of the caucus who are either appointed by the leadership or elected regionally by their colleagues. The *Republican Policy Committee* has functioned as a forum for identifying and articulating party positions on short-term legislative questions and as a center for external party communication. Like the DSPC, its membership is a hybrid of top elected leaders and committee leaders joined by other GOP members who are either appointed or elected. The *Republican Steering Committee*, the successor to the (very differently run) Republican Committee on Committees, makes decisions on committee assignments and leadership with heavy influence from the top party leadership. The *whip organizations* in the Republican Conference and Democratic Caucus are led by an elected majority or minority whip and involve several levels of appointed whips populated by dozens of rank-and-file members. Democrats include a bottom layer of regional whips elected by their peers. The extensive whip organizations primarily serve internal coordination and persuasion functions but have at times had important communications roles as well. Along with these five party organizations, I give some attention to the *Republican Research Committee*, which operated until the GOP took the majority in 1995 and illustrates some important aspects of party operation and participation in the minority.

I largely set aside several other components of the House parties in the discussion that follows. The congressional campaign committees (CCCs), including the Democratic Congressional Campaign Committee (DCCC) and National Republican Congressional Committee (NRCC), are well-established sources of electoral services and resources for the parties' candidates, and they involve participation by caucus members (Clucas 1997; Glasgow 2002; Herrnson 1986; Heberlig and Larson 2012; Kolodny 1998; Kolodny and Dwyre 1998). However, the CCCs operate in multiple realms, working as part of the leadership structure but also as election consulting and research organizations and quasi-political action committees (Herrnson 2009) that are distinct from the rest of the House leadership system and focused on external processes. For this reason, and because they have already received extensive study using an approach similar to the one I use in this research (Kolodny 1998), I leave the CCCs aside in this book. I also give only limited attention to the Democratic Caucus and Republican Conference as organizations. Both have served important coordination functions and involve member participation, but the caucuses do not operate as entities with distinct membership within the caucus (aside from their elected leadership) and they have received focused attention as party organizations elsewhere, both in the modern context (e.g., Dynes and Reeves 2014; Forgette 2004) and across the House's history (Jenkins and Stewart 2008; 2013).

My approach to the study of the core participatory party organizations involves multiple data sources and modes of analysis. I use archived evidence from the papers of 11 former party leaders in the House to construct accounts of the organizations' roles and activity and, where possible, on key decisions and discussions about the organizations themselves. The documentary evidence used in these histories includes internal memoranda and notes, minutes of meetings, leadership vote counts, and analyses, among other types of primary-source evidence (see chapter 2 for more discussion of the archival research). Supplementing these documents with secondary sources, I evaluate how the organizations have served both collective party goals and the goals of individual members. This qualitative evidence is accompanied by quantitative hypothesis-testing on the patterns of participation in each organization and the consequences of that participation for members' career and constituency goals. The quantitative analysis is based on extensive new data sets on organization participation that I have assembled from a combination of archival and secondary sources. I also evaluate data on the staffing of these party organizations, tracking the changes in their staff resources over time.

## Overview and Plan of the Book

The succeeding chapters will lay out the case that our understanding of political parties in the House can be expanded by considering the organizational structures that connect the rank-and-file and the leadership; relying on member participation, these organizations carry out necessary leadership tasks in service of collective party objectives and individual member goals. By delving into examples of party organization operation and the changes in those organizations, the book will illustrate that the party caucus, while centered on chamber organizational and procedural control by the party leadership (Cox and McCubbins 2007; Jenkins and Stewart 2013), has developed a set of structures that facilitate day-to-day work toward collective electoral and policy goals through member involvement. As the quantitative and qualitative evidence will demonstrate, the parties recognize—both in the majority and in the minority—the need to build support through effective exchange of information on party actions, the value of membership-involved communication of a party message, a persuasive process that involves a range of caucus members, and the benefits to members of member participation in party activity. The resulting picture requires an understanding of House parties that goes beyond the top leaders and the powers they are delegated. I argue participation through party organizations is important because of the power delegated to the leadership, and that involvement expands when greater authority begins to flow to the leadership.

In this way, the book provides a new look at a familiar but important topic—the polarization of parties in the modern House. Scholarly and popular accounts have examined both the causes and consequences of rapidly rising polarization in the House, usually with a focus on changing voting patterns, leadership powers, and House procedures (see Theriault 2008 for a review). The emphasis is typically on either the clash of the two parties in the policy process or on the capacity and activity of top party leaders. This book, by contrast, offers a look "under the hood" of the two parties, throwing light on the internal operations of the parties that have changed significantly as the House has polarized. The role of individual members in the life of the House party has shifted, as has control over the internal processes of the party, and these changes have taken place in several stages during the polarizing era of congressional politics. The argument and evidence in this book shows rising party polarization and cohesion first brought about a period of high involvement in the majority and minority parties, but very high polarization, along with strengthening electoral competition, brought a strong form of party government that constrained the role of the rank-and-file in the party, with consequences for both members and for the parties themselves.

The following chapter (chapter 2) elaborates these ideas to provide a framework for interpreting the evidence in the remainder of the book. I offer a participatory perspective on party government, starting with the conditional party government theory and its progeny. I review assumptions about collective party goals and individual member goals and establish the importance of member participation in the principal-agent relationship that creates House party leadership power. I introduce the party functions—coordination, communication, and persuasion—that participatory party organizations facilitate, and I consider the ways in which these functions and member participation change as party government conditions shift. The chapter also considers how and why individual leaders play an important role in driving key organizational changes in the House parties.

Subsequent chapters turn to original evidence and argument on the key party organizations. In chapter 3, I consider party leadership organizations as a venue for rank-and-file member participation. By tracing the rise of the participatory structures in the Republican and Democratic parties through archival evidence, I show how and when the parties have expanded participation and the ways leaders and members have viewed this participation. The archival evidence on participation in this chapter is supplemented by extensive analysis of extended leadership membership rosters from the 1970s through the 2000s to explore who participated and to test hypotheses about how the top elected leadership constituted the party organizations to achieve multiple objectives. I also use the membership data to analyze participation's benefits from the perspective of the rank-and-file member. Through several analyses, I show that participation brings individual benefits for members' career goals and that members vary strategically in how they relate their partisan involvement to their constituents.

The Humphrey-Hawkins, campaign finance, and Republican majority anecdotes all demonstrate the crucial coordination role that extended leadership structures play; this role is the focus of chapter 4. The chapter documents the extensive use of the DSPC and Republican Policy Committees, as well as the whip systems, to coordinate among party members on party strategy and on the party's policy positions. The qualitative evidence shows how changes in party strength, as well as majority status, are associated with differences in the importance and location of coordination activity and openness to developing policy positions within the extended leadership. Yet, coordination of party strategy and maintaining internal communication has required participatory organizations across the time period under examination.

The party's collective policy and electoral goals necessitate linkages between the House caucus and party entities and the public—these external communications functions of the party organizations are the focus of chapter 5. The caucuses' organizations connect members with party officials in other branches and, significantly, with elements of the extended party network that have the potential to affect the caucus' objectives as well as the individual members' goals. More broadly, the party's organizations create and exploit opportunities to communicate political messages to constituencies that will affect the party's electoral goals. Although both of these functions have received some attention in recent years, the account in chapter 5 shows both that the organizational function of communication traces back to earlier decades in the House and that it has superseded coordination as the main role for some parts of the extended party leadership system as electoral competition has strengthened.

Participation in leadership organizations also contributes to the party's direct efforts to build support for legislative initiatives through member persuasion. In chapter 6, I examine the persuasive functions of the extended party organizations. The whip networks make a systematic process of persuasion possible, a process in which leadership participants with connections to individual members assist in expanding party support on votes. I show how this process has changed as party government conditions have strengthened, involving a much larger part of the caucus in much more frequent counting and persuading efforts. This chapter also considers the DSPC and the Republican Steering Committee (and its predecessors) as tools for long-term persuasion. Reviewing the participatory committee-selection function since the 1970s, I show how the role of members has changed and the DSPC and Republican Steering Committee's members have increasingly worked to support collective efforts at long-term persuasion.

Chapter 7 concludes by summarizing the importance of participation for both the leadership's efforts to achieve collective goals and party members' own pursuits. Emphasizing the connections between the theoretical framework and the qualitative and quantitative evidence, the chapter reviews the overall picture of change in the Republican and Democratic organizations as party competition, polarization, and cohesion have increased. I offer some observations about how the study of party participation in leadership organizations can add to future scholarship on congressional parties as well as some comments on how the kind of research in this book—mixed-method research relying on archival evidence—contributes to our understanding of congressional parties and leadership.

# TWO

# Participation in the Party

*A Framework for Understanding
Leadership Organizations*

As former Speaker John Boehner could certainly attest, leading a House party caucus is a challenging job even when the membership is ideologically unified. A generation of scholarship has demonstrated convincingly that party leaders' ability to lead is strongly shaped by the partisan political context; a leader at the head of a cohesive party in a polarized House enjoys more tools for leading the legislative process and more leeway in making effective use of those tools. But whether a particular leader enjoys strong party government conditions or faces a weaker party, the House is not well-designed for leadership by command. Individual members retain their own incentives to act independently. Moreover, the party's objectives and the goals of its members require more of the party, on a day-to-day basis, than simple agenda control. Control over the floor permits the majority party to pursue commonly held policy goals and to block minority party efforts to do the same. For the majority to make effective use of its control, however, it must identify—or work to create—a consensus behind its objectives, and it must enjoy effective communication throughout the caucus about strategic decisions. These connections between the leadership and the rank-and-file ensure leadership actions are faithfully representing the caucus, allow the leadership to make informed decisions about process, and provide greater certainty that the members will make the individual choices necessary to advance collective goals. On the minority side, the electoral incentive to use process and publicity to counter the majority and regain control requires the party to develop a similar set of internal linkages. And for both the majority and minority party, individual members seek and expect extensive opportunities to pursue their individual goals within the party.

House Democrats and Republicans operate not as dictatorships but as participatory parties. The organizations in each caucus involve a large portion of the party's membership in the party's work in ways that serve both the collective party goals pursued by top party leaders and the individual goals held by rank-and-file members. The parties' organizational systems accomplish much of the regular business of the party, business that facilitates the party's use of procedural control (or its attempts to seize it), its efforts to transmit its message and priorities, and the opportunities it provides for its members. This chapter develops this perspective on party organization, reviewing and extending theories of congressional goals and party power to explain why and how the caucuses employ extended leadership structures. I discuss the set of goals at the individual and collective levels that animate the party's regular operation, and I show how conditional party government theory and related arguments link these goals and participatory party leadership structures. Based on this framework, I identify and explain the main purposes served by the extended congressional party leadership. Subsequent chapters will peer into the black box of the modern House Democratic and Republican caucuses to explore how the leadership organizations play these roles on a regular basis and how those roles have changed since the 1970s. In a final section of this chapter, I outline my methodological approach to this investigation, discussing the archival and quantitative research that informs the analysis in the remainder of the book.

## Existing Work on Leadership Organizations

Since at least the publication of Cooper and Brady's influential essay (1981), House parties and leaders have moved onto center stage in congressional scholarship, particularly as party polarization has motivated renewed inquiry into the nature of party power. As legislative scholarship has become more theoretically and empirically focused on congressional parties, the top elected party leadership has played the lead role in the story researchers have told. Speakers, majority leaders, and minority leaders gain and use power, shaping the party's course as they are able in the electorally driven political context.[1] The leadership-centered story is somewhat justified since considerable power is delegated to the elected leadership. Moreover, as I discuss below, recent scholarship has become more sophisticated in considering party leaders as agents who can and do act individually to affect the party's direction (e.g., Green 2010; Strahan 2007).

Less well-understood are the House Republican and Democratic Party organizations. Congressional scholars have occasionally given some attention to the party organizations in the House, but what we know about most of the extended party leadership is quite fragmented—specific to a particular party or political context, or offered in the context of a story about a different aspect of congressional politics. The most convincing accounts of the leadership organizations are in works that seek to explain the gradually growing strength of party leadership in the Democratic majority of the post-reform period. Rohde (1991) and Sinclair (1983; 1995) provide a glimpse of the Democratic whip system, Steering and Policy Committee, and task forces in the 1980s, portraying the leadership structures as inclusive, open, and providing critical tools for internal communication in a diverse majority caucus (see also Loomis 1984). Canon (1989) viewed these Democratic leadership structures in the late 1980s as part of a firmly institutionalized party leadership, with the minority Republican leadership sharing similar features (see also Little and Patterson 1993). Although little scholarship has systematically examined the regular operation of the party organizations, some recent work has turned to the vote-counting operations of the whip systems as a testing ground for understanding party influence, finding important roles for whip counts in shaping House results in the early 1970s Democratic party (Burden and Frisby 2004) and across a larger time frame using archival data (Evans et al. 2003; Evans and Grandy 2009).[2] Related archive-based analysis has provided some sense of the impact of party caucus meetings on party coordination (Forgette 2004) and of the power structure of the steering committees (Frisch and Kelly 2006). Focusing more narrowly on the characteristics of party leaders, a small body of work has presented empirical evidence on the appointment of members into the leadership. Grofman and colleagues (2002) examine the aggregate ideological trends in the extended leadership, and Heberlig and Larson show persuasively that party voting and financial support have been important to members' advancement in appointed leadership positions since the 1980s (Heberlig and Larson 2012; see also Heberlig and Larson 2007; Heberlig, Hetherington, and Larson 2006).

Taken together, this research has provided congressional scholars with a preliminary, but uneven, picture of the House's party leadership organizations. What we lack is a complete and theoretically grounded account of these entities that can explain the changing roles they play in making the contemporary House Democratic and Republican caucuses work. What do members get from a participatory organizational system? What does the top elected leadership get? And why have the organizations been both sustained and significantly changed as the political context in the House has shifted sharply between the 1970s and the 2000s?

## A Participatory View of Party Government in the House

The standard theoretical treatment of parties in the House, generally speaking, begins by viewing power as originally residing with the individual members. Political parties in the chamber exist, and their leaders receive some measure of power, because members find it in their interest to form a long-term coalition and to delegate authority to party leaders who can act to sustain that coalition. Accounts of congressional parties diverge on important details of this relationship (Aldrich and Rohde 2001; Cox and McCubbins 2007; Smith 2007), but the common picture that emerges is one of party leaders empowered as agents of House members, their principals (Sinclair 1995, chap. 1).

The familiar *conditional party government* version of this principal-actor framework provides a starting point for my argument. Conditional party government theory (CPG), as developed by Rohde and Aldrich (Rohde 1991; Aldrich and Rohde 2000b, 2001), begins with the insights of Cooper and Brady (1981), who argued that the power of House party leaders is not primarily based on individual style or skill but rather on contextual factors—electoral circumstances that shape the party's cohesiveness behind a central leader. Aldrich and Rohde elaborated on this initial concept in a series of collaborative and individual publications. The CPG argument enters into the ongoing debate over the existence and nature of party influence by arguing that House parties "will (under certain conditions) seek to use their powers to shift the policy outcomes produced by the body closer to the median position of the party than would otherwise be the case" (Aldrich and Rohde 2000b, 2). Leadership power to do so is delegated by rank-and-file principals to their agents in the leadership; the delegation in CPG is conditional on electorally rooted political circumstances. Where elections produce House party delegations that are more ideologically cohesive internally and more ideologically polarized, the central leadership gains authority to work toward collective policy goals. Power that was decentralized through the caucus flows toward the party leadership. Rohde explained this dynamic in his original formulation of CPG:

> When agreement was present on a matter that was important to party members, the leadership would be expected to use the tools at their disposal (e.g., the Rules Committee, the whip system, etc.) to advance the cause. Chairmen and members on relevant committees would be expected not to be roadblocks to the passage of such legislation. Committee leaders who frequently violated these expectations risked the loss of their positions. Rank-and-file members who frequently opposed the party would be less likely to receive desired committee assignments because of the leader-dominated assignment system. (Rohde 1991, 31)

Conditional party government, then, expects that leaders will use carrots as well as sticks to draw party members toward the party policy position. In addition to the power to reward and punish, leaders also gain greater power to define and structure the legislative agenda to avoid collective action problems and advance policy goals (Aldrich and Rohde 2000b, 5). Conditional party government theory, it is important to note, was developed as an explanation for majority party leadership in the era of Democratic control, although it has been extended to explain later developments in the Republican-majority era, which help to highlight the procedural aspects of CPG (Aldrich and Rohde 2000b; Aldrich and Rohde 2001).

Since the original series of Aldrich and Rohde articles, other scholars have extended and refined conditional party government theory. The initial theory contemplated the electoral roots of party conditions, but it centered on the party's collective pursuit of *policy* rather than electoral goals. Delegation to the party leadership affected incentives and structures that produced desirable, long-run policy outcomes for the party. Subsequently, other authors have drawn the party's collective *electoral* goals into the framework. Smith and Gamm summarize the incorporation of electoral goals into CPG, pointing out that CPG allows room for collective electoral goals even though its original emphasis was on policy. In this view, "legislators believe that effective leaders will help create a favorable image for the party and in doing so enhance their electoral prospects . . . [and] leaders must sometimes pursue strategies that represent trade-offs between the policy and electoral goals of party members" (Smith and Gamm 2009, 144). In a related way, Lebo, McGlynn, and Koger (2007) consider the electoral costs of policy pursuits in articulating their "strategic party government" refinement. In considering electoral consequences, these authors also bring into play the interaction between the minority party and majority party. The party cohesion of the majority is linked to the cohesion of the minority in the Lebo et al. analysis, and, just as importantly, the size of the majority party affects party loyalty. Larger congressional parties are empirically related to weaker party cohesion. This relationship extends the general CPG concept: rank-and-file members are more willing to cede authority to the leadership when party size goes down because the cost of any individual defection goes up (see also Patty 2008; Smith 2007, 206–8). In sum, a "CPG-plus" perspective, drawn from CPG and these later authors, emphasizes that the strength of the House party varies with the willingness of its members to delegate authority to the central leadership to pursue a balance of policy and electoral goals; member delegation, in turn, is conditional on the cohesion of the two individual parties and the polarization between them as well as on the interplay between the relative size and cohesion of the two parties.[3]

The party leadership, then, enjoys delegated authority to accomplish party goals depending on the political context. But delegation is not an all-or-nothing decision. House members are not ceding control to one or a few leaders without further involvement and voice. Congressional scholars could leave the inaccurate impression—particularly in light of the party-versus-preference debate (Smith 2007, chap. 4)—that members' choices begin and end with their decision either to follow personal preferences or to yield to party forces delegated to the leadership. House members, however, can both delegate to the party and actively participate in the party leadership they have created. In doing so, they take advantage of the empowered party to pursue individual goals, to hold the elected party leadership accountable, and to shape the direction of the caucus. From this perspective, House members remain *active* principals in the principal-agent relationship. Just as Strahan (2011) has argued we should see the elected leadership as "causal agents" with independent roles to play, we can also view the rank-and-file as retaining an active role—and the party organizations as providing a mechanism for their activity.

### Active Principals: Delegation and Participation

House members have created congressional parties to advance their individual goals of electoral success and policy making. In CPG-based models, the degree of delegation to the leadership comes from members' agreement levels and the stakes of the conflict with the opposition party; yet there is risk in delegation[4] even under relatively high levels of intraparty agreement and interparty conflict. Because of their individual goals, rank-and-file members have an incentive to mitigate the risk involved in delegation by trying to monitor and influence the actions of the leadership. Especially when delegated authority is on the increase while ideological diversity in the caucus remains, members may be particularly concerned with avoiding agency loss and directing the leadership's priorities and use of power. Stated differently, if members know elected leaders exercise some discretion and have some ability to shape priorities and even preferences (Strahan 2007), then at least a significant subset of members will seek to be involved in what those leaders do and how they do it. These members will be motivated by their own policy or constituency goals to try to shape the collective policy and electoral goods the party produces. The delegation of authority to the top leadership is not absolute.

Individual goals will also motivate members into behaving as active principals in order to achieve personal benefits from the party. When the party leadership has some meaningful control over the agenda, the flow of legislation, and the distribution of selective benefits, some members will seek to employ the party's power and resources for their own individual goals. Participating in party organizations brings members opportunities to seize their share of what the more empowered party leadership has to offer. Reelection, policy, and power goals are all relevant. Electorally, a personal connection to the party leadership could facilitate constituency legislation or allow access to information that will help a member to advance constituency interests. For members who represent districts with lopsided partisan characteristics, involvement also promises to enhance a party-based presentation of self, an idea that chapter 3 examines in more detail. The links to individual power and policy goals are more obvious. For House members with progressive ambition, a position within the extended leadership offers not only party leadership experience and a spot on the leadership "escalator" (Hibbing 1991, 61–62) but also connections with other members that will be valuable when seeking higher positions, especially prestige committee assignments and elected party posts.[5] Members within the extended leadership structure also gain policy and procedural information and the opportunity to affect policy, even if in small ways. David Price (D-NC) has described the personal policy and power benefits of his participation in the Democratic whip system very specifically:

> My own involvement in whip operations has been useful in at least three ways. First, it has let me help mobilize support for measures that I thought were important . . . on which I had worked extensively

in committee. Second, it has made me a partner, albeit a junior one, in leadership undertakings. . . . Finally, it has brought me into discussions of floor strategy and the last-minute alterations needed to maximize votes on various bills. . . . the vote counts and feedback garnered by the whip organization have served as a reality check for committee leaders and have given members like me a means of pushing for needed refinements in advance of floor consideration. (Price 1992, 85–86)

In a similar way, leadership participation can expand members' areas of involvement in a chamber that typically rewards specialization. Paul Wilkinson, executive director of the Republican Policy Committee in the early 2000s, pointed out that members "get assigned to a [standing committee], your one solo powerful committee or your two pretty decently powerful committees, but then you don't have any influence on some things outside of that. But through the Policy Committee, you can give any member with an interest in any topic at least some input into issues" that are outside of their standing-committee specialization. Members benefit, too, from the structured opportunity to pick up information that affects their policy and electoral goals. Republican Policy Committee meetings in the 2000s were mostly members-only with limited staff attendance, allowing members to question and discuss policy issues openly: "Obviously a politician who says he doesn't know something gets in trouble if he says it in public, but [the Policy Committee] was kind of a chance for them to say 'I have no idea about this issue—you tell me what I should think and why I should think it.' [It was] a chance for them to educate each other as well as learn from whoever the guest or guests were."[6]

Not all members will find that their goals are substantially implicated by an empowered party leadership, but many will seek to accompany the delegation of authority to the leadership with involvement in the party to benefit their own goals. As I discuss below, the participatory incentives are different as partisan conditions change, but in both strengthening and strong party government, the party leadership's power is connected to a participatory framework.

### Collective Party Goals and the Participatory Party

A system of participatory partisan organizations serves more than the isolated interests of the individual caucus members. Members empower the top party leadership to pursue collective party goals that the system of party organizations helps to advance. Collectively, the parties in Congress pursue both electoral and policy goals—they seek to *build and maintain electoral majorities* and to *pursue party policy* (Smith 2007; Smith and Gamm 2009).[7] The parties build and maintain electoral majorities through choices in the legislative process—and more overtly electoral activities outside of the legislative process—that publicly increase the value of the party's "brand name." By strengthening the brand, the party has a positive impact on the individual electoral goals of all members linked to the party. Similarly, the congressional parties work to overcome collective action problems that threaten to derail legislative efforts to seek policies party members prefer. The two goals, Smith explains, are "interdependent": the relevance of the two goals to individual members, and therefore to the parties they create, cannot be fully separated, and the party's pursuit of these collective goals will involve a balancing of and sometimes a trade-off between these goals. Participatory party leadership organizations serve both goals directly, and they provide an indirect service toward both goals as well by allowing the leadership to connect members' individual interests in participation to the party's collective electoral and policy objectives.

### Roles of Participatory Party Organizations

In serving collective electoral and policy goals, the party's organizations play several distinctive roles. Through coordination, public communication, and persuasion functions, the caucus organizations provide a set of specific collective goods that advance the big-picture electoral and policy goals. Participation itself forms an identifiable fourth function of the party leadership organizations that benefits the collective goals and yields selective benefits for individual members.[8]

### Coordination

While a typical image of strong party leadership centers on forceful persuasion, even coercion, some scholarship has emphasized the key role of coordination in carrying out party tasks and building party cohesion. Richard Forgette (2004) has observed that the "congressional party organizations do not generally function to instill party enforcement"; instead, the leadership uses the organizations to "transmit strategic information," thereby building "cohesion indirectly through information transmission." In this view, "rather than enforcing compliance in a prisoners' dilemma, party leaders solve a coordination problem of multiple, asymmetric equilibria among copartisans." Because the coordination function is important but conditioned on generally cohesive preferences, Forgette hypothesizes that party organizations may be "more active during times when their enforcement role is least needed, during periods of high preference homogeneity" (2004, 410–11). Coordinating activities include internal communication between the party leadership, committee leaders, and the rank-and-file on party strategies and member preferences as well as efforts to identify positions that can enjoy broad support within the caucus. This sort of participatory coordination work serves the party's interests in the short term as leaders seek maximum information flow on legislative decisions, but it also serves the party's long-run interests in a well-connected party team. Research seeking to demonstrate a direct effect of coordination on party voting unity has yielded some mixed results (Crespin et al. 2014; Forgette 2004; cf. Dynes and Reeves 2014). However, the importance of coordination for the party does not rest on difficult-to-measure short-term shifts in loyalty. Party organizations make long-term investments in linking the membership with the leadership to develop consensus positions and internally communicate about policy and procedure.

## Communication

Party coordination involves effective internal exchange among members of the caucus, but the modern congressional party also engages in elaborate *external* communications strategies. Much of this external communication is oriented toward the party's collective electoral goals, although it can also serve the party's policy objectives. We know the majority and minority parties in both chambers use the legislative process itself for electoral communications—the "vote-a-rama" budget amendment process in the Senate and the minority's use of the motion to recommit in the House are good examples (Oleszek 2011, 74–75; Clark 2012; and see generally Evans 2001; Lee 2009; Sinclair 2006). Beyond the actual lawmaking process, the parties have turned to public strategies for conveying the party's electoral message, both in the majority and in the minority (Malecha and Reagan 2012). As external communications become more important both within and outside of the legislative arena, the party can transmit electoral messages more effectively by making use of its organizational framework to provide legitimacy, resources, and a range of voices in support of its electoral goals.

The partisan organizations of the House connect the caucuses in communication with party actors outside the chamber as well. Parties in American politics involve a broad network of partisan actors who act to set party policy priorities and electoral strategies and to shape public support

(Koger, Masket, and Noel 2009). Whether in the minority or the majority, the parties in the House nurture and use connections with the rest of this expanded party, both in other parts of government and outside of official Washington. The parties' organizations provide a mechanism for linking the expanded political party to the House caucus in order to support the collective goals of the party in lawmaking and shaping an electoral message. Here, the party's communications efforts can also provide direct benefits to individual party members who participate—connections with the expanded party within the party's organizational activity can help members to advance their own goals.

## Persuasion

The persuasive role of congressional parties should be understood to include more than just decisive, last-minute arm-twisting by aggressive party leaders. In pursuit of its collective policy goals, the party leadership pursues a broader strategy of persuasion. Building on an effective network of internal coordination, the leadership relies on a process of persuasion in building support for the party's position on choices before the House. In the Democratic caucus and in the Republican Conference, this persuasive process has come to employ a very large network of party members who channel information and arguments in an effort to secure party goals. This sort of persuasion has become a routinely participatory part of the party's work. At the same time, persuasion can be seen in a much longer term view as an attempt by the party leadership to encourage individual actions that support collective goals, whether through roll-call voting or providing electoral support for the party. Through a changing set of organizational structures, Republicans and Democrats have both used participatory organizations to make decisions about how to distribute the most important selective benefits at their disposal, standing committee seats and committee leadership posts. In this way, the party's decisions about linking benefits to party support have long been shaped by the involvement of many members, not just the top elected leadership or key committee leaders.

Party organizations in the House, then, serve the collective goals of the party that the top party leadership is charged with advancing—and they do so in a way that provides participatory opportunities for the rank-and-file membership. For the elected leadership to effectively meet its expectations, participatory involvement is essential. In a legislative chamber with broad-based parties and strong incentives for individualized elections and legislative behavior (Mayhew 1974), any successful effort at party leadership will, of course, not look like a dictatorship. Central party leadership will advance with the cooperation of many individual caucus members who connect the leaders with the rank-and-file, facilitate the flow of information through the caucus, and legitimize the difficult choices the party has to make. But, as the previous discussion makes clear, the participatory party neither exists simply to make life easier for the top leadership, nor would we expect such an organizational system to be very effective. Individual party members gain from the arrangement. They maintain the opportunity to hold the leadership accountable, particularly when the risks to members of delegation to leaders seem higher. On an even more individualized level, members can use the participatory party system to work toward their own goals of district representation, reelection, policy making, and career advancement. Because participation links the sometimes-diverging individual objectives of the membership and the collective goals of the leadership, we should see party organizations as playing a crucial part in party government in the House.

## Polarization, Party Government, and the Changing Roles of Party Leadership Organizations

In views of House leadership based on conditional party government theory, delegation to the party leadership is not constant over time—members give more authority to the leadership and accept more assertive use of that authority when the policy stakes for the party are high and the party is in greater agreement. In addition, factors that strengthen the electoral consequences of party leadership also contribute to the strength of party government. These influences on delegation to the party leadership should also correspond to the way in which party leaders and the rank-and-file membership interact through participatory party organizations.

When conditions create weak incentives for empowering the party leadership, members will have little impetus for participating in party processes either to advance their individual goals or to shape the way in which the leadership pursues collective goals. As party government conditions strengthen, party organizations take on particular importance. Growing expectations for strong leadership in a caucus that still maintains serious internal divisions creates a set of challenges and opportunities for leaders. The party's leadership must identify common priorities, shape strategy, and build caucus support in the face of some disagreement and uncertainty (see Evans and Grandy 2009; Forgette 2004; Rohde 1991; Strahan 2007). In the terms I outlined above, the party's organizations become particularly important for the leadership's coordination function as the party attempts to place the membership on the same page, to connect committee leaders and the rest of the party, and to foster good internal communication among the party's factions. Similarly, in the strengthening party, participating party members find individual benefit in involvement in the party's decisions and direct access to the party's increasingly important resources. In the strengthening but still diverse party caucus, then, broad-based participation serves the fundamental tasks of the top leadership and benefits the rank-and-file. When party government conditions reach a very strong point, the calculus about the role of party organizations should be somewhat different for members and, in particular, for the top leadership. Although coordination is still a relevant part of the party's task, some of the impetus for broad-based coordination declines as committee actors lose influence to the more centralized party. Just as important, a highly cohesive party facing strong electoral competition has a particular incentive to use its participatory organizations for external communication (for collective electoral goals) and for persuasion (for policy as well as electoral goals) as the party becomes more homogenous and more willing to delegate power to the leadership to persuade through reward and punishment. Participation remains important to the top leadership's work, making its communication efforts more effective and facilitating an efficient persuasive process. For individual members, a very strong party that enjoys more control over the process and over benefits creates strong incentives for participation. However, to the extent that the top leadership influences the membership in participatory party organizations, the combination of strong leadership control and individual member demand may allow the top leadership to create participatory organizations that heavily favor those members who are most loyal to the elected leadership's team. Table 2.1 summarizes these ideas about how the participatory party should operate differently as party government conditions strengthen. This basic set of expectations applies most clearly to the majority party, where conditional party government dynamics are most important, but I will also explore the ways in which these changes affect the House minority.

Under what party government conditions have modern House party organizations operated? The history of the contemporary Republican and Democratic organizations stretches from a time of relatively weak party government in the early 1970s, through a period of strengthening party government conditions, and into an era of very strong party government in the mid-1990s and after. Indicators of these conditions for stronger party leadership include the level of chamber polarization and the cohesiveness of the parties (Aldrich and Rohde 2001). To these core measures of intra-party agreement and interparty disagreement, we can also add an indicator of electoral competition (Smith and Gamm 2009). As discussed earlier in the chapter, the size of the majority party is one measure of the extent to which electoral consequences will weigh in the calculation about party leadership power, potentially for both the majority and minority parties.

Figure 2.1 illustrates these changes with three measures. The first, the median difference, shows the growing gap between the first dimension DW-Nominate scores of the median Republican and the median Democrat.[9] Polarization of the two caucuses grows steadily starting in the early 1980s, reaching a high point by the mid-1990s.[10] Intraparty cohesion, measured by the ratio of majority-party DW-Nominate standard deviation to chamber standard deviation, begins an upswing in the 1970s, plateauing by the late 1980s before further increases in the 1990s. Electoral competition, as measured by the majority's proportion of House seats, rises sharply in the 104th Congress, when narrowly held Republican majorities forced out the long-standing large Democratic majority.

For the party leadership under these changing conditions, party organizations should play somewhat different roles. Although the organizations facilitate coordination, communication, and persuasion through participation across the time period, the caucuses from the late 1970s into the 1980s should find that participatory organizations are especially valuable for coordination as party government strengthens gradually with the parties remaining fairly diverse and standing committees retaining their central role in the policy process. By the end of the 1980s, when party government conditions become quite strong and policy making is more centralized—and particularly in the mid-1990s when intense electoral pressures join

TABLE 2.1. Party Government Conditions and the Roles of Participatory Party Organizations

| Party Government Conditions | Value of Participation for Members | Value of Participation for Leaders |
|---|---|---|
| *Weak* | Limited | Limited |
| *Strengthening* | Access to party resources for career, electoral, &/or policy goals. Accountability for delegated authority. | Open coordination in a diverse caucus; some persuasion and communication. |
| *Strong* | Access to party resources for career, electoral, &/or policy goals. | Communication and persuasion; controlled coordination. |

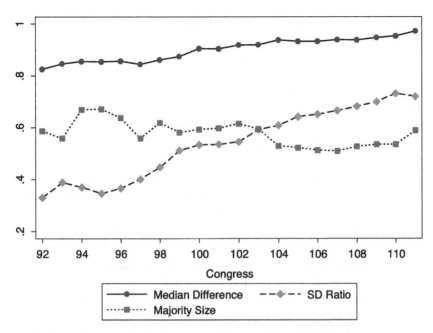

Fig. 2.1. Indicators of Party Government Strength, 92nd–111th Congresses

the mix—the party leadership should rely on the leadership organizations more heavily for external communication and persuasive tasks.

### Leader Agency and Leadership Organization Roles

Thus far, I have argued the interaction of individual goals and collective party goals provides incentives for a system of participatory party organizations. Those organizations become more important for the leadership, particularly for coordination, and valuable to members as party government conditions begin to strengthen. Participatory party organizations remain important under very strong partisan conditions, but because of the somewhat different challenges facing the leadership, the participatory organizations shift in their emphasis toward external communications and persuasive tasks. But one additional element is necessary for a full account of how party organizations function and how and when they experience changes in their roles. Although we should expect to see party organizations change over time with party polarization, cohesion, and electoral competition, some changes to the leadership organizations will be punctuated by turnover in the elected leadership of the caucus. I argue individual party leaders are able to play a key role in choices over party leadership organizations, exercising some discretion about what the organizations do and how they do it within the broader framework of delegated authority.

This claim requires a bit of additional explanation since scholarship on congressional parties and institutions has tended to avoid a focus on individuals. In particular, the agency-based view of congressional parties that dominates the literature and that I have built on for describing the role of leadership organizations does not assign much of an independent role to the party leaders themselves. In his critique of this approach, Strahan has argued "party leadership theories based on principal-agent models" typically assume leaders are "motivated by narrow self-interest of a particular type—ambition to retain a leadership office" and therefore fail to consider "how the politics of leadership might be influenced by leaders' motivations or goals, other than ambition to retain a leadership position" (Strahan 2011, 385–86). Addressing this limitation, Strahan and others (e.g., Green 2007, 2010; Moscardelli 2010; Schickler 2001) have added refinement to agency-based theories of congressional leadership by bringing individual leaders back in. In this view, leaders possess multiple *individual* goals; they do not simply channel the collective goals of the party. And those individualized leader goals can affect the direction of the party, particularly when there is some uncertainty or conflict among rank-and-file members. Leaders "usually will be active and assertive in political situations in which followers are already in agreement about what they want . . . [but] leaders can also be influential in political situations in which followers are divided or uncertain about what they want to see happen in Congress" (Strahan 2007, 11). Since party members are rarely completely united on the specifics of the party's direction, this perspective finds some latitude for individual leaders to make goal-driven choices about process, policy, or both. This perspective is consistent with earlier work emphasizing the role of individual style in the broader political context (e.g., Peters 1997), but it provides an explicit theoretical link between the individualized choices of leaders and the more general building blocks of congressional party power.

In his work on House Speakers, Green sets out a similar argument but expands it to a wider range of goals and leadership situations (Green 2007, 2010). Here, Speakers are not merely narrow agents of the party caucus: "other objectives, derived from constitutional structure and the broader political environment, drive [their] behavior as much as do the preferences and electoral needs of the congressional majority party" (Green 2010, 3). The Speaker pursues a twofold electoral goal—seeking his or her own reelection as well as that of the party's majority—and pursues policy goals that reflect his or her own personal policy preferences in addition to the party's collective policy agenda (Green 2010, 9–10). And Green persuasively shows Speakers acting to advance their own policy preferences (e.g., Newt Gingrich working against particular Republican budget cuts) or district interests (e.g., Tom Foley's active promotion of NAFTA) (Green 2010, 123–24, 127–30). While much of the action Speakers have taken can be linked directly to the party's collective policy and electoral interests, Green demonstrates that the pure agent-of-the-caucus perspective is incomplete, even in cases less exceptional than those that Strahan highlights.

The research discussed above deals primarily with the Speaker, but the argument about leader agency can be directly extended to other leadership posts, including floor leaders, the majority and minority whips, and the chairs of party committees. Like Green and Strahan's Speakers, these leaders are agents of rank-and-file principals and they have strong incentives to seek the party's collective goals. At the same time, they hold their own policy and electoral goals and, particularly for leaders in lower positions in the hierarchy, have personal interests in seeking their own career advancement. The roles and operation of the party committees and whip organizations are defined in part by party rules but also by discretionary choices of the leadership. Some of these choices are made at the highest levels of the party leadership—later chapters will, for instance, show that Speakers spearheaded major changes in the use of policy committees and in the standing-committee selection process. Other meaningful choices, such as the issue focus in the policy committees or the use of the whip system for external communication purposes, are sometimes made by the leaders at the helm of specific party organizations. In short, accounting for the individual agency of elected party leaders helps to explain the timing of some changes that have taken place in the bigger story of party government and the participatory party organizations.

Taken together, the perspectives discussed earlier provide a framework for thinking about how leadership organizations function as a critical part of the Republican and Democratic parties in the House. Members of the House delegate authority to their party leaders to create an effective long-term coalition, but members retain an interest in both monitoring the use of that authority and in enjoying the individual benefits that follow from it. The resulting demand for involvement creates an impetus for participatory organizations as party government conditions grow stronger, and party leaders find, in turn, that participation allows them to more effectively carry out the leadership tasks of coordination, persuasion, and external communication. Very strong party government makes the leadership's coordination task less complex but strengthens the demand for long- and short-term persuasion and for external communication of electoral messages. These shifts do not always occur in linear, gradual ways because the individual goals of elected party leaders observably drive some of the change in how the organizations operate within the caucus.

## A Multi-Method Approach to House Party Organizations

In chapters 3 through 6, I use this framework to examine party leadership organizations in the House since the 1970s. The objective in these chapters is twofold: to demonstrate what party organizations do for the top leadership and for the individual members who participate in them, and to show how and when the organizations have changed in their roles in the caucuses. In pursuing these objectives, I use multiple methods and data sources. In order to evaluate the operation of the party organizations over time, I rely heavily on primary-source documents from the archived papers of former House leaders, including top elected leaders as well as other members with significant involvement in leadership organizations. These papers, supplemented with secondary-source information from contemporary journalism and other writings, allow me to trace the activities of leadership organizations, how they carried out their tasks, and the participatory patterns in those groups. I combine this qualitative approach with extensive quantitative analysis of participation and its returns for party members, based on new data sets of membership in House party leadership organizations since 1975.

### Archival Evidence

Analysis based on archived primary documents was relatively rare in congressional scholarship but has become a bit more common in recent years, particularly in studies of congressional leaders and political parties (e.g., Frisch et al. 2012; Frisch and Kelly 2003; Frisch and Kelly 2006; Green 2006; Harris 2006; Kolodny 1998; Peters 1997). For the research questions in this study, primary-source research is particularly appropriate since I am interested in *process evidence* of the party leadership's activity. In order to tell the story of how party participation served collective goals as well as rank-and-file members' objectives, I need to uncover what the organizations did and compare how they operated at different points in time. The approach to evaluating process evidence of leadership choices and organizational change is necessarily interpretive (Harris 2012), informed throughout by the theoretical framework outlined here and further grounded by quantitative hypothesis testing where the data allows.

The task of evaluating primary process evidence is made more complicated by the uneven practices of retaining party leadership records. Unlike the records of standing committees and other components of Congress, the records of the House party leadership generally remain part of each leaders' personal papers and are preserved—or not—at their pleasure (Society of American Archivists 1992). Fortunately, archived papers are available from some Republican and Democratic House leaders at least through the end of the 1990s.

I have used archived documents from the papers of 11 former members. In examining each member's papers, I focused on files related to the party leadership, reviewing the contents of folders related to party committees and the whip organizations.[11] For standing committee selection records and whip count records, I sampled the files for an understanding of process over time rather than examined them page-by-page since other recent work has undertaken more systematic outcome analysis of those records (Frisch and Kelly 2006; Evans and Grandy 2009). In the leadership files, a range of meeting agendas, minutes, internal memoranda, party publications, membership lists, voting records, and member notes provided a picture of leadership organizations in operation. In addition to leadership files, I examined selected correspondence files for records of communication among leaders and between party leaders and members. Selected issue-related files in some cases provided evidence of leadership organizations' roles and activity on specific issues. In a few cases, the archived schedules of leaders offered evidence of the organizations' routine actions at a particular time. Finally, some staff files retained from staffers involved with the leadership provided memos and records of leadership processes and deliberations. In many cases, the documents used for this project have not been used previously for political science research, to my knowledge.

On the Democratic side, the most important sources are Tip O'Neill's (D-MA) and Tom Foley's (D-WA) papers. The O'Neill papers provided documentation of whip operations, membership, and strategy from the early 1970s through the early 1980s and DSPC membership and activity from 1973 into the 1980s, plus leadership correspondence and staff memos related to the extended leadership and minutes of the Democratic Caucus from the 1970s and 1980s. The Foley papers yielded information on the DSPC's membership and activity from the late 1960s through the early

1990s and whip system documentation from the 1980s, as well as leadership correspondence, staff memos, and Caucus minutes from the 1970s through the early 1990s. Because the very comprehensive Foley records end in the mid-1990s, David Bonior's (D-MI) papers were particularly important for extending my understanding of the Democratic leadership structure closer to the present day. The Bonior files provided some records of whip organization meetings, schedules, communications about and with leadership organization members, and files on the leadership's activity surrounding key contemporary issues. Other information on Democratic leadership came from the papers of Carl Albert (D-OK), Dick Gephardt (D-MO), Jim Wright (D-TX), and Bob Wise (D-WV).

For Republicans, Bob Michel's (R-IL) papers, which are organized for party leadership research, offered extensive records of the minority whip operation in the 1960s and 1970s, records on the Republican Policy Committee and Republican Research Committee (mostly from the 1980s), detailed records of the Committee on Committees, memos on leadership organization strategy and member selection, and some issue-related staff records. In addition, Michel's papers contained detailed lists of extended leadership members and structure during much of the minority period. Mickey Edwards (R-OK), who led the Republican Research Committee in the late 1980s and then the Republican Policy Committee from 1989–93, preserved many records of these leadership organizations from the 1980s and early 1990s. His files provided memos on the objectives and roles of the party committees at a critical time. The papers of Dick Armey (R-TX), while more sparse in their documentation of leadership activity, contained some valuable examples of whip organization and Policy Committee work in the early 1990s and, importantly, after the 1994 election. The Armey papers also contained documentation of GOP extended leadership membership in the 1990s that I have not located elsewhere. In addition to the papers of these leaders, I also consulted the records of former Republican member Bud Shuster (R-PA). Shuster led Republicans on the Transportation and Infrastructure Committee for many years, but he also served on the Republican Policy Committee in the 1970s and led it for one Congress (96th), running unsuccessfully for minority whip in 1980. Because the other archives contained few Policy or Research Committee records prior to the 97th Congress, Shuster's substantial pre-1981 leadership files filled a key gap in the story, particularly for the Republican Policy Committee.

Despite this extensive set of available archives, the primary records still do not cover all of the organizations in each Congress for the main period of this study. Because of these limitations, I have supplemented the primary source evidence with information on participatory party organizations from journalistic sources. This approach, which is in keeping with other recent works on congressional leadership (see, e.g., Frisch and Kelly 2006; Green 2010; Heberlig and Larson 2012; Rohde 1991; Sinclair 2006; Strahan 2007), allows me to consider leadership developments in the thinly documented recent Congresses, to fill in gaps earlier in the time period of the study, and to build context around some of the archival evidence. I rely most extensively on *Congressional Quarterly Weekly Report* (*CQ Weekly*), *National Journal*, and *Roll Call*, and to a lesser extent on *The Hill*, *Politico*, and major national newspapers as documented in the text. Archived internet records of the House parties have also been helpful in reconstructing some of the party organizations' work in the last decade, particularly for the majority Republican Policy Committee, which maintained an unusually detailed public website in the early 2000s.

### Quantitative Analysis

Although I rely heavily on interpretation of archival evidence in the subsequent chapters, many of the core ideas about participation in party leadership are testable through more systematic, quantitative analysis. For each party, I have assembled extended leadership data sets extending from the 94th Congress (1975) to the 110th Congress (2009). Based on archive-sourced lists of party organization members as well as lists found in Washington publications like *CQ Almanac* (see appendix A), these original data sets identify participants in party organizations and allow for analysis of who participates in each type of organization. In addition, the data sets support analysis of member careers in the extended party leadership, the benefits that accrue to participants in party organizations, and the connections between party participation and constituency relationships. Analysis of this data is a main focus in the next chapter on participation in leadership organizations.

# THREE

# Leadership and Membership Perspectives on Party Participation

To even a casual observer, the most striking aspect of the contemporary House party organizations is the scope of member participation in the extended leadership. The extensive reach of the whip organizations and party committees is a development of the last three decades, as the narrowly circumscribed leadership of the 1970s gave way to rapidly growing organizations by the late 1980s and early 1990s. As figure 3.1 depicts, each party's organization had expanded by the late 1990s to include over 100 members—roughly half of the House of Representatives was involved in party leadership in some way. This expansion unfolded differently in the two parties. For Republicans, the leadership structure established in the 1960s was still in place in 1981 at the start of the 97th Congress,[1] and it already involved a substantial portion of the Conference. Gradual growth in the number of leadership posts in the 1980s preceded the Gingrich-led majority's decision to involve many more members in the whip system and other organizations; the number of participating members expanded in the 104th and again in the 105th, despite the abolition of an entire party committee (the Research Committee). Democrats in the early 1970s involved very few members in the leadership—fewer than Republicans in absolute terms and even fewer as a proportion of the caucus. Steady growth in whip system and Democratic Steering and Policy Committee posts in the late 1970s and early 1980s brought a much wider swath of the caucus into

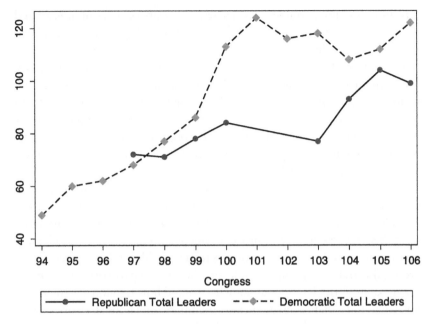

Fig. 3.1. Growth in House Party Leadership, 1975–2000
*Note:* Includes top elected leaders in each party; does not include membership in the congressional campaign committees. Data points for Republicans in the 94th–96th and 101st–102nd Congresses excluded because of incomplete data.

the leadership. But those changes, in total, only brought the Democratic extended leadership in line with the size of the minority's leadership organizations. The late 1980s—particularly the 100th and 101st Congresses—saw the most rapid expansion of the majority leadership as the total number of Democrats involved in leadership approached 120. By the end of the Clinton administration, the two parties' organizations were similarly sized, with Democrats exceeding Republicans in the proportion of the caucus involved.

The expanding scope of the extended party leadership organizations reflects their growing role in providing participatory opportunities that serve rank-and-file member goals even as they facilitate party objectives. As chapter 2 argues, a broadly participatory extended leadership has become necessary for achieving the collective policy and electoral goals of the party, but these participatory opportunities also serve the individual goals of members under stronger party government conditions. For members with intense policy interests, participation in the extended leadership offers the opportunity to take an active role in shaping party decisions about policy directions and floor strategy, particularly in members' areas of interest and standing committee work. Extended leadership activity advances members' power goals by linking them to the elected party leadership, building a foundation for future higher-level leadership activity, and, in some cases, giving them a voice in the caucus's decisions about rewarding or punishing members with committee seats and chairmanships. More broadly, party organizations provide rank-and-file members with ways to enhance their own constituency careers: along with new opportunities to serve constituency interests, members gain a position that they can use to advertise their own power and/or party loyalty.

The many members who become involved in party organizations seem to tailor their party activity to fit their individual goals. Members in the extended leadership can choose a high level of activity in their positions or limit their involvement, and process evidence points toward considerable variation in members' participation. Similarly, evidence from recent Congresses illustrates that rank-and-file members in the party organizations do not make uniform decisions about whether and how to publicize their own involvement to their constituencies—members can choose to work behind the scenes in the leadership or to make their partisan participation part of their presentation of self, in Richard Fenno's terms (Fenno 1978).

The trajectory of the party organizations since the 1970s also demonstrates that the elected party leadership, which exerts considerable control over the membership and activity of the whip system and party committees, uses its choices over participatory opportunities to affect party objectives. In service of party goals, leaders may choose to offer the broadest possible participation, with members from different components of the caucus enjoying roughly equal opportunities to benefit from involvement in the extended leadership. Conversely, under other circumstances, the top leadership may elect to structure party organizations that are weighted toward the leadership's loyalists, using party posts as a loyalty reward and to construct a tightly controlled set of party committees.

In short, participation in these structures has become an element of representation, a way in which rank-and-file members connect themselves and their constituents to the power centers of the modern House—the party caucuses. The top party leadership has strategically shaped and developed these participation opportunities to advance party objectives. This chapter considers the nature of party organization participation from the perspectives of both the members and the party leaders. I begin by tracing when and how the Republican and Democratic leadership developed expansive systems of participatory party organizations. I then turn to quantitative evidence to evaluate how the parties' top leadership has made decisions over the membership of each leadership organization. Analysis of membership rosters in each caucus over time demonstrates that the parties have varied in the extent to which they prioritize loyalty over broad-based inclusion, with changes generally following the party-government expectations outlined in chapter 2. Then, I consider the value of extended leadership involvement from the rank-and-file member's perspective. Evidence on members' involvement in the leadership over time and on the connection between extended leadership work and career advancement shows the significance of work in the party organizations for members' career goals. Finally, I ask how House members relate their party participation to their constituencies. Based on an analysis of members' websites from several Congresses, I show that members vary considerably in their decisions to publicize their party work—some members deemphasize even high-level involvement, while other members make their party leadership roles a central part of their representational style.

### Participation in the Democratic Caucus

In the reform era of the 1970s, House Democratic leaders began to experiment with a more participatory leadership structure. Tip O'Neill's election as Speaker in the 95th Congress marked the rise of a more partisan Democratic leader, but the conditions for strong majority party leadership were weak. Measures of House polarization and cohesion had barely begun to rebound in 1977 from 100-year lows, and the Democrats' share of the House had reached its second-highest point since the 1930s (see fig. 2.1). In this environment, O'Neill faced strong pressures from both the new Democratic White House and the liberal wing of the party from which he hailed, but the basic party government conditions for centralized leadership limited his ability to respond. Building on the reforms begun earlier in the decade, the party gradually strengthened its centralized leadership but did so in a way that encouraged broad involvement in party decisions.

O'Neill's "collegial personality" and political experience (Peters 1997, 212) inclined him toward a style that emphasized backroom procedural operations rather than the public leadership that was becoming common by the Carter era (Farrell 2001, chap. 18; Peters 1997, 217). The fledgling Democratic Steering and Policy Committee of the late 1970s operated in a way that reflected O'Neill's personal preference as well as the needs of a party leadership facing demands for more central coordination and persuasion. As Sinclair (1983) has explained, Democrats initiated a "leadership by inclusion" model in the DSPC. The committee brought a wider range of House Democrats into significant decision making after it was revised in the 94th Congress, and the decision to locate committee assignment decisions in the DSPC responded to demands for participation and access to power in the mid-1970s (Frisch and Kelly 2006, 57). During the Carter era, inclusion on the DSPC also meant a consultative, consensus-building role on the policy side of the committee's activity (see chapter 4). Democratic members were soon seeking out the leadership's appointments to the committee, and the Speaker had to turn away some members who wanted to participate.[2]

In the whip organization, the Democrats similarly expanded the leadership ranks and the involvement of rank-and-file members in party processes. Structurally, the leadership added a number of appointed whip positions in the 92nd–95th Congresses. Ten at-large whips and an additional deputy whip joined the two deputy whip posts already in place at the start of O'Neill's service as majority whip; these new whips reflected some of the caucus' diversity and allowed for broader participation and communication (Dodd 1979, 31). Members solicited appointed whip posts, citing loyalty to the leadership, among other factors, to justify their appointment.[3] By expanding the whip system to favor, at least initially, more junior and more leadership-loyal members (Cooper 1978; Waldman 1980, 390), the party leadership generated new participatory opportunities while also creating a counterweight to the troublesome zone whip system. The Democratic whip process began to involve an early regional count by the elected zone whips with follow-up by the appointed whips to refine and grow the initial base of support.

After the 1980 elections, O'Neill's Democratic caucus used its new participatory structure to respond to a changing political context. The loss of both the White House and the Senate to Republicans increased the importance of institutional capacity within the party for House Democrats, and party government conditions strengthened a bit as the majority's size dropped sharply. With a narrower majority, the threat of defection from the bloc of conservative southern Democrats, and continued demands for participation from a heterogeneous caucus, O'Neill maintained a diverse DSPC in the early Reagan era. He expanded the committee to include chairs of key committees and used his appointment power to increase the proportion of southern "boll weevils" on the committee in 1981 (*National Journal* 1980; *National Journal* 1981; Sinclair 1983, 75).[4]

Participatory opportunities—particularly those controlled by the leadership—grew more rapidly in the whip organization. After the 1980 electoral upheaval, Tom Foley was appointed majority whip in the House, and O'Neill and Foley continued to expand the ranks of the appointed whip system while maintaining the long-standing zone structure. The 44-member whip organization in the 97th Congress was nearly evenly divided between leadership-appointed members and elected zone members, and by the 98th, the number of appointees (26) exceeded the number of elected whips (23).[5] Further expansion at the top of the whip organization in the 99th Congress followed from O'Neill's efforts to maintain support among restive groups in the caucus at the end of his speakership (Barry 1989, 34). During this period, the top leaders apparently worked together to select members for the growing ranks of leader-appointed whips. Memos from 1985, during Foley's tenure as whip, show Foley and his staff considering both how much to expand the system for the 99th Congress and whom to appoint, although several appointments were dictated by the preferences of the Speaker and majority leader.[6]

Under both Wright and Foley's speakerships, Democrats actively sought the appointive at-large and deputy whip posts by soliciting the Speaker directly.[7] The system's expansion through the 1980s reflected this demand from the rank-and-file for participation in the system. These growing participatory expectations arose from policy interests but also from members' personal ambition—*CQ* quoted a Democratic House member in 1985 observing "there's always been ambitious people, but never quite the truckload there is today" (Granat 1985). And Hibbing's mid-1980s rankings of formal-position value place deputy whip posts and prestige committee seats at the same level of prestige (Hibbing 1991, 65).

The Foley memos on the 99th Congress whip system indicate many members had requested deputy or at-large appointments, and they discuss whether to expand the system to accommodate the demand even at the risk of "diluting" the meaning of the whip titles.[8] From its perspective, the leadership continued to recognize the value of an inclusive system. A 1988 memo noted "the Whip Organization still reflects the facts of the 1981 peak period of the Conservative Coalition. There are southern leaders prepared to play a role in the Leadership who can be encouraged through Whip appointments."[9] In this context, the leadership chose continued expansion to meet demand into the late 1980s. By the 101st Congress, the system reached a plateau of roughly 80 appointed whips, about 30 percent of the caucus (fig. 3.2). Within the broadening ranks of the whip system, some appointive whips took on distinct roles of their own. The Democratic Chief Deputy Whips of the 1980s, with their own staff and budget, began

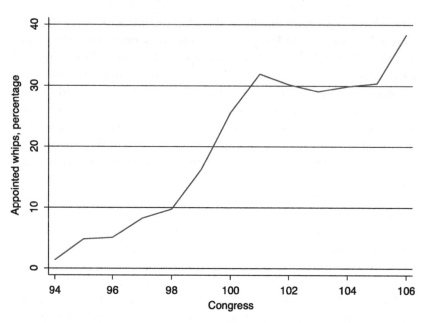

Fig. 3.2. Democratic Appointed Whips as a Percentage of Caucus, 94th–106th Congresses

to take charge of some party communication functions as well as directing the party's strategy and message on major issues.[10]

In both the DSPC and the expanded appointive whip system, then, the Democratic leadership had moved to substantially broaden participation in committee selection, policy and strategic discussions, and short-term whip efforts. In doing so, leaders of the heterogeneous caucus of the 1970s met participatory demands while also reaping the benefits of inclusion as they sought to coordinate, persuade, and respond to stronger expectations for assertive policy leadership. As these expanded majority leadership systems continued into the growing polarization and cohesion of the 1980s, the leadership not only maintained the sought-after opportunities for leadership participation but expanded them rapidly.

Although diverse participation remained an element of the top leadership's considerations into the 1990s, leadership changes and strengthening party government brought about a new emphasis on loyalty in the extended leadership, signaling that participation was becoming a kind of selective benefit, as the analysis later in the chapter shows. In the whip system, David Bonior's long tenure as whip (1991–2001) was a period of continuity in which the large structure established by whip Tony Coelho[11] was continued with both loyalty and representation affecting the leadership's decisions over participation. The size of the appointed whip system dropped temporarily in absolute terms—from about 80 members to about 60—after the loss of the majority control in 1995, although the appointed whips represented almost the same proportion of the party in the 104th as they had in the 101st. Members continued to actively solicit both at-large and deputy whip positions as well as appointed DSPC posts, sometimes tendering promises of loyalty or citing the support of other leaders.[12] After Bonior's 1991 election, a few members included with their notes of congratulations requests for involvement in the whip system, and letters to and from Bonior at the start of other Congresses in the 1990s show members eagerly sought to participate and conversations about appointed whip positions included discussions of members' past work on leadership priorities.[13] One sophomore member, for instance, contacted Bonior after winning reelection in 1994:

> I am writing to remind you of our conversation about my becoming a permanent member of the Democratic Whip Organization as an at-large-whip. I would greatly appreciate your help with this matter. I am sure you recall that I helped whip many bills during the 103rd Congress, even though I was not an official whip. . . . I look forward to discussing this with you in person in the near future.[14]

This request—a successful one—illustrates that, despite the permeability of the Democratic whip system on individual whip counts and at some whip meetings, the appointed posts themselves were of significant value to rank-and-file members. Other evidence shows the leadership in this time period was somewhat selective in its appointments. A 1999 memo shows 16 members requesting new appointments in the 106th Congress were all given whip positions, but many were not given the specific role in the system that they sought.[15] Table 3.1 contrasts the greatly expanded system at this time with the organization from two decades earlier.

Demand for representation within the leadership remained strong in the 1990s, and the top leadership faced specific pressure for inclusion in several ways. The upper ranks of the caucus leadership in the late 1980s and early 1990s were dominated by "white liberal men" (*Congressional Quarterly Weekly Report* 1991; also Burger 1991b). Seeking support for his unsuccessful first bid for Majority Whip in 1989, Bonior apparently faced demands for greater leadership representation of moderate to conservative southerners, and he promised several he would work to achieve that if elected.[16] Pressure from this Democratic constituency and others continued, and, after Bonior's successful 1991 whip election, the leadership made several changes to the whip system in the interest of greater inclusion. Speaker Foley expanded the chief deputy whip post from one position, which Bonior had held, to three (four by the end of the 102nd Congress). The leadership used this expansion to appoint representatives of three under-represented segments of the caucus—southern conservatives, women, and African-Americans—and also gave the new chief deputies automatic seats on the DSPC. Tellingly, though, the leadership responded to these participatory demands without sacrificing its efforts at advancing party goals through a unified leadership: Butler Derrick (D-SC), the new chief deputy representing the remaining cohort of southern conservatives, was both a Bonior loyalist and a far more loyal Democrat than most of his regional counterparts (Burger 1991b; Kuntz 1991). The number of chief deputies continued to grow over time, with eight named in the 109th Congress. (Along with the chief deputies, Democrats in the minority have added to the top ranks of the whip system a "parliamentarian" to monitor majority floor procedure.[17])

The Republican Congresses of 1995–2007 brought some changed incentives for Democratic leaders in their approach to the party leadership organizations, the effect of which can be seen particularly clearly in the DSPC. Party government conditions were now at 100-year highs, and narrow party margins made the stakes of party conflict particularly high. At the same time, loss of majority control (and, later, the White House) created an incentive for Democratic leaders to nurture participatory opportunities as well as capacity for communication and coordination within the House caucus. Initially, under Minority Leader Dick Gephardt, the leadership made changes to the DSPC's structure, dividing the committee into a Steering Committee and a Policy Committee.[18] The change afforded

TABLE 3.1. House Democratic Whip Organization, 94th and 105th Congresses

|  | 94th Congress | 105th Congress |
| --- | --- | --- |
| Appointed Whips | Majority Whip | Minority Whip |
|  | Chief Deputy Whip | Chief Deputy Whips (4) |
|  | Deputy Whips (3) | Deputy Whips (11) |
|  | At-Large Whips (3) | At-Large Whips (47) |
| Elected Whips | Assistant Whips (21) | Regional Whips (24) |
| *Total Whips* | **29 Whips** | **86 Whips** |

*Source: Congressional Quarterly Almanac,* 94th Congress, 1st Session; Dodd (1979); Democratic Whip list, David Bonior Papers, Box 51, Folder 37.

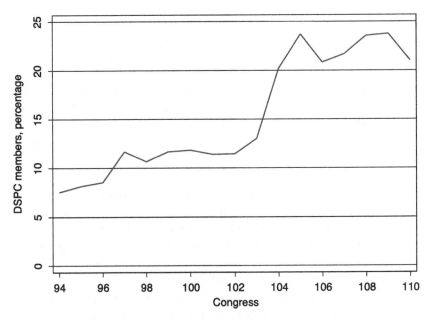

Fig. 3.3. Democratic Steering and Policy Committee Members as a Percentage of Caucus, 94th–110th Congresses

an increased number of available appointive posts to counterbalance the shrinking number of standing committee seats after 1994 (Kahn 1994b; Kahn 1995; Frisch and Kelly 2006, 217), and it provided, at least nominally, a dedicated home for party policy development (Kahn 1994a). The size of the combined committees increased substantially as a proportion of caucus membership (see fig. 3.3). At the same time, each of the two components of the DSPC now had its own set of appointed leaders, thereby expanding higher-level extended leadership opportunities. Under Nancy Pelosi, first as minority leader and later as Speaker, the DSPC was again a unified body with both policy and committee assignment roles, but the DSPC continued to grow in size with 52 members at the start of the Democratic-majority 110th Congress. The post-1994 structural changes to the DSPC reflect the concerns of the leadership and the membership with participatory opportunities in the minority as well as the majority.

The history of the DSPC and Democratic whip organization points very clearly toward the importance of party participation to members in an increasingly partisan House as well as to the top leadership's strategy of retooling the party organizations to meet the needs of strengthening party government. What began as an inclusive strategy under gradually strengthening party conditions evolved—under a similar structure—into a system that better served the party's goals under strong party government. Still, even under the polarized, cohesive, and closely competitive conditions of the mid-1990s, the party retained some internal divisions. The pressures for the top leadership to provide representation to different segments of the caucus continued. As he sought support for another term as Minority Leader, Dick Gephardt (D-MO) would emphasize his record of inclusion in the extended leadership:

> . . . We have made progress over the last two years because we have worked together as a team with an atmosphere of tolerance toward all. I have tried to build consensus through cooperation and inclusion—striving to understand and represent all of the disparate views in our richly diverse caucus. At this time we are confronted by a Republican Party which is monolithic and leadership-dominated. I intend to continue our bottom-up, Members-first policy. Throughout the last Congress, I have tried to be an effective leader by being a good listener, by ensuring that my doors are always open and that every member of our Caucus is heard and heeded. Whether in message meetings, weekly Caucuses, whip meetings, and Caucus and whip task forces, we have sought to insure that people who want to do so can participate to the fullest.[19]

### Who Participates in the Democratic Leadership?

The narrative account above illustrates the importance of leadership participation to many rank-and-file members as well as the strategic considerations that affect the elected leadership's decisions on participation in party organizations. Most of the participatory opportunities are under the control of top leaders, either in positions directly appointed by the leadership or in extended leadership roles that members enjoy *ex officio* with other leader-controlled posts, such as committee chairs. Thus, the question *who participates in the extended party leadership* is largely a question of whom the elected party leaders select; it is a question about their strategic decisions over appointments and organizational structure. The choices they make may reflect an interest in inclusiveness above all, implying that members with different voting records, constituency circumstances, and seniority would be similarly likely to be represented. Alternatively, party leaders may choose to over represent loyal members as a reward or to advance more effective party signaling, or the leaders may wish to reward those with more seniority or favor members in an electorally secure position that will allow greater attention to party activity. Examining these competing hypotheses quantitatively using several decades of leadership rosters highlights both the leadership's choices and how those strategies have changed with evolving party government conditions and individual leadership styles.

### Appointed Democratic Whips

Table 3.2 presents models of appointed whip organization membership. The dependent variable of each logit model is an indicator of appointed whip status for each Democrat in the Congress of record (95th–106th). The independent variables represent key factors related to the representativeness of the membership—party loyalty, ideological centrism in the caucus (indicator variable for middle third of the party's DW-Nominate range), length of tenure, electoral security (share of the two-party vote), as well as an indicator for the south to capture whether this distinctive region within the caucus is overrepresented. (See appendix A for data information).[20]

The results show the whip systems of the O'Neill Democratic caucus embodied the inclusion strategy, with more loyal members no more likely to appear in the appointed whip system than less loyal members. Even as O'Neill and the other leaders of the post-reform period sought a more streamlined, effective, and expansive whip system, they also maintained a heterogeneous network. This pattern changed in the stronger party conditions of the late 1980s when more loyal Democrats were significantly more likely to be appointed whips. By the 102nd Congress, more senior Democrats also were more likely to be whips, a relationship that had never emerged in the earlier period. After the Democrats' shift to minority-party status, the party unity and tenure variables continued to be significant and positive predictors of whip membership through the 106th Congress, the last Congress for which complete data on appointed whips is available. This shift toward greater loyalty among appointed whips does not appear for the regionally elected zone whips, who are not subject to leadership selection (Meinke 2008, 657–59). Finally, in contrast to the loyalty and tenure effects among the appointed whips, the centrist, south, and electoral security measures show no clear trends in their relationship to whip selection over time.

This simple analysis of the whip system's composition provides some quantitative support for portions of the qualitative picture of whip system participation. The system began to take on its modern form under an inclusive model in the late 1970s and early 1980s. Later leaders maintained

TABLE 3.2. Democratic Whip System Unelected Membership, 95th–106th Congresses

| | 95th | 96th | 97th | 98th | 99th | 100th | 101st | 102nd | 103rd | 104th | 105th | 106th |
|---|---|---|---|---|---|---|---|---|---|---|---|---|
| Party Unity | 0.016 | 0.036 | 0.033 | 0.014 | −0.009 | 0.028 | 0.038** | 0.033*** | 0.043*** | 0.025* | 0.040** | 0.045*** |
| | (0.020) | (0.027) | (0.022) | (0.022) | (0.016) | (0.018) | (0.018) | (0.017) | (0.018) | (0.015) | (0.017) | (0.016) |
| Party Centrist | 0.078 | 0.448 | 1.119** | 0.164 | −0.013 | 0.370 | 0.790*** | 0.432 | 0.673** | 0.401 | 0.208 | 0.084 |
| | (0.560) | (0.605) | (0.494) | (0.425) | (0.379) | (0.302) | (0.292) | (0.287) | (0.315) | (0.359) | (0.340) | (0.323) |
| Tenure (log) | −0.164 | 0.264 | −0.119 | 0.210 | 0.146 | −0.064 | 0.114 | 0.393** | 0.744*** | 0.508** | 0.600*** | 0.458** |
| | (0.242) | (0.302) | (0.302) | (0.183) | (0.202) | (0.162) | (0.200) | (0.186) | (0.166) | (0.206) | (0.198) | (0.199) |
| South | 0.327 | 0.370 | 0.534 | −0.265 | −0.235 | −0.059 | −0.002 | 0.021 | 0.140 | −0.145 | 0.423 | 0.344 |
| | (0.538) | (0.569) | (0.644) | (0.601) | (0.453) | (0.369) | (0.347) | (0.325) | (0.332) | (0.371) | (0.367) | (0.355) |
| Vote Share | 0.011 | 0.061*** | 0.037*** | −0.000 | −0.007 | −0.008 | −0.018* | 0.002 | −0.007 | 0.002 | −0.004 | −0.003 |
| | (0.010) | (0.017) | (0.014) | (0.013) | (0.011) | (0.009) | (0.010) | (0.009) | (0.012) | (0.013) | (0.013) | (0.010) |
| Constant | −4.860*** | −11.12*** | −8.190*** | −3.493 | −0.393 | −2.941 | −3.247** | −4.663*** | −5.601*** | −3.959*** | −5.027*** | −4.940*** |
| | (1.528) | (2.745) | (2.167) | (2.221) | (1.688) | (1.803) | (1.641) | (1.662) | (1.784) | (1.437) | (1.606) | (1.485) |
| N | 272 | 268 | 235 | 263 | 247 | 256 | 253 | 264 | 253 | 197 | 202 | 205 |

*Note:* Cell entries are logit coefficients with standard errors in parentheses. Rare-events logit estimation used for 95th–99th Congress models. Extreme party unity outliers ($<25\%$) excluded.

***$p < .01$, **$p < .05$, *$p < .10$, two-tailed tests.

that expanded, heavily appointive network, but both the strengthening party government conditions and the shift to more assertive, centralized leadership goals, beginning with the Wright speakership, led to a modification in the way the leadership filled out the established and elaborate network of whips. In addition to this move toward an expanded and party-loyal team, other evidence shows the leadership began to prioritize fundraising support in selecting whips and other extended leaders in the late 1990s and early 2000s, continuing the pattern of movement toward loyalty using a different measure of member support for the party's collective goals (Heberlig and Larson 2007; Heberlig and Larson 2012).

## DSPC Members

Since its reorganization in the 1970s, the DSPC has included some leadership appointees alongside a larger number of regionally elected and *ex officio* members. Although available data does not allow for a consistent analysis of only appointed membership over time,[21] it is possible to model the full membership as a reflection of leadership decisions over both appointments and the overall structure. Tables 3.3 and 3.4 display a series of rare-events logit models predicting membership in the DSPC across this time period again using unity, centrism, tenure, region, and electoral security as independent variables.

The results present a fairly consistent picture of DSPC membership. In contrast to the evidence from the Democratic whip system, there is no evidence that the leadership has changed the organization's composition systematically with party government conditions. Rather, the full DSPC has almost always overrepresented more senior House Democrats. In the first Congress of the newly empowered DSPC (94th), the relatively small DSPC membership was significantly more loyal and more senior than other members of the caucus. The seniority effect endured through the entire Democratic majority period; as table 3.3 shows, tenure was the one consistently significant predictor of DSPC membership through the 103rd Congress. In several Democratic-majority Congresses, a positive effect for party loyalty reaches statistically significant levels, suggesting a DSPC membership that was significantly more loyal than the rank-and-file in the Democratic caucus (96th, 99th, and 100th Congresses). After the Democrats lost the majority in 1994, the DSPC followed a generally similar pattern (table 3.4), with higher seniority continuing to predict DSPC membership through the 108th Congress. Interestingly, the data also supports contemporary observations that the Pelosi-led DSPC was relatively diverse, with seniority no longer significantly related to DSPC member-

TABLE 3.3. Democratic Steering and Policy Committee, Full Membership, 94th–103rd Congresses

| | 94th | 95th | 96th | 97th | 98th | 99th | 100th | 101st | 102nd | 103rd |
|---|---|---|---|---|---|---|---|---|---|---|
| Party Unity | 0.040** | 0.028 | 0.051* | -0.002 | 0.014 | 0.038* | 0.047** | 0.018 | 0.033 | 0.045 |
| | (0.020) | (0.018) | (0.027) | (0.013) | (0.015) | (0.021) | (0.024) | (0.018) | (0.031) | (0.037) |
| Party Centrist | -0.750 | -0.173 | 0.390 | 0.262 | -0.475 | -0.163 | -0.122 | 0.504 | 0.792* | 0.471 |
| | (0.516) | (0.465) | (0.519) | (0.446) | (0.463) | (0.450) | (0.432) | (0.432) | (0.405) | (0.400) |
| Tenure (log) | 0.849*** | 0.437** | 0.556** | 0.718*** | 0.907*** | 0.750*** | 0.845*** | 0.728*** | 0.733*** | 0.845*** |
| | (0.291) | (0.218) | (0.234) | (0.239) | (0.234) | (0.263) | (0.236) | (0.287) | (0.204) | (0.231) |
| South | 0.681 | 0.490 | 0.742 | 0.249 | 0.595 | 0.650 | 0.412 | 0.395 | 0.706 | 0.374 |
| | (0.618) | (0.542) | (0.493) | (0.482) | (0.451) | (0.448) | (0.466) | (0.476) | (0.461) | (0.438) |
| Vote Share | -0.013 | 0.005 | 0.018 | 0.014 | -0.016 | 0.009 | 0.007 | 0.023 | -0.002 | -0.007 |
| | (0.017) | (0.013) | (0.015) | (0.015) | (0.014) | (0.011) | (0.012) | (0.015) | (0.012) | (0.018) |
| Constant | -5.721*** | -5.584*** | -9.070*** | -4.027** | -3.570** | -7.384*** | -8.265*** | -7.009*** | -6.619** | -7.097** |
| | (2.220) | (1.767) | (3.038) | (1.576) | (1.678) | (2.386) | (2.482) | (2.067) | (2.693) | (3.176) |
| N | 278 | 276 | 272 | 239 | 267 | 251 | 260 | 258 | 267 | 257 |

*Note:* Cell entries are rare-events logit coefficients with standard errors in parentheses. Extreme party unity outliers (<25%) excluded.

***$p < .01$, **$p < .05$, *$p < .10$, two-tailed tests.

TABLE 3.4. Democratic Steering and Policy Committee, Full Membership, 104th–110th Congresses

| | 104th | 105th | 106th | 107th | 108th | 109th | 110th |
|---|---|---|---|---|---|---|---|
| Party Unity | 0.021 | 0.012 | 0.028 | 0.013 | −0.009 | 0.021 | −0.002 |
| | (0.013) | (0.016) | (0.019) | (0.017) | (0.023) | (0.023) | (0.038) |
| Party Centrist | 0.551 | 0.341 | 0.172 | −0.016 | −0.250 | 0.024 | 0.032 |
| | (0.404) | (0.356) | (0.377) | (0.371) | (0.376) | (0.362) | (0.356) |
| Tenure (log) | 0.872*** | 0.835*** | 0.958*** | 0.787*** | 0.503** | 0.186 | 0.304 |
| | (0.225) | (0.219) | (0.263) | (0.266) | (0.225) | (0.258) | (0.212) |
| South | 0.857* | −0.056 | 0.450 | 0.758* | 0.042 | 0.165 | 0.339 |
| | (0.448) | (0.395) | (0.419) | (0.400) | (0.401) | (0.416) | (0.349) |
| Vote Share | −0.008 | 0.001 | −0.001 | −0.004 | 0.004 | 0.029** | 0.022** |
| | (0.017) | (0.014) | (0.011) | (0.011) | (0.011) | (0.012) | (0.011) |
| Constant | −4.488** | −3.551** | −5.331*** | −3.628** | −1.340 | −5.614*** | −3.418 |
| | (1.747) | (1.800) | (1.853) | (1.647) | (2.018) | (2.050) | (3.361) |
| *N* | 201 | 206 | 210 | 209 | 204 | 202 | 235 |

*Note:* Cell entries are rare-events logit coefficients with standard errors in parentheses.
***$p < .01$, **$p < .05$, *$p < .10$, two-tailed tests.

ship in the 109th and 110th Congresses, and only members' own electoral security significantly predicting membership.

## Participation in the Republican Conference

House Republicans developed a substantial system of partisan organizations in the late 1950s and early 1960s, in part to satisfy the participatory interests of members who hoped to shape the minority's policy and electoral direction. Dissatisfaction with the party's electoral defeats and enduring minority status led the party to reorganize the Republican Policy Committee and, later, the separate Research Committee, which joined the existing regional whip organization. The new GOP organizations provided an important center for rank-and-file involvement during a time of limited institutional resources, offering a kind of shadow government in which Republican House members could participate to advance their individual goals (Connolly and Pitney 1994, chap. 3).

The Republican Policy Committee in the minority provides a good example. Surveys of Republican member opinion on the Policy Committee in the 1960s revealed that members valued the participatory functions of the committee and that they generally judged the Committee's effectiveness positively (Jones 1964, chap. 4; Speed 1964, 25). Republicans on the Policy Committee in the 1960s found membership valuable, in part because of the prestige it conveyed to constituents, because of the informational benefits the committee provided, and because it offered a "step up the leadership ladder" (Jones 1964, 101–5). In the last years before Republicans regained the majority in 1995, Connolly and Pitney made similar observations about the GOP leadership organization, noting that "for a Republican craving prestige, a party post provides the best available substitute for the legislative power enjoyed by Democrats" (1994, 46).

Archival records further support this view, documenting the participatory value rank-and-file members saw in the extended leadership of the Reagan-era GOP conference. The minority leader appointed between 7 and 10 members to the Republican Policy Committee during this time, and appointment decisions involved consultation between the Policy Committee chair and the minority leader.[22] Letters to the leadership and internal notes show members actively sought out appointment to the committee.[23] In one illustrative example, Henson Moore (R-LA) sent a lengthy letter to Michel pleading for an appointment to the Policy Committee in the 97th Congress, describing the committee as "one of the most important bodies in the House" because it would "form positions and recommend them to our membership on matters most important to the recovery of our nation, the success of the Reagan Administration, and our hopes to build a Republican majority in the House in 1982." Moore went on to cite numerous factors to support his request for an at-large appointment—including his electoral security, his committee and floor-voting participation, his standing committee background, his "mainstream" and party-loyal voting record within the Conference, and the fact that "no Louisiana Republican has ever served on the Policy Committee."[24] At least for some Republicans, the Policy Committee represented a desirable post that was seen as a reward for loyal behavior and hard work electorally and legislatively.

Along with the Policy Committee, the Republican Research Committee offered a center for interested members of the Conference to participate in party processes with informational, position-taking, and (potentially) career benefits. From its start in the 89th Congress, the Research Committee operated largely on a task-force model, with members of the committee leading task forces to conduct and produce substantive background research on broad issues (Jones 1970, 38, 158–59). The Research Committee, officially speaking, consisted of all members of the Conference, and the task forces of the committee were open to members of the Conference who wished to volunteer. The executive committee of the Republican Research Committee, chaired by a Republican leader elected to the post, consisted of 20 to 30 members, including all of the Conference's elected leadership, several class representatives, and a number of appointees. The leadership appears to have made an effort at representation of the Conference in constituting the executive committee; regions were represented in the appointed membership, and the committee in the late 1980s formally included the chairs of the main Republican caucuses (the Conservative Opportunity Society, the Republican Study Committee, the Wednesday Group, and the "92 Group") in its membership.[25] The Research Committee's task force activity varied from Congress to Congress, and some task forces drew heavy member involvement while others rarely met or yielded only staff-driven research.[26] When task forces were active, though, they drew large numbers of minority party members who sought opportunities for involvement in defined issue areas. In the 100th Congress, 40 percent of the Conference participated on at least one Research task force[27] and a similar proportion was active in the committee task forces of the 102nd Congress (Little and Patterson 1993, 62).

The House GOP whip organization did not expand participatory opportunities during the 1970s and 1980s at the rapid rate embraced by majority Democrats. Following the same basic regional, appointive structure that had been in place for decades, the Republican whip system involved roughly 20 members during this time period (see fig. 3.4). With the sudden expansion of the Conference after the 1980 election, newly elected minority whip Trent Lott (R-MS) added new positions to the structure, opening new participatory opportunities for the larger membership. Two new deputy whips and four additional assistant regional whips kept the whip system's relative size roughly steady as a proportion of the Conference and set the stage for increasing whip-count activity in the 1980s. Later, Newt Gingrich's whip team (in the 101st Congress and after) worked to draw in more elements of the Conference in his effort at broadened public whip strategies. Recruiting members from in and outside of the formal whip organization, Gingrich held weekly "Strategy Whip" meetings of about 25 GOP members.[28]

The oldest component of the House Republican organization—the Committee on Committees—was structured for very broad participation during the GOP minority period and gave the Conference's membership considerable decentralized control over committee assignments. Although the real assignment decisions were centered in a smaller group, the organization represented a long-standing decision by the Conference to locate one of the party's most important decisions in a participatory venue. In the 1970s and 1980s, the World War I-vintage structure of the Committee on Committees prescribed a very large organization with nearly 50

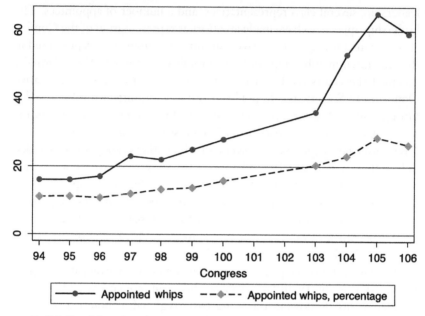

Fig. 3.4. Republican Appointed Whips, 94th–106th Congresses
Note: 101st and 102nd Congresses excluded because of missing data.

members—one for each state having at least one Republican representative, chosen by the members from that state—more than a quarter of the Conference.[29] In voting to approve slates of nominees for standing committees, members of the full Committee on Committees cast a number of votes equivalent to the number of House Republicans elected from their state. The full committee, however, functioned as a rubber stamp for an Executive Committee on Committees, a smaller group of about 20 members (a little over 10 percent of the Conference) who, in most cases, represented "individual multistate groups" and were "chosen by a caucus of each individual multistate group."[30]

Members who participated on the Executive Committee held the real power in the committee selection process from at least the 1950s until the 104th Congress (Masters 1961). Table 3.5 depicts the somewhat byzantine structure of the Executive Committee in the 99th Congress. In this example, 22 executive committee members cast votes equivalent to the total number of Republicans in the House. States with at least five Republican House members received their own seat on the committee, while smaller states had their votes grouped together according to the number of members from the state. Small-state groups with 18 or more votes were given two seats on the Executive Committee, with the designated votes split between the two representatives.[31] This structure allowed small-state representatives a voice, but it preserved the concentrated influence for Executive Committee members from the largest states, and it had the effect of giving some disproportionate regional influence to the Midwest and the East (see also Frisch and Kelly 2006, 46–51). Overall, in contrast to the

TABLE 3.5. Republican Executive Committee on Committees, 99th Congress, and Republican Steering Committee, 105th Congress

| 99th Congress: Executive Committee on Committees | 105th Congress: Republican Steering Committee |
| --- | --- |
| *Leadership* | *Leadership* |
| Minority Leader | Speaker (3 votes) |
| Minority Whip | Majority Leader (2 votes) |
| | Majority Whip |
| *State Representatives* | Speaker's Appointees (2 x 1 vote) |
| California (18 votes) | Conference Chair |
| New York (15 votes) | Policy Committee Chair |
| Ohio (10 votes) | NRCC Chair |
| Pennsylvania (10 votes) | NRCC Past Chair |
| Texas (10 votes) | Appropriations Chair |
| Illinois (9 votes) | Budget Chair |
| Florida (7 votes) | Rules Chair |
| Michigan (7 votes) | Ways & Means Chair |
| New Jersey (6 votes) | |
| Virginia (6 votes) | *Regional Representatives* |
| Indiana (6 votes) | California |
| North Carolina (5 votes) | Cotton South |
| 4-member States (2 x 8 votes) | East North Central |
| 3-member States (2 x 15 votes) | Great Plains |
| 2-member States (2 x 9 votes) | Mid-Atlantic |
| 1-member States (11 votes) | Atlantic Coast |
| | Tidewater South |
| *Class Representatives* | West South Central |
| Freshman Class (1 vote) | West |
| Sophomore (1 vote) | Small State Representative |
| | *Class Representatives* |
| | Freshman Class |
| | Sophomore Class (2 x 1 vote) |
| *Total Members*: 23 | *Total Members*: 26 |
| *Total Votes*: 186 | *Total Votes*: 29 |

*Source*: Executive Committee on Committees, 27 Dec 1984, Michel Papers, Leadership Series, Box 7, Folder: 99th—Committee on Committees—Executive Committee; Steering Committee Notice, Office of the Speaker, 15 Oct 1998, Armey Collection, Legislative Series, Box 55, Folder 4.

*Note*: All members of the Steering Committee (105th Congress) cast one vote except where noted in the table.

post-reform Democratic committee selection process, committee assign-ments in the GOP remained centered in a process that was not only par-ticipatory but also subject to little top-down leadership control.

In somewhat different ways, each of the minority-era House Repub-lican organizations linked members' individual participatory interests to broader party goals. The structure of these organizations remained largely constant from the 1960s until the GOP won the majority in 1994; this system permitted a very large portion of the Conference to participate. As figure 3.1 shows, in the early 1980s, the absolute number of Republicans in the Research Committee, the Policy Committee, the Executive Com-mittee on Committees, and the whip organization roughly matched the number of Democrats in the DSPC and Democratic whip system—despite the much smaller size of the Republican membership. Rank-and-file GOP members who did not enjoy access to the same committee or subcom-mittee chair positions and staff resources could receive policy, career, and electoral benefits from formal involvement with the party organization.

### Participation in the Republican Majority

Seizing the majority in the 104th Congress, the Gingrich-led Republican Conference implemented major changes to its organizational structure that permanently changed the locus of member participation in party leadership. The leadership disbanded the Research Committee, ending the policy-development participation its task forces had provided for a large group of minority members, particularly in the last decade of the Republican minor-ity. The Republican Policy Committee continued with a large membership, even growing in 1995 to keep pace with the increased size of the Confer-ence (see fig. 3.5). The majority Policy Committee, with a narrower role in the Conference, offered more limited benefits for members, but members continued to request appointment and the leadership used appointments to reward active members.[32] In the same wave of changes, the Republican Committee on Committees became the Republican Steering Committee and lost the considerable autonomy it had enjoyed in the minority. The Steering Committee still served as an entree into leadership activity, how-ever. As chapter 6 discusses in more detail, the restructured Steering Com-mittee grew in absolute terms (see fig. 3.6) and changed in structure to place much more decision-making influence with the top leadership.

The younger and more energized membership of the new majority Republican Conference still would benefit from participation in the party, but the energetic center of this broad-based participation was now in the

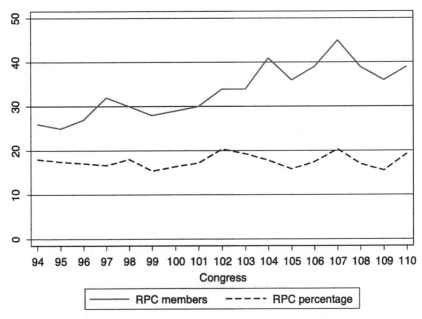

Fig. 3.5. Republican Policy Committee Membership

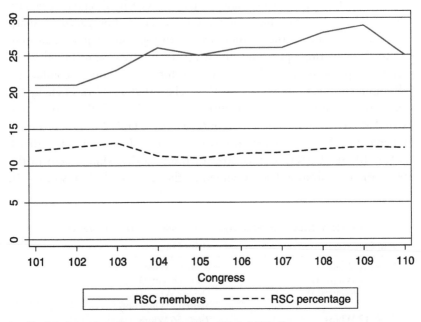

Fig. 3.6. Republican Steering Committee, 101st–110th Congresses
Note: Data reflects Committee on Committees before 104th Congress, Steering Committee for 104th–110th Congresses.

whip organization. During the previous decade, Trent Lott and Newt Gingrich had overseen an increase in whip activity, and Gingrich had increased the profile of the Republican whip organization, but the structure and process still closely resembled the minority whip of the 1960s and 1970s—and it stood in sharp contrast to the extensive, inclusive Democratic whip system. The new majority's needs and the demands of the vocal rank-and-file led the new Speaker and the majority whip (Tom DeLay, R-TX) to reinvent the Republican whip system. The freshmen (73 in total) and class-of-1992 sophomores constituted more than half of the Conference and yielded a majority that was, as Sinclair has observed, "both unusually homogenous ideologically and determined to enact major policy change" (Sinclair 2006, 123; also Fenno 1997). This determined and ideological majority, though, also rested on a much narrower margin than any in modern House history, the smallest majority since the last Republican-controlled House in 1953–54.

The whip organization for this new majority involved a very large base of members, although the membership analysis below shows that it was not a particularly representative group. DeLay's new broad and efficient whip organization included a Chief Deputy Whip (Dennis Hastert, R-IL), 13 deputy whips, and 40 assistant whips overseen by designated deputy whips.[33] Altogether, the whip system grew at a rate that outpaced the sharp increase in the size of the Conference. With the chief deputy managing day-to-day counting operations, the whip system drew on its broad-based membership and developed a fast routine for vote counting, conducting full counts in several hours (Cohen 1995; Hastert 2004, 120). Then, by the start of the second Republican-majority Congress in 1997, the whip system expanded further to include a total of 66 whips, as table 3.6 shows—nearly 30 percent of the Conference, compared to about 20 percent in the 103rd. As Roy Blunt (R-MO) took control of the majority whip system in the 2000s, the organization had expanded further to a total of 76 whips—16

TABLE 3.6. House Republican Whip Organization, 94th and 105th Congresses

| 94th Congress | 105th Congress |
| --- | --- |
| Minority Whip | Majority Whip |
| Regional Whips (4) | Chief Deputy Whip |
| Assistant Regional Whips (12) | Deputy Whips (16) |
| | Assistant Whips (48) |
| Total: **17 Whips** | Total: **66 Whips** |

Source: *Congressional Quarterly Almanac*, 94th Congress, 1st Session; *Congressional Quarterly's Politics in America 1998*.

deputy whips and 60 assistant whips, including 11 freshman members. By this time, the whip system was tightly controlled by the top leadership, and member participation in the system was almost exclusively behind the scenes. In a practice that soon became common for both Democratic and Republican whips, the Republican majority whip now kept the full whip roster as a tightly held secret (Crabtree and Billings 2002; Remini 2006).

Republicans in the majority found that the intersection of party goals, as shaped by Gingrich's particular choices, and the individual interests of members required continuing participation opportunities, even in a Conference with a far more centralized power structure. For a party focused on moving an ideological agenda and maintaining a narrowly held majority, a large and reliable whip system provided a necessary leadership tool that also offered many rank-and-file members opportunities to gain policy and process information and advance career goals. And with a majority strongly led from the center, the coordination opportunities the Research and Policy Committees had provided before 1995 were no longer a major part of the participation activities offered in the Conference.

### Who Participates in the Republican Leadership?

The GOP organizations, like their Democratic counterparts, are constituted in part by appointment and in part through positions held *ex officio* or chosen by election from a Conference subgroup. As in the Democratic case, analysis of Republican organization membership can shed light on how both leadership appointment decisions and the structural design of organizations affect the representativeness of the extended leadership. Since the 1994 election marked a sudden shift in Republican organizations, in contrast to the secular change in Democratic organizations from the 1970s through the 1990s, the analysis of the GOP allows the opportunity to see how majority status and the new leadership affected representation and participation in the party.

### Republican Whips

In contrast to the Democrats, who have long elected their regional whips, the Republicans have always appointed all of the whips below the minority or majority whip. Tables 3.7 and 3.8 display models of GOP whip organization membership for the 94th Congress through the 107th Congress (the last for which appointed whip lists are available). These models are structured similarly to the models of Democratic organizations above, except for the regional variables, which test for representational differences in the southern and western regions that were increasingly important to the party.

The results in table 3.7 show that the immediate post-reform era minority whip systems were generally representative of the Republican Conference. With primarily regionally based representation, the whips did not differ significantly from the Conference except on tenure in the 95th and 96th Congresses, where higher seniority predicted whip membership, and on party loyalty in the 96th. This tradition of a representative Republican whip system generally held through the 1980s and even into the first two Congresses when Newt Gingrich was minority whip.[34]

Changes started with the 103rd Congress (table 3.8) when the GOP whip organization began to look more loyal and more senior than the rest of the rank-and-file. But after the 1994 election, Republicans appointed about 50 new whips, and only a few whips who had served in the 103rd Congress were returned to the system. During the rest of the 1990s, the whips were significantly more *junior* than the rest of the Conference, and they were significantly more loyal to the party in the 104th, 106th, and 107th Congresses (105th Congress, $p = .15$, two-tailed). As figure 3.7 illustrates, the whips in the 104th Congress were overwhelmingly drawn from the cohort of GOP members elected in or after 1992—the group that was the driving force in the new majority (Rae 1998). In the following two Congresses, that cohort only became more dominant in the Republican whip organization. By the 107th Congress, tenure no longer has a negative effect on membership in the logit model, but this result reflects both the "aging" of the early-90s cohort and the truncated available whip list for the 107th Congress, which excludes the lowest-level whips.

The overall picture of the House Republican whips from the mid-1970s through the early 2000s is one of change from a small, regionally based group of appointees—who served to represent the cohorts and degrees of loyalty within the party well—to a much larger organization of mostly junior loyalists. The shift to a disproportionately loyal whip organization came later for the Republicans than for Democrats; it did not coincide neatly with the strengthening party government conditions of the 1980s, and instead it followed the rise of more sharply partisan leadership and narrow majority control in the 1990s. Blunt's focus on the loyalty of Republican whips in the 2000s (see chapter 6) provides a strong reason to assume the trend of a significantly more loyal whip organization has continued in later Congresses for which full whip rosters are not yet available.

TABLE 3.7. Republican Appointed Whips, 94th–102nd Congresses

| | 94th | 95th | 96th | 97th | 98th | 99th | 100th | 101st | 102nd |
|---|---|---|---|---|---|---|---|---|---|
| Party Unity | 0.002 | 0.032 | 0.036** | 0.026 | 0.002 | 0.023 | 0.018 | 0.011 | 0.023 |
| | (0.016) | (0.020) | (0.017) | (0.017) | (0.014) | (0.014) | (0.014) | (0.017) | (0.025) |
| Party Centrist | -0.054 | -0.571 | -0.120 | 0.163 | -0.044 | -0.155 | -0.128 | -0.394 | -0.786 |
| | (0.554) | (0.582) | (0.579) | (0.489) | (0.547) | (0.523) | (0.484) | (0.590) | (0.774) |
| Vote Share | 0.013 | -0.011 | 0.014 | 0.019 | 0.011 | 0.018 | 0.021 | 0.011 | -0.023 |
| | (0.028) | (0.018) | (0.020) | (0.020) | (0.018) | (0.018) | (0.014) | (0.018) | (0.019) |
| Tenure (log) | 0.271 | 0.569** | 1.103*** | 0.153 | 0.068 | 0.311 | 0.191 | -0.473 | 0.320 |
| | (0.229) | (0.281) | (0.328) | (0.339) | (0.316) | (0.347) | (0.299) | (0.297) | (0.236) |
| South | 0.138 | -0.228 | -0.437 | -0.063 | 0.333 | -0.255 | -0.026 | 0.136 | -0.461 |
| | (0.601) | (0.596) | (0.668) | (0.588) | (0.639) | (0.548) | (0.500) | (0.599) | (0.672) |
| West | 0.189 | -0.093 | 0.091 | 0.080 | -0.114 | -0.699 | -0.322 | -0.162 | -0.951 |
| | (0.695) | (0.682) | (0.716) | (0.624) | (0.726) | (0.694) | (0.657) | (0.722) | (0.872) |
| Constant | -3.041 | -4.111** | -7.157*** | -5.460*** | -2.723** | -4.889*** | -4.621*** | -2.851* | -2.357 |
| | (2.278) | (1.921) | (1.693) | (1.817) | (1.383) | (1.428) | (1.524) | (1.672) | (2.647) |
| N | 137 | 139 | 152 | 185 | 158 | 173 | 171 | 168 | 158 |

*Note:* Cell entries are rare-events logit coefficients with robust standard errors in parentheses. Excludes elected party leaders.

\*\*\*$p < .01$, \*\*$p < .05$, \*$p < .10$, two-tailed tests.

## Republican Policy Committee

The Policy Committee's membership consistently has been a mix of top Conference leaders, regionally selected representatives, and leadership appointees. The committee has grown, especially since 1994, as the party has expanded the list of appointees, the number of represented regions, and the standing committee chairs included in membership. In the earlier years of the Policy Committee, its representativeness was a point of contention, with members concerned in particular about how well the elected and appointed members represented the more junior members of the Conference (Jones 1964). The committee's structure, in the 1960s and more recently, indicated a concern with maintaining representation for leadership, regions, and more junior members; however, the increase in appointive members, particularly in the early 1990s, suggests that the leadership has sought to exert more control over the committee's membership, either to affect its activity or to use the posts as reward, or both.

The logit analyses in tables 3.9 and 3.10 provide a look at the Congress-by-Congress representativeness of the Policy Committee between 1975 and 2008. In the late 1970s, when the committee was relatively small but dominated by the leadership and its appointees, committee members had significantly higher party loyalty and greater seniority than other Conference members. In the 97th Congress, as the committee expanded somewhat

TABLE 3.8. Republican Appointed Whips, 103rd–107th Congresses

|                | 103rd | 104th | 105th | 106th | 107th |
|----------------|-------|-------|-------|-------|-------|
| Party Unity    | 0.049** | 0.059* | 0.038 | 0.060** | 0.120** |
|                | (0.024) | (0.035) | (0.026) | (0.030) | (0.056) |
| Party Centrist | −0.316 | 0.445 | 0.281 | 0.196 | −0.186 |
|                | (0.442) | (0.352) | (0.332) | (0.338) | (0.429) |
| Vote Share     | 0.016 | 0.032** | 0.008 | 0.012 | −0.016 |
|                | (0.015) | (0.014) | (0.015) | (0.010) | (0.016) |
| Tenure (log)   | 0.637*** | −0.931*** | −0.727*** | −0.452* | 0.678** |
|                | (0.192) | (0.276) | (0.242) | (0.258) | (0.308) |
| South          | −0.743 | −0.485 | −0.399 | −0.221 | −0.093 |
|                | (0.493) | (0.415) | (0.386) | (0.391) | (0.497) |
| West           | −0.754 | −0.267 | −0.588 | −0.271 | −0.409 |
|                | (0.576) | (0.462) | (0.437) | (0.449) | (0.578) |
| Constant       | −6.978*** | −7.873** | −3.807 | −6.645** | −12.682** |
|                | (2.238) | (3.304) | (2.481) | (2.678) | (5.251) |
| N              | 170 | 228 | 221 | 212 | 211 |

***$p < .01$, **$p < .05$, *$p < .10$, two-tailed tests.

†Dependent variable data for 107th Congress is incomplete; see text for discussion.

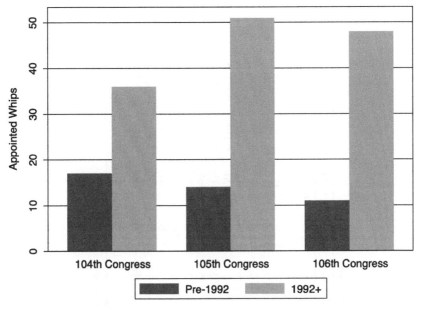

Fig. 3.7. Electoral Cohorts in the 1990s Republican Whip System

to include more ranking committee members and freshmen and sopho-more class members,[35] committee members' loyalty was not significantly different, on average, from other GOP members; after the 97th, Policy Committee member seniority also was not significantly different from that of the rank-and-file. From the 98th Congress through the 102nd, the Pol-icy Committee was, as a whole, roughly representative of the Conference on party loyalty, tenure, and electoral security, as well as in the proportion of the committee from the increasingly important southern and western regions.

As later chapters will demonstrate, by the early 1990s, Republicans began to use the committee less for coordinating among party members on positions and strategy and more for partisan messaging and, later in the majority, for building connections with the administration and outside groups. As these changes unfolded, the committee returned to overrepre-sentation of more party-loyal members. Policy Committee members were significantly more loyal than other members in the 103rd through 108th Congresses. More senior members were significantly overrepresented in the 103rd and 104th, as well as in the 108th. The general skew toward a more loyal and more senior membership fades in the latest Congresses,

TABLE 3.9. Republican Policy Committee Full Membership, 94th–103rd Congresses

| | 94th | 95th | 96th | 97th | 98th | 99th | 100th | 101st | 102nd | 103rd |
|---|---|---|---|---|---|---|---|---|---|---|
| Party Unity | 0.033** | 0.023 | 0.043** | 0.013 | 0.006 | 0.009 | 0.007 | -0.019 | 0.015 | 0.037* |
| | (0.016) | (0.015) | (0.018) | (0.015) | (0.013) | (0.014) | (0.014) | (0.012) | (0.018) | (0.022) |
| Party Centrist | 0.004 | 0.367 | -0.344 | 0.009 | -0.358 | 0.202 | 0.520 | 0.635 | 0.503 | 0.370 |
| | (0.458) | (0.465) | (0.468) | (0.432) | (0.471) | (0.471) | (0.456) | (0.443) | (0.386) | (0.394) |
| Vote Share | -0.019 | 0.035* | 0.000 | 0.021 | 0.014 | 0.007 | -0.016 | -0.004 | 0.008 | -0.006 |
| | (0.031) | (0.019) | (0.015) | (0.016) | (0.017) | (0.018) | (0.014) | (0.015) | (0.011) | (0.014) |
| Tenure (log) | 0.539** | 0.740* | 0.860*** | 0.679** | 0.441 | 0.567 | 0.607 | 0.026 | 0.110 | 0.625*** |
| | (0.256) | (0.391) | (0.297) | (0.299) | (0.343) | (0.393) | (0.382) | (0.343) | (0.242) | (0.238) |
| South | -0.189 | -0.493 | 0.112 | -0.555 | 0.013 | 0.166 | 0.016 | -0.064 | -0.590 | -0.318 |
| | (0.526) | (0.568) | (0.521) | (0.492) | (0.538) | (0.512) | (0.508) | (0.523) | (0.459) | (0.430) |
| West | -0.371 | -0.875 | 0.321 | -0.116 | -0.092 | 0.030 | -0.537 | -0.461 | -0.593 | -0.887 |
| | (0.639) | (0.749) | (0.558) | (0.512) | (0.543) | (0.533) | (0.595) | (0.603) | (0.528) | (0.590) |
| Constant | -3.350 | -6.538*** | -6.075*** | -4.698*** | -3.266** | -3.647** | -1.970 | 0.094 | -3.052* | -4.865** |
| | (2.616) | (1.939) | (1.948) | (1.617) | (1.424) | (1.541) | (1.490) | (1.539) | (1.849) | (2.092) |
| N | 144 | 146 | 160 | 193 | 167 | 181 | 179 | 176 | 166 | 178 |

Note: Cell entries are rare-events logit coefficients with robust standard errors in parentheses.
***p < .01, **p < .05, *p < .10, two-tailed tests.

with no significant patterns distinguishing the membership in the 107th, 109th, and 110th Congresses (save an overrepresentation of the South in the 110th, the first minority-Republican Congress). A separate analysis of only the *appointed* Republican Policy Committee members (not shown) during the same time frame revealed few patterns of significant difference between the appointees in each Congress and other rank-and-file House Republicans.[36] One notable exception to the general representativeness of the at-large appointees is in the 104th Congress, where the 12 leader-appointed Policy Committee members were significantly more loyal than other members.

In short, the Republican Policy Committee's structure has encouraged fairly representative participation, but the committee has, at times, over-represented loyalists and more senior members. These patterns of participation can be read as consistent with the trends in the committee's activity that will be further explored later in the book. The Policy Committee of the late 1980s and early 1990s, which looked like the Conference on these key dimensions, was used to produce and signal positions on the minority's short-term positions; broad participation was important to the leadership's use of the committee as well as to its members' own goals. As that role fell away and the committee focused on communicating partisan messages to (and receiving them from) outside audiences, the committee's overall composition leaned toward more loyalty and seniority.

TABLE 3.10. Republican Policy Committee Full Membership, 104th–110th Congresses

|  | 104th | 105th | 106th | 107th | 108th | 109th | 110th |
|---|---|---|---|---|---|---|---|
| Party Unity | 0.094*** | 0.094** | 0.075** | 0.076* | 0.118** | 0.041 | −0.010 |
|  | (0.036) | (0.048) | (0.033) | (0.044) | (0.056) | (0.040) | (0.027) |
| Party Centrist | −0.474 | −0.301 | −0.082 | −0.389 | 0.416 | 0.390 | 0.521 |
|  | (0.390) | (0.391) | (0.380) | (0.359) | (0.365) | (0.365) | (0.360) |
| Vote Share | 0.000 | −0.005 | −0.016 | 0.000 | 0.004 | −0.001 | −0.012 |
|  | (0.012) | (0.019) | (0.012) | (0.013) | (0.013) | (0.015) | (0.017) |
| Tenure (log) | 0.418* | 0.380 | 0.382 | −0.056 | 0.571** | 0.203 | 0.242 |
|  | (0.223) | (0.259) | (0.291) | (0.246) | (0.227) | (0.206) | (0.242) |
| South | −0.259 | −0.058 | −0.335 | −0.389 | −0.337 | 0.395 | 1.256** |
|  | (0.401) | (0.440) | (0.399) | (0.423) | (0.455) | (0.470) | (0.505) |
| West | −0.404 | −0.010 | −0.695 | −0.103 | −0.193 | −0.534 | 0.437 |
|  | (0.497) | (0.505) | (0.507) | (0.471) | (0.523) | (0.638) | (0.643) |
| Constant | −10.272*** | −10.206** | −7.300** | −8.076* | −13.742** | −5.866 | −1.019 |
|  | (3.453) | (4.660) | (3.018) | (4.174) | (5.489) | (3.613) | (2.558) |
| N | 236 | 228 | 220 | 220 | 228 | 232 | 200 |

*Note:* Cell entries are rare-events logit coefficients with robust standard errors in parentheses.
***$p < .01$, **$p < .05$, *$p < .10$, two-tailed tests.

## Republican Committee on Committees (Steering Committee)

Tables 3.11 and 3.12 provide quantitative support for the conclusion that the restructuring of the Steering Committee in 1995 represented an important change in this party leadership organization. The familiar set of predictors from the other models of membership are used here to predict whether a GOP member is a member of the Executive Committee on Committees (97th–103rd Congresses, table 3.11) or the Republican Steering Committee (104th–110th Congresses, table 3.12). In the minority, under the Executive Committee on Committees structure, the committee's members showed consistent and statistically significant differences from the rest of the Conference on only one factor: seniority. As would be expected on a decentralized leadership committee consisting mostly of members selected within states (or state groupings) by the membership, along with some top party leaders, the Executive Committee on Committee's representatives were significantly more senior than the rank-and-file.[37] The only other factor that significantly predicts membership in the minority period is southern regional status in just two Congresses, the 97th and the 100th. Then, beginning with the Republican majority's reformed Steering Committee in the 104th Congress, party loyalty joined seniority as a significant predictor of membership, and this pattern held until Republicans lost majority control in the 110th Congress (table 3.12). By structuring the committee to include

TABLE 3.11. Republican Executive Committee on Committees, 97th–103rd Congresses

|  | 97th | 98th | 99th | 100th | 101st | 102nd | 103rd |
|---|---|---|---|---|---|---|---|
| Party Unity | 0.003 | –0.000 | 0.007 | 0.023 | 0.003 | –0.007 | 0.038 |
|  | (0.019) | (0.018) | (0.017) | (0.019) | (0.017) | (0.017) | (0.023) |
| Party Centrist | 0.033 | 0.242 | –0.393 | –0.104 | 0.460 | 0.375 | –0.021 |
|  | (0.620) | (0.622) | (0.594) | (0.574) | (0.468) | (0.462) | (0.454) |
| Vote Share | –0.013 | 0.017 | 0.027 | 0.012 | –0.004 | 0.003 | 0.007 |
|  | (0.017) | (0.017) | (0.024) | (0.019) | (0.015) | (0.014) | (0.017) |
| Tenure (log) | 1.532*** | 1.606*** | 1.755*** | 1.803*** | 0.759 | 1.095** | 0.809** |
|  | (0.505) | (0.558) | (0.585) | (0.560) | (0.467) | (0.491) | (0.331) |
| South | 1.012* | 0.591 | 0.865 | 1.004* | 0.863 | 0.708 | 0.258 |
|  | (0.603) | (0.590) | (0.676) | (0.562) | (0.583) | (0.547) | (0.489) |
| West | 0.132 | 0.564 | 0.227 | 0.479 | 0.339 | 0.714 | 0.283 |
|  | (0.942) | (0.769) | (0.902) | (0.767) | (0.751) | (0.621) | (0.615) |
| Constant | –4.015** | –5.781*** | –7.263*** | –7.912*** | –3.481** | –3.820** | –6.896*** |
|  | (1.784) | (2.031) | (2.167) | (2.489) | (1.739) | (1.776) | (2.311) |
| N | 193 | 167 | 181 | 179 | 176 | 166 | 178 |

*Note:* Cell entries are rare-events logit coefficients with robust standard errors in parentheses. Dependent variable is membership in Executive Committee on Committees for 97th–100th Congresses and the reformed Committee on Committees for 101st–103rd Congresses.

***$p < .01$, **$p < .05$, *$p < .10$, two-tailed tests.

all elected leaders and key committee chairs as well as hand-picked representatives of the Speaker, Republicans effectively created a committee made
up of senior loyalists. In a period when financial and legislative demonstra-
tions of loyalty were increasingly important to the majority, the party structured a committee selection mechanism that could control the distribution
of committee seats accordingly. Participation would hold substantial value
for the power goals of members on the Steering Committee, but seniority
and loyalty set the stage for involvement after the 1994 election.

## Party Leadership Participation and Member Careers

The discussion of membership changes and participation in House party
organizations demonstrates that members have sought out party posts, see-
ing the value for personal goals. The leadership, in turn, has expanded and
maintained the leadership organizations even as they have shaped them
to changing collective and leadership goals. This dynamic raises another
important question: how do extended leadership positions figure into
members' House careers? When are they likely to enter the leadership
in order to gain career benefits, and do they tend to remain in the leadership for multiple terms once they enter? More fundamentally, is service in
the party's organizations associated with advancement to more desirable

TABLE 3.12. Republican Steering Committee, 104th–110th Congresses

|  | 104th | 105th | 106th | 107th | 108th | 109th | 110th |
|---|---|---|---|---|---|---|---|
| Party Unity | 0.182*** | 0.223** | 0.118*** | 0.178** | 0.187*** | 0.114* | 0.025 |
|  | (0.057) | (0.090) | (0.043) | (0.081) | (0.070) | (0.059) | (0.033) |
| Party Centrist | −1.179** | −0.024 | 0.234 | −0.483 | −0.650 | 0.323 | 0.908** |
|  | (0.522) | (0.486) | (0.428) | (0.503) | (0.474) | (0.426) | (0.427) |
| Vote Share | −0.000 | 0.010 | 0.007 | 0.030* | 0.028* | 0.000 | 0.015 |
|  | (0.016) | (0.025) | (0.013) | (0.016) | (0.015) | (0.015) | (0.018) |
| Tenure (log) | 0.892*** | 1.182*** | 1.024** | 0.868** | 1.140*** | 1.293*** | 0.945** |
|  | (0.324) | (0.392) | (0.420) | (0.392) | (0.350) | (0.438) | (0.479) |
| South | −0.438 | −0.152 | −0.317 | −0.532 | −0.154 | −0.292 | 0.063 |
|  | (0.558) | (0.604) | (0.524) | (0.645) | (0.500) | (0.513) | (0.558) |
| West | −0.905 | −0.339 | −0.438 | 0.014 | 0.474 | 0.522 | 0.715 |
|  | (0.648) | (0.661) | (0.587) | (0.586) | (0.575) | (0.515) | (0.637) |
| Constant | −19.322*** | −24.735*** | −14.543*** | −21.881*** | −23.268*** | −14.852*** | −7.310** |
|  | (5.336) | (8.708) | (4.129) | (7.804) | (6.830) | (5.581) | (3.085) |
| N | 236 | 228 | 220 | 220 | 228 | 232 | 200 |

*Note:* Cell entries are rare-events logit coefficients with robust standard errors in parentheses.
***$p < .01$, **$p < .05$, *$p < .10$, two-tailed tests.

posts—in particular, prestige committee seats and top (elected) party leadership posts?

In his account of House careers from the 1950s–1980s, John Hibbing observed "there are practically as many paths through the formal positions of the House as there have been members" (Hibbing 1991, 71). In the Republican and Democratic leadership organizations, widely varying career paths have continued to be the norm. Many members enjoy sequential appointments in leadership positions, beginning as a junior appointee to a party committee and advancing to other positions later in their careers. For example, Ed Pastor (D-AZ) received a DSPC appointment in his sophomore term (103rd Congress) and again from the 105th–108th Congresses, and he joined the whip system as an appointed deputy whip in the 106th Congress and rose to a chief deputy whip position by the 111th Congress. Other members are selected into the leadership later in their careers: Ralph Regula (R-OH) served from the 93rd through the 97th Congresses before becoming a member of the Republican Policy Committee in 1983 and, subsequently, a member of the Republican Committee on Committees (later, Republican Steering Committee). Similarly, Pat Schroeder (D-CO) entered the Democratic leadership in her fifth term in 1981 as an appointee to the DSPC, where she served for two Congresses, and she served as an at-large whip from the 97th–99th Congresses. Schroeder later received a more selective appointment to a deputy whip position, where she served the party until she left the House after the 104th Congress.

James Walsh (R-NY) illustrates that some members build a foundation for legislative work in their extended leadership career: Walsh participated as a Republican Policy Committee member in his second and third terms (101st and 102nd Congresses), as a Theme Team[38] member in the next Congress, and then as an appointed whip from the mid-1990s to the mid-2000s as he also gained power as an Appropriations subcommittee chair/ranking member. For future Speaker Dennis Hastert (R-IL), behind-the-scenes work in multiple extended leadership positions paved the way for his unexpected rise to the top elected leadership post. Hastert entered the Republican extended leadership in his second term (101st Congress) as a Republican Policy Committee and Committee on Committees member, and he added an appointed whip position to those two posts in the 102nd and 103rd Congresses. After helping Tom DeLay win the majority whip post in 1994 (Hastert 2004), Hastert served as chief deputy whip for two terms until ascending to the speakership in 1999.

Cliff Stearns (R-FL) provides a final, contrasting example, showing that some members have more meandering trajectories in the extended leadership. Stearns was put on the Republican Committee on Committees during his freshman and sophomore terms (101st and 102nd Congresses), and then he joined the Republican Research Committee and served as a regional whip in the 103rd Congress. Stearns' career as a whip ended with the overhaul of the whip system in 1995, though, and he joined the Republican Policy Committee for five terms. As Stearns rose to a more significant legislative role as an oversight subcommittee chair (Energy and Commerce), he left the party leadership rather than continue in an extended leadership role as many members have done.

### Seniority and the Extended Leadership

Most members in the extended leadership have served several terms in the House before their selection, but the patterns of tenure in the party organizations have varied over time and between the parties. The average House tenure (in terms) of a party organization member has ranged from about four for Republicans in the 104th Congress to about seven for Democrats in the 103rd, and the average tenure for an organization member between 1975 and 2000 was 5.5 terms, slightly higher than the average tenure for all members. These figures conceal some important trends, however. Many members in both conferences enter the extended leadership as more junior members and remain for multiple terms. In the Democratic caucus in particular, longevity in the party organizations grew during the late 1980s and early 1990s as the large extended leadership system became institutionalized. Table 3.13 shows the average number of terms in extended leadership for Democrats with House tenures of three, four, and five terms. In each subgroup, the average time in the leadership tended to rise between the 99th Congress (1985) and the 104th (1995).

Another way to view members' careers in party organizations is through

TABLE 3.13. Mean Previous Congresses in Leadership Organizations for Democratic Organization Members, by Completed Terms in House

| Congress | Tenure: 3 Terms | Tenure: 4 Terms | Tenure: 5 Terms |
|---|---|---|---|
| 99th | 1.7 (10) | 1.4 (14) | 1.5 (10) |
| 100th | 1.0 (11) | 1.6 (16) | 1.7 (12) |
| 101st | 1.2 (25) | 2.0 (10) | 2.3 (16) |
| 102nd | 1.3 (8) | 1.9 (24) | 2.8 (10) |
| 103rd | 1.9 (8) | 2.2 (5) | 2.1 (23) |
| 104th | 1.3 (6) | 2.6 (7) | 3.5 (4) |

*Note:* Number of cases for each mean value in parentheses.

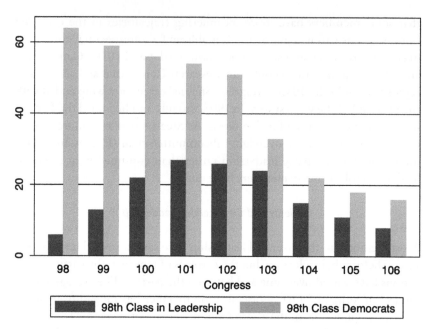

Fig. 3.8. Involvement in Democratic Party Leadership Organizations, 98th Congress Class (Elected 1982)

the leadership participation of House members in a cohort. In figure 3.8, I track the involvement of members from a large Democratic freshman class at a time when the leadership had grown to substantial size—the Democratic class of 1982 (98th Congress). Over their first few terms, the Democratic cohort entered the extended leadership at a sharply increasing rate. Few freshman Democrats were involved in the 98th Congress, but about half of the remaining members were in leadership organizations by the 101st Congress. Later, as retirements and defeat weeded out the class in 1992 and 1994, the vast majority of remaining members were part of the leadership system. The overall picture is one of a cohort that is drawn into leadership participation relatively early in their careers and remains involved over time.

### Leadership Careers: Arriving Early, Staying Late

These examples and descriptive analyses establish a few general trends. First, members follow differing paths through the extended leadership, with some entering and exiting the organizations after only short periods or serving nonconsecutive terms. But many members serve many consecutive terms in the extended leadership after they are selected. Second, members tend to enter at a relatively early point in their House careers, and the length of service in the leadership, even for more junior members, grew in the 1980s and 1990s.[39]

More thorough quantitative analysis further establishes these patterns at the level of the individual member career. Table 3.14 includes two types of models of members' involvement in the Republican or Democratic party leadership system. The first and simplest approach is a pooled logit model (models 1 and 2) of each member's first selection (failure) into a party committee or whip system. The model includes all members in each Congress who did not participate at $t - 1$, and the dependent variable indicates whether or not each member experiences a failure at $t$. The models cluster standard errors on member id and include a series of dummy variables (not displayed) for each Congress. For both Democrats and Republicans, the

TABLE 3.14. Entry and Membership in House Party Leadership Organizations

| | (1) Entry: Democrats, 95th–106th Congresses | (2) Entry: Republicans, 97th–106th Congresses | (3) Membership: Democrats, 95th–106th Congresses | (4) Membership: Republicans, 97th–106th Congresses |
|---|---|---|---|---|
| Party Unity$_{t-1}$ | 0.225** | 0.208* | 0.292*** | 0.086 |
| | (0.090) | (0.126) | (0.072) | (0.076) |
| Party Centrist$_{t-1}$ | 0.282* | 0.463* | 0.415*** | 0.210 |
| | (0.163) | (0.246) | (0.119) | (0.148) |
| Tenure (log) | −0.753*** | −0.729*** | 0.421*** | 0.398*** |
| | (0.134) | (0.274) | (0.086) | (0.125) |
| Vote Share | 0.0003 | 0.003 | −0.001 | 0.003 |
| | (0.005) | (0.009) | (0.003) | (0.004) |
| Available Posts | | | 0.025*** | 0.005 |
| | | | (0.003) | (0.005) |
| Nonleader Terms | | | −0.483*** | −0.818*** |
| | | | (0.028) | (0.071) |
| Constant | −0.988** | −0.761 | −2.785*** | −0.523 |
| | (0.417) | (0.710) | (0.332) | (0.526) |
| *N* of Observations | 1,452 | 517 | 2,485 | 1,481 |
| *N* of Members | | | 587 | 419 |

*Note:* Cell entries for (1) and (2) are logit coefficients with first entry into party leadership organizations as the dependent variable; cell entries for (3) and (4) are population-averaged logit models with membership in party leadership organizations at *t* as the dependent variable. Robust standard errors in parentheses. Top party leaders and members with party loyalty scores <30% are excluded. Individual Congress dummies not displayed for (1) and (2).

***$p < .01$, **$p < .05$, *$p < .10$, two-tailed tests.

logged tenure variable is a strong negative predictor of first entry, suggesting members in both caucuses tended to experience their first selection into the leadership system earlier in their careers, even when other factors are accounted for, and more senior members who had never participated were less likely to enter than their junior colleagues. In each party, higher loyalty scores in the previous Congress increase the likelihood of a member being selected in the current Congress. Members who were party centrists in the prior Congress were also more likely to be selected ($p < .10$, two-tailed).

The second set of models (3 and 4) in table 3.14 are population-averaged pooled logit models (Zorn 2001) predicting whether a member is or is not involved in the party's organizations at time $t$. Following Beck, Katz, and Tucker's (1998) approach, the models account for duration dependence with an indicator of the length of time (number of Congresses) a member has spent outside the leadership at $t$ (labeled "nonleader terms"). Unlike the models of first failure, these models include all members in each Congress and account for whether they are included in the extended leadership. An additional variable (labeled "available posts") accounts for the size of the leadership system at $t$ since any member's likelihood of involvement is affected by the growing size of the leadership system.

Model 3 shows that, for Democrats between the 95th and 106th Congresses, loyalty, seniority, and ideological centrism in the caucus all increase the likelihood of participation in the extended leadership. In contrast to the model of first entry, where lower tenure predicted initial selection, the analysis with all members in each term shows that members with more seniority are more likely to be involved in the leadership. In addition, the variable for "nonleader terms" adds to the story of member careers: its significant and negative effect shows that longer periods of time outside the extended leadership decrease the chances of entering the leadership in the next Congress. For the GOP in the 97th through 106th Congresses,[40] party loyalty and centrism have positive coefficients, but their effects are not statistically significant. Both seniority (positive) and time out of the leadership (negative) dominate the story of overall membership for Republicans. These models further the general conclusion on member careers in the leadership: members tend to enter relatively early, but participation in the system overall is skewed toward more senior members as members who are involved tend to remain involved over time.

### The Career Rewards of Leadership Participation

Members participate in the extended leadership to advance several types of individual goals, but the tendency for members to enter the system relatively early in their careers raises the possibility that a formal "place at the table" advances one goal in particular: members' ambitions to rise to more powerful positions in the House later in their careers. Members who seek positions on powerful standing committees may be advantaged by the connections within the caucus that they have built in the party organizations. Their work in the leadership also allows them to demonstrate that they are team players worthy of the party's limited prestige-committee resources. If this is the case, then members who have served in the extended leadership should be more likely to receive prestige committee appointments, even when other factors are controlled.

I test this possibility using committee assignment data from the 95th through 107th Congresses.[41] I define prestige committees to include Ways and Means, Appropriations, Rules, and Commerce (Energy and Commerce).[42] The dependent variable in the models in tables 3.15 and 3.16 is an indicator of whether a member who was not a prestige-committee member at $t - 1$ transferred to a prestige committee at $t$. Existing research establishes that party loyalty is a factor in prestige committee transfers and request success (Cox and McCubbins 2007; Frisch and Kelly 2006; Heberlig 2003; Maltzman 1997; Smith and Ray 1983), so the models include a variable for party loyalty. Following standard practice, they also account for tenure with a squared term to capture curvilinear effects (Cox and McCubbins 1993), and I also include an indicator of party centrism. In these pooled models, the loyalty and

TABLE 3.15. Democratic Prestige Committee Transfers, 95th–107th Congresses

|  | (1) | (2) |
|---|---|---|
| Party Unity$_{t-1}$ | 0.349*** | 0.318*** |
|  | (0.112) | (0.111) |
| Extended Leader$_{t-1}$ |  | 0.521** |
|  |  | (0.213) |
| Party Centrist$_{t-1}$ | 0.427** | 0.412** |
|  | (0.195) | (0.195) |
| Tenure | 0.228 | 0.162 |
|  | (0.357) | (0.366) |
| Tenure$^2$ | –0.066 | –0.063 |
|  | (0.043) | (0.044) |
| Constant | –2.969*** | –2.837*** |
|  | (0.717) | (0.729) |
| N | 1,778 | 1,778 |

*Note:* Cell entries are rare-events logit coefficients with robust standard errors in parentheses. Individual Congress dummies omitted.

***$p < .01$, **$p < .05$, *$p < .10$, two-tailed tests.

centrism variables are lagged, and Congress dummy variables (not displayed) account for Congress-specific effects.

The first column of table 3.15 (model 1) depicts a standard model of prestige-committee transfers for Democrats. In keeping with existing findings on Democratic prestige assignment, voting loyalty is a significant and positive influence on the likelihood of a prestige transfer, but member seniority is not a significant factor. Democratic party centrism in the previous Congress also increases the likelihood of a prestige transfer. The model in the second column (model 2) shows that an extended leadership post in the previous Congress significantly increases the likelihood of a prestige committee transfer, even as the effects from the basic model hold. For Republicans (table 3.16), party unity is a positive predictor and tenure, in contrast to the Democratic models, has a curvilinear effect on Republican prestige assignments, with seniority increasing and then decreasing the likelihood of transfer. These relationships hold when party participation is included, and membership in a party leadership organization at $t$ − 1 increases the likelihood that a member will receive a prestige committee transfer at $t$. These findings tell a clear story: alongside conventional factors, participation in the extended leadership boosts members' chances of selection onto a power committee. Although this result partly reflects the ambition of those who would seek both leadership posts and prestige assignments, it points to the value of party leadership participation in building a House career.

TABLE 3.16. Republican Prestige Committee Transfers, 97th–107th Congresses

|  | (1) | (2) |
|---|---|---|
| Party Unity$_{t-1}$ | 0.339*** | 0.305** |
|  | (0.131) | (0.133) |
| Extended Leader$_{t-1}$ |  | 0.667*** |
|  |  | (0.207) |
| Party Centrist$_{t-1}$ | 0.270 | 0.286 |
|  | (0.218) | (0.219) |
| Tenure | −0.765*** | −0.802*** |
|  | (0.114) | (0.115) |
| Tenure$^2$ | 0.035*** | 0.036*** |
|  | (0.008) | (0.008) |
| Constant | −0.158 | −0.301 |
|  | (0.454) | (0.464) |
| N | 1,145 | 1,145 |

Note: Cell entries are rare-events logit coefficients with robust standard errors in parentheses.

***$p < .01$, **$p < .05$, *$p < .10$, two-tailed tests.

Party leadership organizations are a potential stepping stone to an even bigger prize: a top party leadership post.[43] Analyzing the relationship between earlier party organization activity and successful leadership bids is more difficult since the number of members entering the top leadership in the modern period is quite small. However, the bivariate relationship between party organization membership and successful entry into the top leadership provides at least a crude picture of the connection. The crosstabs in table 3.17 include all members who were not part of the top party leadership team in the previous Congress, and they break down those members according to their involvement in the extended leadership in that Congress and whether they enter the top leadership in the current Congress. The majority of both Democrats ($\chi^2$ = 19.06, $p$ < .001) and Republicans ($\chi^2$ = 14.38, $p$ < .001) who assume a top leadership post for the first time were involved in extended party leadership organizations in the preceding Congress. For members of both caucuses, the typical path into the top ranks of the party includes service in a party leadership organization.

## The Constituency and Party Leadership Organizations

The expansive system of party leadership posts provides participatory opportunities that serve the top leadership's goals under varying party gov-

TABLE 3.17. Leadership Election and Prior Extended Leadership Status

*Democrats*

| | Extended Leader in Previous Congress? | | |
| --- | --- | --- | --- |
| Top Leader? | No | Yes | |
| No | 2,098 | 1,163 | 3,261 |
| | 99.71% | 98.31% | 99.21% |
| Yes | 6 | 20 | 26 |
| | 0.29% | 1.69% | 0.79% |
| | 2,104 | 1,183 | 3,287 |
| | 100% | 100% | 100% |

*Republicans*

| | Extended Leader in Previous Congress? | | |
| --- | --- | --- | --- |
| Top Leader? | No | Yes | |
| No | 1,472 | 970 | 2,442 |
| | 98.99% | 96.9% | 98.15% |
| Yes | 15 | 31 | 46 |
| | 1.01% | 3.1% | 1.85% |
| | 1,487 | 1,001 | 2,488 |
| | 100% | 100% | 100% |

ernment conditions, and the posts are demonstrably useful to individual members for access to the policy process and as a stepping stone to positions of greater power and prestige. This now-commonplace part of the Washington career may also have relevance to members' constituency careers. Party leadership participation, at least for some members, may itself serve as a marker of representation that members can offer to the constituency: presentation of partisan activity can become part of members' "home style," particularly in a political environment that is more polarized both in Washington and in the constituency.

Richard Fenno's conception of home style describes members as seekers of constituency trust (Fenno 1978). Through the stages of their careers, members develop strategic methods of self-presentation and explanation of Washington activity that forge lasting representational connections with key elements of the constituency. In Fenno's early work, set in the 1970s era of weak parties, the role of partisanship in home style received little attention, but in later work, Fenno has described partisanship as an important component of self-presentation for some members. Describing the home style of a conservative and issue-oriented junior member, David McIntosh (R-IN), Fenno shows how party activity becomes part of home style rather than an activity to be pursued once leeway is built through other means. McIntosh's House career included early involvement in party leadership roles, and his district self-presentation centered on his loyalty as a Republican partisan (Fenno 2007, 190–201). For a member like McIntosh, the effort to show constituents that "I am one of you" through home style becomes, in significant part, an effort to show that "I am a good Republican (or Democrat) like you."

The assumption here is that members will make strategic decisions about whether and how to incorporate party leadership activity into home style. As with other home style choices, this decision should be contingent, among other things, on constituency factors and on the member's own mix of goals. The analyses above demonstrate that members with varying tenure and electoral security are involved in the party leadership, but those who do participate should be more likely to present and explain that work when partisan constituency cues are stronger and when the member's own decision making reflects a strongly ideological orientation.

### Evidence of Constituency Connections

Tracing the links between party leadership organizations and constituency is a difficult task since many of the communications between members and constituents are ephemeral and best captured through Fenno-style direct observation. We can observe first, on an organizational level, that the parties have sometimes sought to publicize and frame their members' work for constituency consumption. Dick Gephardt and David Bonior, for instance, issued press releases at the start of the 105th and 106th Congresses on the election or appointment of individual members of the whip team, with details on the positions as well as quotations from the members casting their party service in constituency terms. In 1998, freshman Brian Baird (D-WA) included the following explanatory statement linking party and constituency in Gephardt's press release announcing his election as a regional whip:

> When I ran for this seat, I promised to do my utmost to help the people of the Third District; that's always at the forefront of my mind. The opportunity to serve as regional whip will allow me to interact with many more of my colleagues than would a typical new Member of Congress, and I fully intend to make sure that every person I talk to understands the needs and priorities that we have in Southwest Washington—like transportation, trade, education and economic development.[44]

This pattern of press releases for advertising and explaining positions has continued through the most recent Congresses, with news of members' leadership positions appearing both on their personal webpages[45] and in local press.[46] At the same time, both parties appear to be cautious in their efforts to publicize their members' involvement: for at least the last decade, the default for the dozens of lower-level whip posts is secrecy, with neither party releasing even a complete list of participants.

The clearest systematically available evidence of members' *independent* efforts to connect representation and party leadership activity is in their own decisions to include party activity on their congressional websites. Member communication through electronic media and franked mail has proven to be a solid source for analyses of self-presentation and home style when Fenno-style observation is not feasible (Cormack 2013; Grimmer 2013; Gulati 2004; Lipinski 2004; Niven and Zilber 2001; Yiannakis 1982). Here, I assume members make strategic decisions over the information included in prominent locations on their websites and some members in the extended party leadership will choose to emphasize and even explain their partisan involvement. This type of self-presentation and explanation, however, will be avoided by some members who do not choose to link their partisan activity with the constituency. Stated differently, if party leadership participation is of value to members for representational purposes, we should see evidence that some members fold it into their home style. But, since participation in party organizations serves other goals as well, this aspect of Washington activity may be conspicuously absent from the connections other members make with their constituents.

The data to evaluate this hypothesis is coded from the websites of listed party organization members in the 111th and 112th Congresses. I searched the official House websites of all members in each Congress who were publicly identified in *CQ's Politics in America* as holding extended party leadership posts.[47] I searched the pages of each member's site for mentions of their individual party organization involvement and for explanations of that work. In most cases, members who presented and/or explained their involvement did so alongside their lists or explanations of committee and caucus participation or as part of their biographical narrative.[48] I gathered additional examples from other recent Congresses to supplement the systematic data collection on the 111th and 112th.

### Examples of Presentation and Explanation

Some examples from the websites illustrate the stories House members tell about their partisan involvement and its relationship to representation. Many members who present their party leadership participation describe their role on the same plane with their standing committee or caucus memberships, emphasizing the prestige of their position.[49] This was the case with Joe Wilson (R-SC):

> Joe serves on the House Armed Services Committee—where he serves as Chairman of the Subcommittee on Military Personnel—the Committee on Education and the Workforce, and the Committee on Foreign Affairs. He was appointed by the Republican Leader to the highly influential Republican Policy Committee and works as an Assistant Republican Whip. He is Co-Chair of the Composites Caucus, the Bulgaria Caucus, the Kurdistan Caucus, and the Americans Abroad Caucus. He . . . also serves on the Congressional Caucus on India and Indian Americans. (113th Congress)

On the Democratic side, Karen Bass (D-CA) offered a similar story, describing her party involvement alongside other meaningful Washington work:

She was selected by Democratic Leader Nancy Pelosi to serve on the prestigious Steering and Policy Committee, which sets the policy direction of the Democratic Caucus. Representative Bass is also playing a leadership role in the Congressional Black Caucus (CBC), where she serves as Whip for the 113th Congress. (113th Congress)

Following this pattern of emphasizing the prestige of leadership appointment, G.K. Butterfield (D-NC) explained that he "was appointed by Speaker Nancy Pelosi and Majority Whip, Congressman Jim Clyburn, to serve as one of eight Chief Deputy Whips responsible for helping to formulate Democratic policy and insuring the passage of legislation by maintaining good communication with members." He went on to connect the constituency with the prestige of his position, noting that he was "the first Democratic member of Congress from North Carolina to serve as a Chief Deputy Whip" (110th Congress).

Like Butterfield, some members involved in the party leadership provide some context for constituents to understand the extended party leadership role. In perhaps the most striking recent example, Diana DeGette (D-CO), a Democratic chief deputy whip, provided a dedicated page on her House site explaining the history and function of the whip system in some detail under the heading "What's A Whip?" Elsewhere, DeGette noted:

> . . . as a whip, she works to ensure passage of key pieces of legislation and orchestrate opposition to Republican legislation that is antithetical to Democratic values. Steadily rising in the Democratic Whip organization since her first term in Congress, U.S. Rep. DeGette previously served six years as Regional Whip and two years as the Democratic Floor Whip. (113th Congress)

In a similar way, Frank Pallone (D-NJ) stressed the importance of his activity for advancing party goals and values:

> Pallone holds an important leadership position within the House Democratic Caucus. As the Communications Chair of the Democratic Policy Committee [DSPC], the New Jersey congressman plays an active role in developing and implementing the Democratic Party's message. In this capacity, Pallone coordinates the party's message on the floor of the House of Representatives. (113th Congress)

In each of these examples, we see members who find the party label to be an important part of their self-presentation outside of the campaign context, presenting and explaining their party positions as evidence of their loyal service to the party that connects the member and the reelection constituency.

Other members involved in the extended leadership offer explanations that make the constituency connection to their party work more explicit—these members do not appear to assume that party service alone is evidence that "I am one of you." Tim Ryan (D-OH) fused his extended leadership involvement and his committee assignments to show how his Washington activity advanced localized interests:

> In 2006, Ryan was chosen by House Speaker Nancy Pelosi to join the Democratic Steering and Policy Committee, which is responsible for nominating Democratic Members to serve on House Committees and advising the Speaker on policy. That same year, the Steering and Policy Committee appointed Ryan to the powerful House Committee on Appropriations where he serves on the Subcommittee on Labor, Health and Human Services, Education, and Related Agencies ("Labor-HHS") and the Subcommittee on Energy and Water Development, and Related Agencies ("Energy and Water"). . . . Ryan's primary focus remains on the economy and quality-of-life of his Northeast Ohio congressional district. He works closely with local officials and community leaders to advance local projects that enhance the economic competitiveness of Northeast Ohio and help attract high-quality, high-paying jobs. (110th Congress)

Joseph Crowley (D-NY) offers an example of members who cast their party leadership participation as a way for their states and/or districts to have a place at the table of power. Crowley's website put forward an exceedingly detailed explanation of his Washington activity, and he set his work in a localized context, discussing his personal roots in his Bronx/Queens district and emphasizing the links between his work and New York. He placed his whip position front-and-center in this discussion, explaining it even before he explains his Ways and Means and Foreign Affairs committee posts:

> In January 2003, Congressman Crowley was selected to serve in the Democratic House Leadership in the prestigious position of Chief

Deputy Whip, making him the highest-ranking New York Member in the caucus party leadership. Congressman Crowley uses his seat at the leadership table to promote sound policies to improve public education, make healthcare more affordable, and protect Social Security for working families in the Bronx and Queens. Congressman Crowley has consistently worked and will continue to work with his colleagues in the Democratic Caucus to promote the Democratic agenda. (110th Congress)

Greg Walden (R-OR) similarly explained his whip role in the context of a lengthy, district-focused discussion of his legislative work:

> . . . He also serves on the House Resources Committee where he chairs the Subcommittee on Forests and Forest Health, a post fitting for a representative with nine national forests in his district. Additionally, Greg is a Deputy Whip, one of only 17 in the House of Representatives. This position allows Oregonians to have a strong voice within House leadership and involves Greg in regular meetings to plan and discuss the House of Representatives' course of action. (109th Congress)

The substance and context of these leaders' explanations illustrate some members' effort to connect their extended leadership functions directly to tangible constituency interests. These members strategically explain their personal leadership power as a positive reflection on the district and a force for advancing the district's particular issue interests and needs.

Many members appear to find that party leadership participation is a more uncomfortable fit for their home style. Deborah Pryce (R-OH), a very involved and relatively high-ranking GOP leader in the 2000s, explained her party leadership activity in detail *in the context of her bipartisan approach*. Pryce introduced her website's biographical sketch by noting that she "first came to the United States House of Representatives in 1993 and has since established herself as a strong leader who has earned the respect of members on both sides of the aisle." She later explained that she:

> . . . also holds the title of Deputy Whip. In this role she is responsible to gauge the support of fellow Republicans for legislation on the House floor and work with other members of leadership to shape strategy on issues. Pryce's background as a prosecutor and judge and her reputation as a consensus builder have served her well in all of

these leadership roles and have earned her the title of "Peacemaker." (109th Congress)

Pryce linked this and other leadership activity to her issue work, which she in turn connects to the constituency. Despite her strong involvement in Republican leadership, she overtly deemphasizes the partisan aspect of her leadership and emphasizes the issue and constituency consequences.

Other extended leadership members do not attempt to present and explain their leadership roles, conspicuously avoiding any mention of relatively prominent party leadership posts even when they choose to present their Washington activity in detail. Wayne Gilchrest (R-MD) explained that he "is most often described as an independent voice for his constituents on Capitol Hill" whose "willingness to champion issues and vote his conscience regardless of party affiliation has earned him respect from both sides of the political spectrum" (110th Congress). He went on to detail his issue concerns, committee work, and involvement in a range of caucuses in some detail, but unlike many of his colleagues, he never mentioned his membership on the Republican Policy Committee or attempted to link it to constituency interest.

### Quantitative Evidence of Presenting Partisan Participation

These examples suggest that members adopt varying approaches to publicizing their party leadership participation; in turn, the variation implies that participation has perceived value for constituency goals for a subset of members while others participate in service of other goals and avoid potentially challenging efforts to tell persuasive stories about party work to the reelection constituency. My analysis of member websites in recent Congresses provides some more systematic evidence on who communicates partisan work to the constituency.

Presentation of party work is indeed variable—among those members who were publicly listed in *CQ Politics in America* as extended party leaders in the 111th, 112th, and 113th Congresses, more members avoided mention of their leadership role than mentioned it. Figure 3.9 shows that between 30 and 40 percent of the listed party leaders mentioned and/or explained their party activity on their official websites. The majority of listed members made no mention of their work, even though all members in recent Congresses provide at least minimal description of some Washington work, including standing committee assignments.

Although the number of observations is small, some simple analysis of

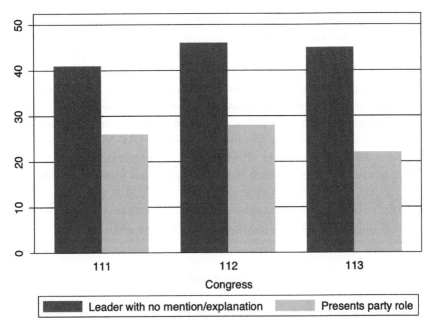

Fig. 3.9. Presenting Partisan Leadership Activity on Official Websites

*Note:* Totals based on coded website content from extended leadership members who were listed in *Politics in America.* Excludes top elected leaders in both parties, and excludes RPC members for 113th Congress for comparability.

the differences between members who do and do not present their party activity is possible. I take the decision to present party activity as an indicator of a member's willingness to incorporate partisanship into home style. I expect that members who do so will be more electorally secure and will represent districts that are more strongly partisan, as indicated by the party's share of the vote in the last presidential election. Members who present should also be those who take a more polarized position in voting behavior and those who have shorter terms of House service. On the latter point, because Fenno describes constituency connections as path-dependent strategic choices (see Fenno 2000), I assume those members who are in the extended leadership and are more junior will have made early-career decisions to pursue an active career in the party and they therefore will be more likely to incorporate that activity into their self-presentation.

In table 3.18, I compare listed extended leaders on these characteristics in the Democratic-controlled 111th Congress and the Republican-controlled 112th Congress, grouped according to whether they do or do not present their partisan activity on their websites. The results suggest a relationship between three factors—district partisanship, electoral security, and tenure—and extended leaders' decisions to present their party participation. Participants in the extended leadership who presented that activity on their websites were from more partisan districts and were more electorally secure (although that relationship does not reach statistical significance in the 112th Congress). Members in both Congresses who presented partisanship were also more junior, by several years on average. Ideological extremism (as measured by the absolute value of DW-Nominate scores), however, has an inconsistent effect across Congresses and is not statistically significant. It is also worth noting that party has some relationship to this choice. A higher proportion of Democratic leaders mentioned their activity in both Congresses, although that relationship is statistically significant only in the 112th Congress ($\chi^2 = 7.6454, p = .006$).

## Conclusion

The wide range of evidence in this chapter illustrates that participation in the extended party leadership serves the power, policy, and constituency representation goals of House members. In turn, top party leaders have used leadership participation in different ways under weaker and stronger party leadership conditions to advance party goals. Generally speaking, participation is used by the party's leadership to draw a broad and representative segment of the caucus into policy and strategic decisions, but under stronger party government, participation has become more selective. Democratic leaders in the 1970s and early 1980s expanded the DSPC and the whip organization to respond to demands for participation by the rank-and-file and to facilitate the party's efforts to move a more cohesive policy agenda within a large and still-diverse caucus. Democrats encouraged more involvement in committee selection, policy and party

TABLE 3.18. Mean Comparisons of Partisan Presentation, by Selected Characteristics of Listed Extended Leadership Members

|  | 111th Congress | | | 112th Congress | | |
|---|---|---|---|---|---|---|
|  | No Mention | Mention | $p$ | No Mention | Mention | $p$ |
| Ideological Extremism | .469 | .494 | .247 | .510 | .470 | .819 |
| District Pres. Vote | 61.634 | 66.115 | .068 | 59.152 | 68.714 | <.001 |
| Member Vote Share | 69.731 | 82.308 | <.001 | 67.218 | 70.630 | .128 |
| Member Tenure | 18.146 | 14.615 | .070 | 16.522 | 13.357 | .092 |

*Note:* Cell entries represent difference-of-means tests between listed leaders who present and do not present party activity on their official websites, with one-tailed $p$ values reported. Top elected party leaders excluded. 111th Congress: $N = 65$. 112th Congress: $N = 72$.

strategy, and whipping efforts. As partisan battles intensified in the 1980s, the party further increased the size of its extended leadership but selected more loyal members to participate, at least in the large appointive whip network. On the Republican side, Conference members used the elaborate system of minority party committees during the 1970s–1980s as a locus for involvement when the party's access to institutional resources was limited. A relatively large proportion of the Conference participated meaningfully in committee selection and in policy and strategic decision making. Once the GOP moved into the majority in the 1990s, participatory opportunities became quite extensive, but organizations other than the whip system became less important centers of activity as party power centralized. Republican party leaders created a leadership system that heavily favored junior loyalists, particularly during the period of divided government and small GOP majorities during the late 1990s.

From the member's perspective, the empirical evidence shows that leadership participation plays an important role in advancing career goals. Members follow widely varying paths through the extended leadership, but the analysis in this chapter highlights a tendency for members to begin participation in party organizations early in their House careers and to remain in the party leadership for multiple terms. Notably, shorter House tenure predicts *first entry* into the leadership for those who have not previously participated, but longer tenure in the House increases the likelihood that any member will be among the extended leaders in a given Congress. The evidence also paints a clear picture of the role that party participation plays in members' advancement within the chamber. When other important factors are accounted for, involvement in party leadership organizations increases the chances that a House member will transfer onto a prestige committee, and most members who take the first step into the top ranks of the party leadership do so from a position in the extended leadership system.

This chapter has also highlighted the role leadership participation plays in constituency representation for some members. I have argued that party involvement is part of a partisan self-presentation for some rank-and-file members, although less than half of the Republican and Democratic extended leadership members publicly advertise their roles. Members who do present their partisan participation are, on average, more junior, more electorally secure, and represent more partisan districts. And, in explaining their activity to their constituents, members vary in how they link their Washington work to constituency goals. Some members stress the prestige of their position, while others use it as evidence of their loyalty to the party, and still others attempt to show how party participation directly advantages the geographic constituency's interests.

# FOUR

# Coordination in Party Leadership Organizations

"There is great dissatisfaction with the current whip system. This is partly the result of lack of full knowledge by the membership at large of what is currently being done. However, it is clear that input to the system is uneven. Information often comes in too late and is not completely accurate. Some of the regional whips do a fine job while the work of others is less than adequate. In some cases, people who do not even support the legislation are used as whips. To help solve this problem, I suggest that the whip information-gathering structure should be centralized. All polling of members on key legislation should be made from one office by a small staff working directly under the control of the Whip. . . ."

—William Brodhead (D-MI), 1975[1]

"By controlling the chamber's intelligence operation, [Majority Whip Tom] DeLay helps determine what decisions his superiors make. The 71-person whip team meets formally on a weekly basis, and the 16 deputy whips gather almost daily. That's where his power lies."

—*Roll Call* (Eilperin and Vande Hei 1997)

"The most important commodity around a legislative body is information."

—A Democratic whip (quoted in Sinclair 1995, 128)

The congressional parties operate as collective bodies attempting to serve the goals of the party as a whole and the objectives of the individual member. In its efforts to do so, the party in the House majority enjoys control over procedure and, as a result, the chamber agenda; meanwhile, the minority retains its prerogatives in limited elements of the process (e.g., motions to recommit). Both the majority and the minority distribute selective benefits (e.g., campaign resources) that encourage members to support the party position. Although agenda control constitutes the major source of majority caucus power and both caucuses encourage loyal behavior through selective benefits, the parties in the House have found that achieving their objectives requires more: specifically, the use of internal structures to support coordination among members. Coordination, as chapter 2 explains, includes communication from the leadership to members about party positions and strategy, communication from members to the elected leadership about preferences and intentions, and efforts to identify or negotiate workable caucus plans on policy or strategy. In addition to providing information flow on specific matters, these coordination activities have the secondary effect of building a sense of partisan "teamsmanship" that contributes in a general way to party-regarding behavior (Lee 2009, 2011). All of these forms of coordination have become necessary in order for majority and minority parties to achieve collective goals, and they rely on a participatory party structure for their effectiveness.

As the quotations on the whip systems of the 1970s and 1990s illustrate, the party organizations' capacity for and effectiveness in coordination has varied over time, although both weaker and stronger caucuses in the majority and in the minority have found the coordination function necessary. The evidence in this chapter will show that caucuses under moderate but strengthening party government conditions have made extensive use of party organizations to identify and coalesce around common objectives. For more cohesive parties under stronger party government conditions, as Forgette (2004) argues in his study of full caucus meetings, party coordination brings necessary information to members that in turn can have observable secondary persuasion effects, increasing party support. The sections below will examine how the two caucuses have used the participatory party organizations, particularly the policy committees and the whip organizations, to facilitate coordination between the 1970s and the 2000s in changing ways.

## Coordination in the Democratic Caucus

During the 1970s reform era and the years following it, House Democratic leaders faced a substantial challenge. As previous chapters have discussed, the large majority included broad ideological diversity and, increasingly, demands for more assertive and progressive policy leadership, especially after the 1974 post-Watergate midterms. The caucus responded with some organizational and procedural changes that empowered the leadership but increased member involvement (see chapter 3; also Rohde 1991; Sinclair 1995), and the top leadership began to employ these innovations to provide much-needed coordination in the form of two-way communication between leaders and the rank-and-file.

The Democratic whip system gradually became better organized for this kind of coordination, starting in the early 1970s. The formal whip process of the 1960s and earlier centered on regionally selected zone whips who reflected the ideological pluralism of the caucus and allowed for only limited persuasion. Documents from the late 1960s and early 1970s show that zone whips could limit even the basic information-gathering function of the whip office. Notes from Hale Boggs' tenure as whip (87th–91st Congresses) indicate that southern zone whips often refused to provide full information from their polling, passing along only numbers of supporters and opponents without identifying them by name; at least one zone whip apparently refused to communicate at all.[2] The problem continued into the early reform era when Tip O'Neill would face his own set of intractable conservative zone whips[3] and whip counts of varying accuracy.[4]

The 40-year-old structure and operation of the Democratic whip institution began to change in the early 1970s. With more assertive central leadership under O'Neill—first as majority whip and later as Speaker—joining the other changes in the caucus, the whip system gradually became a more tractable tool for the elected party leadership to share and gather information. The expanded set of appointed whips created a core of extended party leaders with some inherent loyalty to the leadership. As structural changes improved the whip system's capacity for internal coordination, the O'Neill whip system began to develop more systematic information flows. A staff memo to O'Neill (in 1971 whip files) shows the whip office sought to improve the accuracy of whip counts by tracking the performance of regional whips, as well as the voting patterns of all Democrats; it also considered ways to improve communication to the membership on major legislation.[5] The reform period saw enduring changes on both fronts. First, the whip office began to conduct routine retrospective assessments of whip count accuracy and of support among whips and members overall—records of voting were not regularly kept under earlier whips (Ripley 1964, 576).[6] Second, the whip office became a tool through which the leadership disseminated various kinds of information that served the interests of both members and the central leadership. Some of these were simple services, such as the distribution of cards displaying a schedule of recess dates for the session or providing "speech cards" with prepared speeches and talking points on Democratic accomplishments for district work periods (the latter began in 1973 under whip John McFall).[7] Both of these services, of course, helped rank-and-file members with electoral efforts while advancing party goals by encouraging attendance at key votes and the dissemination of a cohesive Democratic message. Even more fundamentally, the whip office at this time developed new tools to communicate party positions and scheduling on a regular basis. Whip notices conveyed information on the week's calendar of legislative business,[8] and whip advisories, distributed on nearly a daily basis in session, summarized upcoming legislation, Democratic achievements, and leadership actions (including DSPC endorsements).[9]

Consequential changes came to the regular meetings and whip process as well. O'Neill began to transform the existing tradition of weekly "whip coffees," which he inherited from Hale Boggs,[10] into a routine way for the top leadership to communicate with whips and the broader membership (Farrell 2001, 296). O'Neill took attendance and kept minutes of the whip meetings, and the meetings served several purposes. Records of the 1971–72 meetings show that the leaders and whips frequently discussed upcoming legislation, prospects for victory on votes, whip counts, and even the wording of whip check questions.[11] O'Neill also used the meetings to cajole and excoriate the whips over responsiveness and counting problems and to sort out disagreements over scheduling issues.[12] In the early-1970s whip system, then, we begin to see the emergence of the Democratic party's participatory coordination efforts—the tools that would be necessary as the caucus gradually delegated more procedural authority to the central leadership but sought to be involved in the use of that authority.

Coordination in the expanding Democratic leadership structure went beyond the whip system; reform-era Democrats also employed the reconstituted DSPC, with its broadened base of participation and its newfound visibility and power as the committee on committees (see Frisch and Kelly 2006). The first DSPC of 1973 and 1974 (93rd Congress) was substantially more active than the predecessor it resembled; members met 28 times over the two years, issuing resolutions about both legislation and procedural matters and meeting with outside figures for discussion of policy and electoral politics.[13] The DSPC of the 94th Congress established a pattern of meaningful policy activity, despite taking on committee assignments for the first time. Meeting 38 times, the committee reviewed legislative proposals and considered resolutions after consulting with key members, rejecting at least one major resolution.[14] The committee created task forces and ad hoc committees to address key policy areas, with demonstrable success in coordinating on Democratic agenda items for this Congress.[15] The DSPC was responsible, via a task force headed by Jim Wright (D-TX) in cooperation with Senate Democrats, for framing a detailed congressional Democratic program on energy and the economy in early 1975 (Stewart 1975, 21).[16] The records of the DSPC's meetings during its second Congress show discussion among participating members could be substantive and frank—for instance, the committee conducted a wide-ranging debate in January 1975 on the majority's response to intelligence oversight failures, initiating steps that led to the creation of the Select Committee on Intelligence.[17]

This meaningful movement toward coordination in the party organization did not occur without conflict and concern. Some members viewed the revised whip organization as inadequate for the coordination role they envisioned, and the DSPC received criticism as a committee that "neither steers nor sets policy" and "spends too much time considering extraneous matters such as presentations by economists and pollsters" (also see the Brodhead quotation at the start of this chapter).[18] Meanwhile, the top leadership proceeded with considerable caution in formalizing roles for members to help shape legislation and strategy. Majority Leader Tip O'Neill and Chief Deputy Whip John Brademas (D-IN) made an effort early in 1973 to give the DSPC some independence from Speaker Carl Albert's office. O'Neill unsuccessfully tried to persuade Albert to name Brademas to lead the DSPC, ostensibly to save Albert the time-consuming task of managing the new body.[19] Both Richard Bolling (D-MO), a Democratic Study Group (DSG) activist and member of the new committee, and John Barriere, executive director of the DSPC, reacted scornfully to this proposal. Both men argued the committee needed to be under Albert's direct control. Barriere warned Albert that if the DSPC "is to be an effective tool and your tool, like [the] Policy Committee in the Senate, you must not only be in ultimate charge, you must be on top of things constantly."[20] Albert seemed to warn of the DSPC's limited, leadership driven role in his comments at the inaugural meeting of the committee in April 1973:

> If [the DSPC] is to play a vital role in the operations of the Democratic Party and in the House, it must, on one hand, be vigorous and dynamic and advocate progressive legislation. At the same time, however, it should not undertake objectives which might be laudable but not obtainable. It should remember at all times that it is an agent of the Democratic Caucus and its role should be to provide

aid, guidance and leadership to the Caucus, but not to endeavor to dictate to the Caucus.[21]

Though the DSPC had broadened responsibilities and membership, it remained the Speaker's "tool," both because of his leadership of the committee and because half of the committee's members were either Speaker appointees or members *ex officio* from the leadership. The early debate over control of the committee reflects an ongoing tension that has shaped the DSPC—the committee was formed in part to respond to participatory needs of the Democratic membership, but the committee was never a decentralized decision-making body, and Democratic leaders' pursuit of collective party goals and their own power have led them to maintain substantial control over the committee's operation.[22] This conflict in the design of the DSPC, though, is what also gave it potential as an effective venue for members and leaders to communicate on party action, and the committee actively assumed that role in the late 1970s. DSPC rules at this time required meetings twice a month in session, and the committee met more than 50 times in the 95th Congress.[23] When the DSPC was not addressing crucial committee-assignment business, the typical meeting centered on discussions of short-term strategy and policy. With a membership relatively representative of the large and diverse Democratic caucus, the committee allowed O'Neill to access the views of the membership and to test legislation on a "microcosm" of the caucus after standing committee work and before floor consideration. The frank DSPC discussions informed the Speaker's strategic decisions about proceeding with legislation, serving as "a barometer of the House," according to Peter Kostmayer (D-PA) (Cohen 1978).

During the active legislative sessions of 1977 and 1978 (the first Carter Congress), standing committee chairs and DSPC members routinely discussed committee timing and floor strategy. Records of the DSPC's activity show the organization was a mechanism for working with committee leaders and using the committee process to the leadership's advantage, but not necessarily for centralizing policy functions that otherwise would be with the committees. Strategic discussions in the committee also involved reports from the Speaker or whip organization on vote counts.[24] Substantive discussions of upcoming major legislation frequently led to DSPC resolutions urging Democratic support for measures: the committee passed 18 resolutions during the 95th Congress, 16 of which dealt with specific legislative action.[25] Minutes of many other DSPC meetings show the party regularly used the meetings to disseminate information about legislation moving toward the floor. Standing committee chairs reported in detail on legislation, justifying the content of bills and compromises necessary to sustain them, and explaining potential threats to their success. Not all legislation that received extensive coordinating discussion in the DSPC resulted in a formal endorsement—in many cases, standing committee leaders simply used the DSPC as a forum for sharing information that would help members to understand the party's objectives and what was needed for the party's legislation to succeed.[26]

A June 1979 DSPC meeting provides a focused example of what O'Neill's committee undertook during the Carter era. The meeting began with a presentation by Vice President Mondale on the administration's bill creating a Department of Education; committee participants voiced concerns and Mondale defended the measure. O'Neill updated the committee on pending campaign finance legislation, providing whip data and announcing that the bill would be pulled because of a lack of support. Majority Leader Jim Wright (D-TX) addressed the committee about energy policy problems from policy and political perspectives, and Henry Reuss (D-WI) provided information about a committee bill dealing with some of the energy issues Wright raised. The committee also dealt with routine business—unanimously filling two committee vacancies and approving spending authorizations for suspension votes.[27]

In sum, the DSPC was serving the party's coordination interests by facilitating leader-committee chair communication, by encouraging open consideration among members of majority party strategy, and by providing clear formal communications to the rank-and-file on the party's positions. The DSPC's coordination was particularly important in a period when strengthening demands for assertive policy action in a still-factionalized caucus made centralized leadership challenging.

If the DSPC of the 1970s emphasized broad-based coordination among many party figures—top leaders, committee chairs, members of the extended leadership, and leadership staff—the DSPC in the Reagan era took on a somewhat more circumscribed role. For a time, the Caucus as an organization functioned as a forum for open, contentious debate on strategy and legislation. In spring 1981, for instance, the full caucus considered and debated the party's response to Reagan's first budget proposals over the course of several weeks.[28] Caucus meetings had the advantage of openness to all members, and Gillis Long (caucus chair, D-LA) closed the caucus to nonmembers after the 1980 elections, making the caucus meeting a plausible place for the heterogeneous party to air differences and grievances (Granat 1983). The DSPC continued to communicate party policy (in addition to its regular committee-on-committees duties) and to serve as a venue for committee leaders and the party leadership to discuss and coordinate short-term strategy.[29] As one DSPC staffer explained in a 1980s interview with Little and Patterson, the DSPC ". . . is an arm of the leadership . . . to make sure that the committees and leadership are in sync" and its "greatest resource is to keep in touch with committees, keep them prepared, and get them ready for the floor" (1993, 52).

The limited coordination role of the DSPC during the Reagan administration was not satisfactory to all Democrats. As he prepared to leave the House in late 1982, Richard Bolling praised the stronger leadership structure but suggested the DSPC should be moved into a more centrally driven coordination and persuasion role as "the executive committee of the House Democratic Caucus" (Cohen 1982a). At the other end of the spectrum, junior members in the 1980s sought a reinvigoration of the DSPC in building broad policy consensus, and at the start of the 99th Congress, Tip O'Neill promised more policy activity for the committee (Granat 1984; Riehle 1984), and Wright made a similar avowal early in his tenure (Hook 1986).

Instead, the DSPC underwent centralizing changes as Wright took over the speakership and shifted the committee's membership and staff toward party and personal loyalists; these changes further diminished the DSPC's meaningful role in coordinating strategy and policy. Reorienting the DSPC allowed Wright to consolidate control over the committee assignment process, a crucial tool for his leadership (Frisch and Kelly 2006, 213), although individual members of the DSPC remained relevant in the assignment process and used the role to their political advantage (Calmes and Gurwitt 1987; Kosterliz 1989). The record of the DSPC's activity in the late 1980s suggests the committee was not policy focused under Wright: a meticulous journal of the DSPC's activity between the 1988 election and mid-1990 shows that the committee met only 15 times, dealing with assignment-related business and little else at each meeting.[30] Meanwhile, the DSPC staff's well-established role in providing in-depth policy analysis apparently faded under Wright, with the loyalist DSPC staff providing "political, not technical, services," according to Connolly's Wright-era interviews (Connolly 1991, 6). The DSPC remained important in the House Democratic leadership system, but its role and power was now almost exclusively focused on controlling committees through the assignment process. The DSPC, as John Barry wrote, "belonged to Wright" (1989, 83).

Under Tom Foley, the pattern of assignment-centered DSPC meetings that began under Wright continued, but Foley's goals involved dialing back some of the partisan conflict that Wright and his Republican opponents had fueled (Biggs and Foley 1999; Rohde 1991, 184–85), and some of the changes Wright had made to the DSPC were reversed. Foley does appear to have returned a serious policy component to its staff work, with the staff producing extensive briefing books for the Speaker on issues and committee work.[31] DSPC staff worked with committee chairs to engage in planning for the party's agenda,[32] and maintaining a "window on the inner workings" of major committees appears to have been one of Foley's objectives in selecting the membership of the DSPC (Burger 1991a). By the end of the Democratic majority period in the early 1990s, the DSPC provided a limited set of coordination functions for the leadership. The DSPC helped the top leadership to gain information and plan both policy and strategy, but this work involved more staff activity than member-centered coordination.[33]

As an active forum for information exchange, the whip organization began to take over the role it had previously shared with the DSPC. As the whip system expanded further in the 1980s and became more institutionalized, regular whip meetings ultimately took on more of the coordination function for Democrats. By the mid-1980s, whip meetings were a well-established opportunity for whips, as well as other members, to debate issues and strategy. "Those are very electric meetings," one staffer told *CQ*, "very often there are screaming matches" (*Congressional Quarterly Weekly Report* 1985). As Sinclair outlines, these engaging whip meetings served to communicate complex or unexpected strategic maneuvers to the membership, to clarify party positions for the rank-and-file, to allow the leadership to draw on information held by the many lower-level whips, and to give whips and other members "a shot at influencing their leaders and a basis for assessing whether the leadership is, in fact, acting as a faithful agent" (Sinclair 1995, 122–27, quoted p. 126).

Chapter 3 showed that Speaker Wright and Majority Whip Coelho made centralizing changes in the way the whip system was constituted. In terms of its key coordination role, the whip system continued to provide extensive communication with the membership to serve both collective and individual goals, including a wide range of published political and policy material. But, as Rohde notes, the whip system's weekly meetings became—in Dan Rostenkowski's words—"a tool for total control" under Coelho in contrast to the earlier, more open-ended meetings (Rohde 1991, 107).[34] Other accounts similarly suggest that the weekly whip meetings took on a less open, more controlled feel, although members still did seize the whip-system venue to question and challenge the leadership (Barry 1989, 144–46, 199–200, 280–81, 455). Although coordination had moved from the more deliberative forum of the DSPC to the more controlled whip system, some participatory basis for intraparty communication was still needed in the stronger party government conditions of the late 1980s.

The organizational structure for coordination in the Democratic caucus continued in a similar fashion into the minority period after 1994. Under David Bonior, the whip system's routines for facilitating communication through whip meetings continued (Price 2004, 195); scheduling records from the early 1990s show the caucus held whip meetings every Thursday in session, with each week's open whip meeting preceded by a "pre-whip" meeting of key leaders, and Bonior also met formally with chief deputy whips, zone whips, and deputy whips.[35] Later, under Steny Hoyer, the reorganization of the large whip network gave to a large set of appointed whips—the 28 members designated as "senior whips"—primary responsibilities for the weekly short-term strategy meetings and keeping "the pulse of the caucus," further institutionalizing this coordination function in the extended whip system (Billings 2003b; quoted from Wallison 2003).

While the whip organization continued to hold the main responsibility for information flow between the leadership and the membership, Nancy Pelosi—first as minority leader and later as Speaker—did employ the DSPC for some coordination purposes, but Pelosi seems to have personalized this aspect of the committee's role. Pelosi's style favored both centralized leadership as well as regular consultation with a group of personal loyalists (Peters and Rosenthal 2010, Dennis and Palmer 2010), and secondary sources suggest that she constituted the DSPC with an eye to creating a loyal "inner circle" to use as a "sounding board" that still represented the diversity of the caucus (Billings 2003a, 2003c, 2003d; Dennis and Hunter 2011; Kimitch 2007; Yachnin and Newmyer 2007).

### Coordination in the Republican Conference

The roots of House Republicans' organizational tools for coordination date back somewhat earlier than the Democrats'. In the seemingly "permanent minority" of the 1960s and 1970s (Connelly and Pitney 1994), Republicans had developed intraparty tools to encourage development of policy and strategy to counter the better-resourced majority. Jones' extensive interview-based research (1964; 1970) presents a detailed picture of the midcentury developments in Republican organization, particularly in the Republican Policy Committee. The minority Republican Policy Committee was a venue for communication and coordination within a diverse coalition (Jones 1970, 30, 154; Jones 1964, 101).[36] In this sense, the Republican leadership's use of the Policy Committee in the 1960s has parallels with the O'Neill-era Democrats' use of the Steering and Policy Committee, with its regular weekly meetings serving a role not unlike that of the 1970s DSPC and 1980s Democratic whip meetings (Jones 1964, 63, 68; Jones 1970, 155). Jones presents evidence to suggest a substantive role for the committee in the Kennedy era, showing that its official policy positions (28 in the 87th Congress) had an impact as communications devices within the Conference. Policy Committee position issues were associated with much higher levels of GOP voting agreement than on roll calls overall (1964, 88). At a minimum, the Policy Committee was successful at singling out important issues on which the party could coalesce to present a united front against the majority—and the organizational framework for this coordination was especially valuable given the minority's limited access to institutional resources.

As the Democrats proceeded in fits and starts toward a more cohesive and assertive caucus in the 1970s, the House GOP used the now-established coordinating function of the Policy Committee to formulate and express a coherent minority response to the Democratic-driven agenda. Under Policy chairs Del Clawson (R-CA) and Bud Shuster (R-PA), weekly meetings of the committee focused on response to the current House legislative agenda, and the committee generated policy positions based on deliberation informed by representatives from standing committees responsible for the week's agenda items (*National Journal* 1977). In the second session of the 96th Congress (1980), the Policy Committee met 32 times, issued 25 official policy statements, and identified 54 key roll-call votes.[37] The committee's policy positions were based on the two-way flow of information between leaders and the membership as Policy Committee members made an effort to represent the views of the rank-and-file on questions before the committee. Bud Shuster, as a regular member of the Policy Committee in the 95th Congress, polled the members in his region on specific issues by distributing reply cards. Members indicated their views on pending legislation and on whether the Policy Committee should stake out an official Republican position on those bills.[38] Policy statements, in addition, sometimes drew fine distinctions based on divisions within the Conference. A June 1980 statement, for example, explained the committee's strong endorsement of the Motor Carrier Act of 1980 (H.R. 6418) but indicated "the Policy Committee is aware of disagreement among Members with reference to Section 8, and takes no position on amendments to be offered to that section."[39]

The minority Republican Conference was actively using the whip organization for intraparty communication in the 1960s and 1970s as well, with a small network of whips providing intelligence to the leadership about member positions. Under the minority whip, Republicans had one deputy whip and three (later four) regional whips overseeing a series of assistant regional whips (three to six per region).[40] With its small regional structure, the Republican whip system was a limited tool, but the party did make effective, if sporadic, use of it for internal communication. In a formal count, the Republican whip distributed questions to the members of the whip organization who returned responses and information directly to the minority whip. In some cases, questions were posed and answers transmitted in writing.[41] Notably, the Republicans favored whip question wording that signaled information-gathering rather than persuasion. Instead of asking questions to which the party-correct answer was always "yes," Republicans usually asked their members neutrally worded questions: "Would you vote for or against the creation of a Department of Urban Affairs?" or "How will you vote on the combined debt-oil tax deferral legislation?"[42] When Republicans held the White House in the 1970s, the whip system's coordination of the House GOP aided the administration's legislative strategy. Republican President Gerald Ford held a very weak political hand after the 1974 elections, and Ford chose a veto strategy that, at least in placing short-term limits on Democratic policy change, proved successful in 1975 and 1976. The information flow from the House Republican leadership was central to this approach, with Michel's whip organization fielding veto-override-related questions 13 times in 1975 alone. The Ford White House used House Republicans, and the whip organization in particular, as its firewall against override attempts (Conley 2002).

Late in the Republican minority period, the Republican Policy Committee was particularly active as a center for strategic coordination. William Connelly's unpublished interview-based research on the Republican Policy Committee provides one view of how the committee functioned in the mid-1980s; Connelly observes that the committee "served to facilitate communications generally among House Republicans" over immediate agenda items (Connelly 1988, 15).[43] In providing short-term policy information to members and providing a sense of the rank-and-file positions to the leadership, the committee *ratified* House Republican policy, in the view of Dick Cheney (R-WY), a chair of the Policy Committee during the mid-1980s (Connelly 1988, 16). As it had for the preceding two decades, the committee provided a venue—as a meeting closed to the public but open to members of the Conference—that made it valuable to leaders and the rank-and-file. Connelly's respondents described the Republican Policy Committee, *inter alia*, as a "safety valve," a "lightning rod," and a "screaming platform" (1988, 12–15).

Archival evidence shows the committee engaged in systematic coordination activity in the late 1980s, particularly under Policy Committee chair Mickey Edwards (R-OK). In the 100th Congress, the Conference described the committee's roles to include holding "policy meetings on a need basis to air views on issues of concern to the Conference," issuing "policy statements on issues and disseminat[ing] the statements to the Members and the press," and considering "resolutions or other matters brought before the Republican Conference and referred to the Policy Committee and report findings on such subjects to the Leadership and the Conference."[44] Elaborating this framework, Edwards described the role of the committee's substantive activity as "decide," "develop," and "disseminate." In other words, the Republican Policy Committee would consider and mediate between policy options on selected issues, develop "a consensus Republican position" on some key matters, and "attempt to influence the public debate outside the institution" on those issues.[45] In choosing issues, the focus was on subjects "actually moving through the legislative process," and not on very long-term matters, which traditionally were the venue of the Republican Research Committee.[46] Following this framework, the Republican Policy Committee's central activity was deliberation on and production of coherent near-term policy positions (*National Journal* 1989). Some of the committee's activity also took a broader view of the issue agenda for a congressional session, in contrast to the reactive model of the late 1970s and early 1980s. For instance, the committee held forums in 1990 on the agenda for the session, and it helped to produce a lengthy document on leadership issue priorities for the 101st and 102nd Congresses. In another example, the committee in 1994 held several open forum meetings to consider issue positions for the midterm elections.[47] The committee's work in the late minority period explicitly linked internal coordination and external communication of the party's agenda, serving both collective policy and electoral goals.

The Edwards committee met routinely in two forms: weekly, the committee met in a forum open to Conference members to "hear the views of any member of the Conference who wishe[d] to address items on the agenda," and then the formal membership of the committee would meet in executive sessions "to reach the decisions based on input from members of the Conference."[48] Mickey Edwards formalized this pattern in the 101st Congress,[49] and the committee continued to meet fairly regularly in this fashion well into the 1990s. Data from 1990, for instance, shows the committee met 21 times in open forum and 14 times in executive session in a six-month period.[50] The open-forum sessions were attended by GOP members beyond the Policy Committee's formal membership, and topics discussed ranged widely, with the leadership communicating on strategy, members discussing forthcoming agenda items and procedure, and attendees considering positions on upcoming issues—following the familiar coordination and team-building pattern seen in previous decades in both the Republican Policy Committee and its DSPC counterpart. An early 1989 committee meeting, for example, included information on Newt Gingrich's (R-GA) strategy against Speaker Jim Wright, as well as discussion of a Republican task force on the savings and loan crisis, among other topics. About 50 Republican members attended the meeting.[51] In another example, at a late 1990 meeting, Minority Leader Michel addressed budget negotiations, Bill Archer (R-TX, ranking member on Ways and Means) discussed supporting President Bush's veto of the Textile, Apparel, and Footwear Trade Act, and Tom Delay (R-TX) explained his resolution "calling for the House to postpone adjournment until the House . . . agreed upon a budget for FY91." On other occasions, the Policy Committee met to address legislative strategy on issues such as budgets, health care, and family and medical leave.[52] The committee also took on an overt role in coordinating the minority's strategic use of the (newly public) discharge petition procedure in the 103rd Congress (Jacoby 1993).

The increased strategic coordination activity of the Policy Committee was joined in the late 1980s by a strengthened strategic role for the whip system. Newt Gingrich's election[53] as whip over Edward Madigan (R-IL) by a two-vote margin in 1989 marked a turn in the Conference toward a more procedurally aggressive partisanship. *CQ Weekly* described the Gingrich victory as "an expression of seething impatience among House Republicans," prioritizing assertive partisan leadership over competent, behind-the-scenes intelligence gathering (Hook 1989b; also Harris 2006). Leading the whip organization, Gingrich essentially maintained the system he inherited from Trent Lott for counting and persuasion (see chap. 6), but he expanded the whip's strategic role. Gingrich sought personally to establish a central position in policy development and political strategy (Hook 1989a), and he shaped the whip organization accordingly. Among other changes, Gingrich expanded the important chief deputy whip post, previously held by Madigan, to two positions. Gingrich assigned Robert Walker (R-PA), a Conservative Opportunity Society cofounder and long-time Gingrich ally, to serve as his assistant in whip operations on the House floor, and he chose the more moderate Steve Gunderson (R-WI) to assist in longer-term policy roles (Connelly and Pitney 1994, 42; Elving 1989). In doing so, the new minority whip built necessary connections to other segments of the Conference—Gunderson had helped to found the moderate "92 Group" caucus—but maintained close control over whip operations.

Although the Republican whip organization took some additional coordination responsibilities, the Policy Committee of the late 1980s maintained its substantive role in coordinating short-term party positions. Detailed records of the Policy Committee's official positions are available for a number of Republican-minority Congresses, including the 101st and 102nd Congress under Mickey Edwards' chairmanship.[54] These records reveal the types of issues on which the committee took public positions and allow some very basic analysis of how the committee's positions related to floor voting results. The Republican Policy Committee issued 26 resolutions or statements[55] in 1989, the first session of the 101st Congress. Seventeen House floor votes were clearly associated with one of these committee positions. As table 4.1 shows, the committee positions are selective in that they do not address all high-profile, controversial issues from the session. Some of the 1989 policy positions highlight the committee's efforts to support the new Bush administration's legislative agenda, including its statement on defense policy and resolutions in support of capital gains tax cuts and the White House's drug control strategy. Other resolutions and statements reflect either the minority party's work to define a coherent alternative position or the minority's short-term reactions to the majority's maneuvers or difficulties—e.g., the resolution supporting one standing committee's bill in conflict with another. Voting patterns on the 17 floor votes demonstrate that the committee's formal positions tended to address issues that were, not surprisingly, party unity votes by the traditional definition (more than half of one party opposing more than half of the other party). But beyond that general observation, note that much of the committee's activity centered on issues that split off a substantial minority of either the Democratic caucus or the Republican Conference. On a number of issues, Republicans were nearly unified but Democrats were split, as on the GOP minimum wage alternative, the repeal of catastrophic health care, the capital gains tax compromise, and the Nicaraguan elections bill. In these instances, the Policy Committee's actions appear to support the party's collective efforts to communicate a public message while muddling the majority's message. In many other cases, the GOP had a sizable internal minority opposed to the party position, and the Policy Committee's activity (as in the campaign finance example discussed in chapter 1) likely played a role in coordinating Republican members around a cohesive position on a potentially difficult issue. Overall, the committee's formal actions at this time suggest an effort to serve multiple collective interests of the Conference as a whole, as defined by top leaders, and not those of one particular leader or faction—a conclusion that is reinforced by the voting agreement of the minority leader, minority whip, and Policy Committee chair on all 17 votes.[56] The Policy Committee was coordinating on issues that sometimes divided the caucus but on which the top leadership team was entirely unified.

The examples in table 4.1 show the committee identified issues of considerable existing or potential Republican Conference agreement to signal through official resolutions and statements; no more than about one-third of House Republicans voted against the Conference majority on these Policy Committee items. Republican agreement on these issues is higher than on other 1989 party votes. On average, 83.3 percent of Republicans voted together on the 1989 votes related to Policy Committee positions, while only 78.9 percent voted together on average across all party unity votes ($p = .10$). The committee's signaling did not elevate GOP agreement beyond typical levels for high-profile votes: 82.5 percent of Republicans voted together on CQ Key Votes on average in 1989 ($p = .42$). The set of issues the committee chose, however, is quite different from the set of key votes CQ identified in 1989. This evidence suggests a committee effort to define a clear, short-term Republican set of positions on which at least a large majority of the Conference could agree.

The full Policy Committee was not always a successful forum in the 1980s minority for *developing* detailed legislative proposals, as Connelly emphasizes in his interview-based account of the period (1988, 28). The Republican Research Committee, by contrast, sometimes provided an organizational home for coordinating policy development in the Conference. Its task-force system of longer-term policy consideration was uneven in its activity (and, in many cases, was largely staff-driven),[57] but the Research Committee task forces did serve to communicate detailed policy information within the Conference in addition to publicizing the minority party's positions (see chap. 5). The 1988 drug bill provides an illustration of the committee's internal policy development role. Congress and the president moved toward an election-year omnibus drug bill in 1988, near the end of the 100th Congress, and the Republican Research Committee

TABLE 4.1. 1989 House Republican Policy Committee Resolutions/Statements

| Date | Resolution | Total Votes | GOP Votes | Dem. Votes |
|---|---|---|---|---|
| 2/24/89 | Calling for "measured consideration" of H.R. 5, Foreign Ownership Disclosure Act | — | — | — |
| 3/14/89 | Supporting Earned Income Tax Credit | — | — | — |
| 3/15/89 | Opposing Oberstar bill on Eastern Airlines (Roll-call: H.R. 1231 passage, 3/15/89) | 251–167 | 21–152 | 230–15 |
| 3/16/89 | Statement on Minimum Wage Principles (Roll-call: Goodling amendment to H.R. 2, 3/23/89) | 203–221 | 159–17 | 44–204 |
| 4/25/89 | Calling on Federal Reserve to avoid high interest rates | — | — | — |
| 5/2/89 | Supporting capital gains tax cuts | — | — | — |
| 5/2/89 | Supporting repeal of Section 89 of Internal Revenue Code—nondiscrimination provisions of 1986 Tax Reform Act (Roll-call: Previous question on rule for FY1989 supplemental, preventing Gekas amendment, 5/24/89) | 218–205 | 0–173 | 218–32 |
| 5/2/89 | Supporting spending cuts in FY1991 budget resolution (Roll-call: Passage, H Con Res 106, 5/4/89) | 266–160 | 107–64 | 159–96 |
| 6/6/89 | Condemning Tiananmen Square violence | — | — | — |
| 6/6/89 | Opposing Gonzalez amendment in committee to H.R. 1278 requiring banks to fund Affordable Housing Program (Roll-call: Bartlett amendment, 6/15/89) | 209–212 | 166–6 | 43–206 |
| 6/6/89 | Supporting off-budget financing for H.R. 1278—Financial Institutions Reform, Recovery, and Enforcement Act (Roll-call: Rostenkowski amendment, 6/15/89) | 280–148 | 30–146 | 250–2 |
| 6/6/89 | Opposing Frank housing provisions of H.R. 1278 | — | — | — |
| 6/15/89 | Opposing Family Medical Leave Act (Roll-call: Passage, 5/10/90) | 238–190 | 39–136 | 199–54 |
| 7/12/89 | Supporting Agriculture committee version of Tongass Timber Reform Act and oppose Interior committee version (Roll-call: De La Garza substitute, 7/13/89) | 146–271 | 112–55 | 34–216 |

| Date | | | | |
|---|---|---|---|---|
| 7/24/89 | Statement on defense policy (Roll-calls on H.R. 2461: Synar Stealth bomber amendment, Spratt Mobile MX amendment, Frank Midgetman amendment, 7/26/89) | 259–161 | 49–124 | 210–37 |
| | | 224–198 | 21–151 | 203–47 |
| | | 168–255 | 60–113 | 108–42 |
| 8/4/89 | Statement on Campaign Reform Package from Republican Policy Committee | — | — | — |
| 9/21/89 | Supporting Repeal of Catastrophic Health Care Coverage (Roll-call: Donnelly amendment to H.R. 3299, 10/4/89) | 362–67 | 164–10 | 198–57 |
| 9/21/89 | Supporting EITC for child care (Roll-call: Edwards amendment to H.R. 3299, 10/5/89) | 141–286 | 134–41 | 7–245 |
| 9/21/89 | Supporting Ways and Means Compromise on capital gains (Roll-call: Rostenkowski amendment to H.R. 3299 deleting tax cut, 9/28/89) | 190–240 | 1–176 | 189–64 |
| 9/21/89 | Supporting president's national drug control strategy | — | — | — |
| 9/21/89 | Supporting Drug War Bond Act | — | — | — |
| 10/3/89 | Supporting passage of budget reconciliation (Roll-call: Passage, H.R. 3299, 10/5/89) | 334–91 | 146–28 | 188–63 |
| 10/3/89 | Supporting H.R. 3385 on elections in Nicaragua (Roll-call: Passage, 10/4/89) | 265–156 | 165–11 | 100–145 |
| 10/17/89 | Supporting drug control strategy | — | — | — |
| 10/17/89 | Supporting H.R. 3402, The Polish and Hungarian Democracy Initiative of 1989 (Roll-call: Passage, H.R. 3402, 10/19/89) | 349–49 | 128–36 | 221–13 |
| 10/25/89 | Opposing rescinding budget sequestration until passage of reconciliation and appropriations bills. | — | — | — |

*Source:* Information on Republican Policy Committee resolutions and statements from Mickey Edwards Collection, Legislative Series, Box 81, Folders 25 and 26. Party splits calculated from Voteview (2013).

helped to formulate a minority draft bill in a task force. The Republican proposal, which emphasized stronger legal sanctions on the drug trade and drug users, shaped a series of Republican amendments added to the majority-preferred bill before House passage, and the Research Committee supported the floor debate with a position paper addressing arguments about the constitutionality of the GOP criminal law provisions (Lawrence 1988a, 1988b, 1988c).

The Policy and Research Committees produced internal communications that supported members' informational needs as well as the leadership's interest in transmitting strategy; the Republican whip system in the late minority era, like the majority Democratic organization, had stepped up its efforts to serve member needs in this way as well. Although Republicans in the minority seem to have relied more heavily on the Conference than on the whip for producing information,[58] the whip's office under Gingrich (and later in the majority) was providing detailed short-term information to Republican members.[59]

### Decline of Short-Term Coordination in the Policy Committee

The Republicans' 1994 victory brought the party into House majority status for the first time in four decades, and the new leadership imposed major changes on the extended leadership system. The new Republican majority would need internal coordination in the form of two-way information flow and collaborative negotiation over policy and strategy perhaps even more than the minority Conference did, particularly since the party had increased substantially in size. Speaker Gingrich and the new leadership team, in keeping with their centralizing approach to leadership in the 104th Congress (e.g., Aldrich and Rohde 2000a, 2000b; Fenno 1997; Sinclair 2006; Strahan 2007), drew the coordination function largely under the aegis of the top leadership, mostly through the tightly controlled whip system. The Conference jettisoned the Republican Research Committee entirely,[60] and the Republican Policy Committee took on other roles and became less relevant to routine party strategy.

Some of the changes were already underway prior to the 104th Congress, as the Policy Committee early in Clinton's first term began to emphasize communication of partisan messages. Even as the Policy Committee grew in size and, a bit later, gained its own staff lines for the first time, the coordination function on short-term legislative matters in the Policy Committee declined, and external communication of broad positions emerged as its main focus. Evidence from leadership files and from the committee's website suggests that open committee forums became infrequent and the Republican majority leadership focused the Policy Committee on executive session meetings, as well as staff work.[61] Under the direction of Policy Chair Christopher Cox (R-CA) in the late 1990s and early 2000s, the committee did use the process of developing big-picture policy statements as a way to both educate interested members and resolve some disagreements within the party,[62] so an element of coordination remained despite the changes.

In a few instances, the majority Republican Policy Committee played a visible role in the party's immediate legislative business, under top leadership control. In the 104th Congress, Republican leaders pursued a strategy of attaching policy "riders" to the House's annual appropriation bills to implement controversial policy choices efficiently. Under a plan by Majority Leader Richard Armey (R-TX), the Policy Committee reviewed and approved the controversial policy amendments (Evans and Oleszek 1997, 123; Burger 1995). The leadership also used the Policy Committee in the 105th Congress to debate and develop strategy for controversial Republican legislation to reform ethics rules and processes (Eilperin 1997a; Eilperin 1997b).[63] The majority party also chose the Policy Committee as a venue for battling internally over the specifics of campaign finance reform proposals (again) in 1996 and 1997 (Hume 1996a; Hume 1996b; Keller 1997). Aside from the legitimating role on policy riders and the unusual team-building function on the internally divisive questions of ethics and campaign funding, the contrast in the substance of the Policy Committee's activity between the late 1980s and the late 1990s is quite sharp. Short-term strategic coordination declined, and policy messages and connections with the larger party network became important concerns, as chapter 5 outlines.

The whip system, flexible meetings of top leaders and staff, and GOP task forces provided majority leadership-controlled platforms for near-term Conference coordination. In particular, Tom DeLay's greatly expanded whip organization offered coordination to the majority in the form of deliberation and discussion among members, communicating strategy, and gathering intelligence. Initially, DeLay took charge of the whip organization with some restrictions from above: Gingrich limited the resources available to the whip organization in the 104th Congress, maintaining minority-era funding levels for the whips in the 104th Congress (Burger 1994b). In the following Congress, though, DeLay received a major increase in budget and staff support and further expanded the membership of the whip network. DeLay's large whip organization met weekly, with deputies meeting much more frequently in session (Eilperin and Vande Hei 1997). In essence, the Republican majority whip system had grown to replicate its Democratic majority predecessor in size, institutional resources, and its role in two-way information sharing. As it did, it took on more of the responsibility for strategic communication, just as the Democratic whip system had done relative to the DSPC.

Although little primary evidence of DeLay's intelligence-gathering operation is available, a whip count in the Armey papers provides an instructive glimpse into the process in the 104th Congress and the internal coordinating information it generated.[64] The July 1996 tally asked members about their support for H.R. 3580, the Worker Right to Know Act, introduced by Harris Fawell (R-IL). The Right to Know Act "would require labor unions to get a signed agreement from any employee before accepting or requiring the payment of union dues for actions other than collective bargaining, such as political contributions" (Cassata 1996). In the count, whips informed members that "consideration is being given to bringing the Worker Right to Know Act to the floor" and asked "at this time, do you favor or not favor this bill?" Although Republicans were strongly in support of the bill—the whip count showed 195 members in favor, 31 opposed, and 7 undecided—the issue was problematic for Republican opponents, and the whip process transmitted specific objections to the leadership. The whip report included notation on the specific reactions of some members, including one who labeled the action a "dumb idea" and another who "would rather not have to vote on this bill." This whip effort supplied detailed intelligence not only on positions but on members' specific concerns, and both the whip question and the responses are targeted *specifically toward the leadership's decision about scheduling strategy*, not just its assessment of support for passage. In this case, the leadership chose to join the Right to Know Act with its campaign finance proposal—another internally divisive issue—into legislation that ultimately failed on the House floor with substantial Republican opposition.

As the "listening sessions" example in chapter 1 illustrates, the Republican whip system has continued to function as the organizational center for two-way communication within the Conference since the 1994 changes. The regular whip counting process has continued relatively unchanged since that time (Kane 2013), but McCarthy responded to the fragmentation within the Conference by renewing whip organization activity that vents and responds to member concerns. At the same time, the Conference has not returned to using the Policy Committee as a more decentralized participatory platform for serious coordination work, keeping it in a diminished role on near-term policy matters since the initial return to the majority in 1995.

## Party Organization Staff and Coordination

Any discussion of the House leadership organizations needs to consider the importance of staff to the organizations' work. Although the organizations are fundamentally serving leader and member goals through participation of members, leadership staff has been central to these organizations since they began to emerge in their modern form in the 1970s. Organization staff has become important for external communication and supporting persuasion, but the staff has had a particularly notable effect on coordination. As the Humphrey-Hawkins example in chapter 1 nicely illustrates, the party leadership staff works to keep components of the leadership and standing committees connected as well as to encourage coherence across the elements of the participatory party. The staff, in turn, have come to represent a tangible resource of the leadership organizations that are a benefit to involved members (Glassman 2012), particularly for those who rise to high-ranking extended leadership positions, such as chief deputy whips and the Republican Policy Committee chair. Like the rest of the party leadership staff (Peterson, Reynolds, and Wilhelm 2010), the party organization staff has grown rapidly since the 1970s. Figure 4.1 displays the rising expenditures for party organization staff (in constant dollars). Although the majority party has enjoyed a slight advantage over time, both parties' organizational resources have expanded at a similar rate.

In the O'Neill-era Democratic caucus, the staff of the DSPC supported that organization's coordination role and helped the Speaker to oversee, first, a sprawling legislative agenda in the late 1970s and, later, a caucus pressured by a politically powerful opposition White House. DSPC staff kept the Democratic leadership apprised of standing committee activity in considerable detail, tracking the progress of major and minor legislation and monitoring the content of committee hearings.[65] The staff's written work at this time heavily emphasized legislative substance and coordinating internal strategy—coordinating a still-divided majority and working against a strengthening conservative policy coalition.[66] DSPC staff also devoted some effort to longer-term planning of the party agenda.[67] By the late 1980s, under Jim Wright, the DSPC's staff grew by about 50 percent (see fig. 4.2), and Wright became known for his personal use of the party organization's staff. Wright "used staff as an extension of himself . . . not as advisers," and seized a prominent piece of Capitol Hill real estate to house the expanded DSPC staff (Barry 1989, 69–71). But the staff continued to serve a coordination role, particularly by keeping party leaders abreast of developments in the committees.[68] Although the DSPC staff numbers

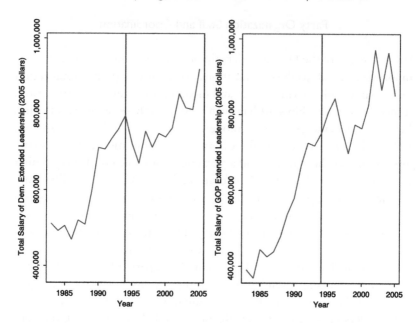

Fig. 4.1. Salary Expenditures of House Party Leadership Organizations, 1983–2007

Note: Includes statutory and lump-sum staff. Vertical line marks the divide between Republican and Democratic majorities. (See appendix A for data source information.)

fell back to pre-Wright levels under Tom Foley, the staff did considerable policy work for the leadership and coordinated with committees,[69] supporting Foley's objective of maintaining a "window on the inner workings" of the standing committees (Burger 1991a). In the minority in the 1990s, the DSPC staff grew again, but the staff began to shift toward more communications activity, as chapter 5 explains.

As the whip organizations have expanded and taken on most of the routine coordination role, the whip staff has grown as well, with both parties typically designating staff not only for the majority or minority whip's office but also for the chief deputies. Since the early 1980s, the Democratic whip organization has maintained roughly 20 total staffers supporting its operations. The thickening of the chief deputy whip layer in the 1990s corresponded to a major increase in the staff allocated to the chief deputy majority whips—the staff increased from 5 in the 100th Congress to 8 in the 103rd, and 15 staffers were serving the chief deputies by the 106th. As the Republican whip system became more elaborate and more important

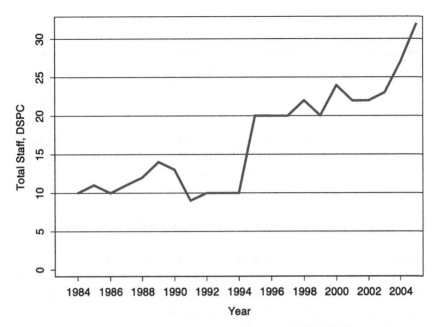

Fig. 4.2. Democratic Steering and Policy Committee Staff, 1983–2005
(Data from author's tabulations from various editions of the quarterly *Report of the Clerk of the House* *[through 1994] and Statement of Disbursements of the House* [after 1994]. Staff listings for the DSPC are not included in the *Report of the Clerk* prior to 1983.)

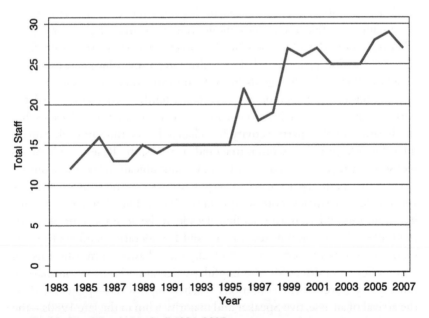

Fig. 4.3. Republican Whip Staff, 1984–2007
(Data from author's tabulations from various editions of the quarterly *Report of the Clerk of the House* [through 1994] and *Statement of Disbursements of the House* [after 1994]. Total includes staff to the majority or minority whip and to the chief deputy majority/minority whips.)

for coordinating the majority party's efforts, its staff also jumped in size in the 1990s. The large staff Tom DeLay employed in the late 1990s was sustained through Blunt's tenure as whip and even into the Republicans' return to the minority in 2007, as figure 4.3 shows. In short, while the story of House party organizations is primarily one about involvement of party members in the power exercised by the leadership, the expanding staff resources of these organizations reflects their increasing importance to the coordinating functions of the parties.

## Conclusions: Coordination in the Extended Party Leadership

The evidence in this chapter demonstrates that the modern party caucuses in the House rely on their organizational framework to forge informational connections among individual members and between members and the leadership. To provide incentives for supportive behavior on key measures and achieve collective policy objectives—the subject of chapter 6—or to create a cohesive message to communicate outside the House for electoral benefits—a main concern of the next chapter—the party leadership must first understand what policy positions are acceptable to the membership, work with members in key positions to shape and move the legislation, and communicate within the caucus about strategic plans. The leadership, in addition, enjoys the added benefit of indirect persuasion that results from the coordination process and the resulting teamsmanship, and members benefit in their individual goals from the information they acquire.

Republicans and Democrats have consistently used elements of the party organization to facilitate coordination over the past four decades, but the location of that party activity has changed over time in each caucus. The Republican Policy Committee (and, at times, the Research Commit-tee) served the party's needs for two-way communication routinely during the minority period, particularly so as policy divisions and strategic maneu-vers divided the parties more sharply in the 1980s. The Democratic major-ity found the DSPC, during its first decade, to be an important place for the leadership, key committee leaders, and Democratic members to com-municate. But both conferences gradually turned away from robust use of their policy committees for meaningful, participatory information sharing. Once party government conditions reached high levels—punctuated by the arrival of an assertive Speaker and majority whip in the late 1980s—the DSPC moved into a narrower role and some coordination moved to the larger but increasingly loyalist whip organization. Faced with majority status for the first time, Republicans made a similar move in 1995 under a centralizing leader in a polarized House. At a greater distance from the strong central leadership, the Policy Committee no longer regularly served key short-term coordination needs, but an enlarged, strengthened, and loyal whip system filled in its place. For both Republicans and Democrats, the policy committees worked well to coordinate party and standing committees as long as the latter remained crucial to policy and process (Aldrich, Perry, and Rohde 2013), but the controlled whip organization was better suited to a leadership-centered approach.

The overall picture is one in which the caucuses found their policy committees valuable tools when internal demands for more assertive policy and procedural leadership grew and participation allowed members to maintain involvement in a strengthening party leadership. But more homogenous parties facing close electoral combat encouraged a more controlled approach to coordination. This approach still relies on the party organizations—even during Gingrich's first Congress, the Conference's communications were not run solely from the Speaker's office. But leaders of cohesive parties in a polarized chamber have preferred a large but loyal whip system to carry the coordination function.

# FIVE

# External Communication and
# Party Leadership Organizations

The congressional party's coordination activity, as the previous chapter demonstrated, is concerned with facilitating communication within the caucus. In order to advance party legislative goals as well as the individual goals of the rank-and-file, House leaders have used party organizations to gather information from members, to share information internally, and to encourage communication among party leaders, committee leaders, and the rank-and-file. This form of communication—in the service of internal coordination—is joined by an *external* communications role for the party organizations. As I will show, the external communications function of congressional party organizations has a relatively long history, but it has become much more important in the electorally competitive, strong-party-government era of the 1990s to the present. The parties in the House have at least two distinct constituencies outside of the chamber with which they seek to communicate through participatory organizations: the potential reelection constituency for the party's members and the expanded network of party actors.

The communications role of party organizations is oriented, first, toward conveying the party's priorities and messages to a broad constituency to affect election outcomes and to build constituency support for policy initiatives. Congressional research of the last decade has placed renewed theoretical emphasis on the importance of collective electoral goals and the party image (e.g., Lee 2009; Smith 2007), and some work on the congressional parties has stressed the growing "PR" function of congressional

114

leadership (Lee 2011; Malecha and Reagan 2012, 68–88; Sinclair 2006, 263–83). House party leaders facing an ongoing battle for control of the chamber since 1994 have given new attention to communicating a clear public message about the party's identity and agenda. In this environment, both the majority party and the minority party have an incentive to use resources at their disposal to project messages and to connect their internal efforts at coordination and persuasion to this external messaging. These activities are not entirely new innovations in recent Congresses, though, as the evidence shows participatory organizations in the earlier post-reform period also engaged in some external communications efforts.

The second focus of external communication, the expanded party network, encompasses a range of party-related actors who work together, formally and informally, toward party objectives. According to Koger, Masket, and Noel, the modern party is defined by the scope of these actors, who "join' the party when they begin communicating with other members of the network, developing common strategies and coordinating action to achieve shared goals" (2009, 637). Both information and political support flow through this network (Desmarais, La Raja, and Kowal 2015; Grossmann and Dominguez 2009; Koger, Masket, and Noel 2009, 2010; Masket 2009), which includes interest groups, media outlets, campaign professionals and consultants, political staffers in government, partisan activists, as well as the formal organizations of the political parties (Bernstein and Dominguez 2003; Koger, Masket, and Noel 2009). This expanded party network is necessary to the goals of congressional party leaders. On the policy side, parties in the House should recognize the strategic importance of support from party actors outside Congress—leaders can advance their efforts to move (or stop) legislation by working with entities in the expanded party that can affect the goals of individual party members and the party's reputation more broadly. We have known for some time that outside group leaders can and do shape the political environment for successful congressional policy making (see Arnold 1990, esp. chap. 5). The scope of the modern expanded party network does not diminish its importance for legislating (Grossman and Dominguez 2009), and we should expect House leaders to use the chamber's party organizations to attempt to channel and make use of this resource. On the electoral side, the expanded party network provides resources in the form of endorsements and campaign support for the party's candidates (Dominguez 2005; Grossmann and Dominguez 2009; Masket 2009). And, to the extent that ambitious rank-and-file members of the caucus see benefits for their individual goals in connections with the expanded party, the House party leadership should also see value in offering links with outside actors as a selective benefit of participating in party leadership organizations.

In this chapter, I review evidence for the parties' externally directed communications through extended leadership organizations. I first evaluate the party organizations as participatory centers for publicly communicating electorally oriented messages. I then consider the connections party leaders have forged with the expanded party network, both in earlier years and in more intensely partisan recent Congresses, emphasizing how these efforts serve the party's collective goals as well as the interests of some rank-and-file members. Throughout, the evidence from archival and secondary sources supports the conclusion that the House leadership in both parties has made greater use of the party organizations for external communications since the late 1980s and, in particular, since the 1995 Republican takeover. The communications role followed the directions of the congressional parties in general, and it was well suited to fill the gap left as strong party leadership moved some party organizations away from coordination functions.

## Communicating an Electoral Message

In her most recent account of congressional party activity and polarization, Sinclair observes that "Members of Congress . . . have come to expect their party leaders to participate effectively in national political discourse, influencing the terms of the debate so as to further their members' immediate legislative goals and to protect and enhance the party's image" (2006, 265). This message communication—or "PR politics" in Sinclair's terms—has become central to the role of the elected party leadership in the majority and in the minority. For the House majority, this external communication serves to frame the majority's accomplishments to build electoral support. For the House minority, whose positions are institutionally disadvantaged in Washington policy debates, the party's external communications are a core part of its majority-building work: they define the party brand and build support for the minority's agenda against the current majority's. The leadership in both cases has relied on the organized party leadership structure and its members to communicate party messages. In addition, as the caucuses have made less use of some organizational components since the 1980s for coordination, the communications role has predominated for those elements of the system. A review of the external communications activity in several Democratic and Republican party organizations highlights these trends.

## Democratic Steering and Policy Committee

In the 1970s, the DSPC served as a key component of the majority's short-term policy coordination. Even then, the majority used the committee, at times, for a participatory approach to communicating a party message when it lacked the agenda-setting power of the White House. In the 94th Congress, a DSPC Task Force on Information, led by John Brademas (D-IN), issued detailed briefs on Democratic legislation and political messages.[1] During Ronald Reagan's first term, the DSPC's role shifted more noticeably in the direction of communication. Although the caucus rules on the committee's role remained the same,[2] the majority now used the DSPC in conjunction with other caucus efforts in part to counter Reagan's agenda-setting platform. During 1981 and 1982, House Democrats engaged in a wide-ranging effort to formulate and disseminate an alternative Democratic agenda on the economy (Herrnson and Patterson 1995). The Democratic Caucus oversaw a series of seven task forces on the economy with the goal of pushing the Democratic party to "run a national campaign of its own" by shifting from "thinking legislation" to "thinking politics" by building "political issues" in the House for the midterm elections.[3] The DSPC, under Richard Bolling's (D-MO) supervision, was then responsible for using the task force products to synthesize a coherent policy alternative. After the Democratic resurgence in the 1982 elections, the DSPC again served in a similar clearing-house role as the House Democrats developed and publicized alternative policies (Cohen 1982b; Cohen 1983).

Later, when Democrats were in the House minority in the 1990s and 2000s, the committee's work had some similarities to the early-80s party-in-opposition role. During the 1990s, the committee was a source of political materials in support of Clinton initiatives and in opposition to the GOP majority (Simendinger 2000; Wildavsky 1997). Specialized staffers for the Policy Committee ("steering" and "policy" roles were organized under separate co-chairs for a time) worked on both short-term messaging and long-term policy development in conjunction with key members (Kahn 1995; *National Journal* 1995). By the 106th Congress, the Policy Committee employed at least a dozen staffers who had designated issue specialties, providing the House Democrats with substantial resources for articulating an alternative policy agenda in the minority.[4] The Policy Committee's role in the Gephardt-led minority period, then, was as a heavily "staff-driven shop" (Billings 2003d) that served the issue communication needs of the leadership in opposition.

In recent years, particularly since House Democrats returned to the minority in 2011, the DSPC has been a visible platform for the minority leadership and members to participate in public hearings on its legislative priorities (Hunter 2011b; Millman 2011). In one example, discussed in chapter 1, Georgetown law student Sandra Fluke spoke to the DSPC on women's health issues after the chair of Oversight and Government Reform prevented Democrats from calling Fluke to testify about contraception coverage.[5] But this was only the most widely reported and controversial of the Democrats' many DSPC hearings on core caucus priorities in the 112th and 113th Congresses. (The committee held a few hearings in the Democratic-majority 111th Congress on key issues as well.) Table 5.1 lists major public DSPC hearings from 2011 through early 2014, showing that these hearings tended to focus either on issues "owned" by the party or on challenges to the majority's management of salient issues. These hearings resembled standing-committee hearings in format, with statements by minority leader Pelosi, DSPC members, and other Democrats, and question-and-answer exchanges with carefully chosen witnesses. Some of the DSPC hearings attracted substantial participation from the caucus, with as many as 25 members involved.[6] For the Democratic minority, the DSPC gave an aura of institutional legitimacy to the party's efforts to frame a public message for its collective electoral goals, and it allowed Democratic members to participate in support of the party's message as well as their own position-taking.

TABLE 5.1. Examples of Democratic Steering and Policy Committee Hearings, 112th–113th Congresses

| Hearing Topic | Date |
| --- | --- |
| Future of the Affordable Care Act | 1/18/2011 |
| Job creation and infrastructure | 2/2/2011 |
| Jobs, innovation, and energy | 2/28/2011 |
| Risks of default to the economy | 7/7/2011 |
| Small business and job creation | 10/4/2011 |
| Entrepreneurship and job creation in the "supercommittee" | 11/3/2011 |
| Women's health and contraception | 2/23/2012 |
| Gas prices and speculation | 4/4/2012 |
| Paycheck Fairness Act | 5/30/2012 |
| Gun violence prevention | 1/16/2013 |
| Sequestration and the federal workforce | 2/21/2013 |
| Race and justice in America | 7/30/2013 |
| Long-term unemployment benefits | 12/5/2013 |
| 5-year anniversary of the Lilly Ledbetter Fair Pay Act | 1/29/2014 |

*Source:* C-Span.org; DemocraticLeader.gov.

## Democratic Whip Organization

The whip organization in the Democratic caucus illustrates the role of the modern, institutionalized whip system in using the legislative process to advance a public communication strategy. For Democrats, the whip organization allowed coordination of a floor-messaging strategy as this kind of activity became a more routine part of House leadership efforts in the 1980s. The majority chief deputy whip's office, empowered with its own staff and budget, took charge of the majority's use of one-minute speeches under Bill Alexander (D-AR) in the early 1980s. The staff developed a database of key members for delivering one-minute speeches, analyzed the past impact and effectiveness of Democrats' one-minutes, and made some effort to focus the content of the speeches on electorally useful issues.[7] This more direct effort to craft a public message joined the whip system's long-standing role in disseminating issue-specific talking points and pre-written speech notes to help members to communicate the party's message in the district.[8]

In the 1990s, David Bonior made several changes to the structure and operation of the extensive whip organization in an effort to improve messaging, particularly after the party lost the majority. With an eye toward supporting the Steering and Policy Committee's work to publicly communicate Democratic alternatives after the 1994 losses, the minority whip reoriented the top levels of the appointed whip structure. The four chief deputy whips in the 104th Congress had specific, rather than general, roles; Bonior assigned one to supporting policy research, two to linking policy development to committee and subcommittee strategy, and one to coordinating communications (Kahn 1995).

Partisan communications were also advanced by the minority whip's work to coordinate around key issues and persuade members to support party positions. In the 106th Congress, the Democrats faced a GOP majority held by very narrow margins, and the minority used the whip organization simultaneously to push against Republican policy agenda items *and* to advocate publicly for Democratic alternatives. The Bonior whip organization went beyond whipping floor votes to targeting other tools for messaging. On one major issue—the health care Patient's Bill of Rights—the whip organization pursued a complex strategy, whipping members through a whip task force to support a discharge petition on a Democratic-favored bill (sponsored by John Dingell, D-MI),[9] coordinating 168 signatures on the petition on the first day. The minority whip also used a discharge-petition strategy on the minimum wage in 1999, when Democrats sought to place pressure on Republicans and take advantage of their popular position.[10]

### Republican Policy Committee

On the other side of the aisle, the Republican Policy Committee has played a role in external communication throughout its long history in the Conference. The committee itself had its beginnings, in fits and starts, in the post-World War II period as a way for the Republican minority to more effectively develop and then advertise policy positions. In his early study, Charles Jones noted "much of what the House Republican Policy Committee does can be attributed to the efforts of a frustrated minority trying to become the majority" (Jones 1964, 138). Through the 1960s, the Policy Committee continued to focus on party position taking, and it refined its efforts to publicly communicate the Republican alternative more effectively (Jones 1970, 159–60), particularly when the party was both in the minority and out of the White House.

Under the large Democratic majorities of the 1970s, a major focus of the Policy Committee's work was articulating opposition to specific Democratic legislative proposals and providing arguments for alternative Republican policies. The committee's 24 policy statements in 1977[11] include a statement in opposition to Democratic revisions to the Hatch Act (H.R. 10), a call for support of the motion to recommit on the Tax Reduction and Simplification Act of 1977 (H.R. 3477), and arguments for specific changes needed for Republican support of the Clean Air Act amendments of 1977 (H.R. 6161).[12] The statements represent the committee's public framing of the issues it deliberated upon. During the 1980 election season, the committee issued numerous public statements attacking the opposition generally or outlining an alternative agenda for electoral purposes. In September 1980, for instance, the committee's members endorsed a series of "Republican Pledges" for the election and prepared boilerplate press releases on a Carter administration defense policy issue for Republican House challengers to use in their local races.[13]

In this early period, then, the Republican Policy Committee linked its work on short-term policy coordination to electoral communication, and it also served as a source for purely electorally oriented material for the minority party. Under Dick Cheney's (R-WY) chairmanship in the early 1980s, this split role continued. The Policy Committee was a center for talks about integrating leadership plans with Conservative Opportunity

Society (COS) ideas and making conservative ideas "more politically salable" (Cohen 1984), thus connecting substantive policy directions with external communications. At the same time, the Cheney committee also used its research activity to analyze data on PAC contribution patterns in the 1984 election in order to highlight the disproportionate corporate PAC contributions to Democratic incumbents and to cast the Democratic majority as "fraudulent" (Cohen 1985).[14]

As chair later in the 1980s, Mickey Edwards (R-OK) made a concerted effort to take the dual roles of coordination and communication seriously. A Conference document from this time period described the Policy Committee's role to include holding "policy meetings on a need basis to air views on issues of concern to the Conference," issuing "policy statements on issues and disseminat[ing] the statements to the Members and the press," and considering "resolutions or other matters brought before the Republican Conference and referred to the Policy Committee and report findings on such subjects to the Leadership and the Conference."[15] As chapter 4 outlined, the Edwards committee engaged in significant coordination activity, but public communication was also a central feature of the Policy Committee's approach, and Edwards' staff assembled a plan to communicate Republican positions via the committee.[16]

By the very end of the Republican minority era, though, the committee's official statements took on a more partisan tone, appearing to be more overtly for public political consumption than committee products from the late 1980s (or even a decade earlier) had been. In other words, the connection between internal coordination and public communication faded, with the committee's apparent emphasis moving to electoral messaging. In the last congressional session before the 1994 Republican takeover, the Policy Committee issued 23 official policy statements. Most responded to the White House and congressional majority's agenda items in a short-term fashion, but the content shows the movement toward external messaging. The titles of the policy statements, which included "Rigged Rule for the EPA Bill" and "Child Pornography: Dirty Pictures and Dirty Politics in the House of Representatives," illustrate the shift.[17] Some of this change may have resulted from the congressional party's response to the loss of the White House after 12 years in 1993. Although the Republican Policy Committee, it seems, was less central to the minority's response to the loss of White House resources than the Democratic Steering and Policy Committee had been for the Democrats in 1981, the Republican Policy Committee played a visible and overtly message-oriented role—for instance, by pressing the Democratic majority on procedural issues and reforms that were an important part of the Republican brief against Democratic control (Foerstel 1993a, 1993b).

Although the Policy Committee's rules publication in the majority period of the 1990s-2000s continued to describe the committee as "the House majority's principal forum for discussion of specific legislative initiatives," the majority committee's function is better captured by other text in the rules document: "Many issues that call for a clear statement of majority policy are not properly addressed (or cannot be timely addressed) by legislation. The Policy Committee . . . is uniquely well suited to issue such statements after careful deliberation and opportunity for all Members to be heard."[18] Under chair Christopher Cox (R-CA), the committee met frequently and issued sharply worded statements on major issues. It continued the trend from the late minority period of offering broad positions with partisan political aims, such as a 1999 policy statement on "The Clinton-Gephardt Abandonment of Social Security" and a 1997 statement on "How The ABA Became a Left-Wing Lobbying Group."[19] Many policy statements contained detailed substantive material that would be useful to the membership even as they also helped to push the party's issue framing—a 2002 statement on the estate tax, for example, was headlined "Throw the Death Tax From the Train!" but also provided a good executive summary of evidence in support of conservative arguments on the issue.[20] The Republican Policy Committee, then, remained quite active in the GOP majority of the 1990s and 2000s, but as short-term coordination became less important, the committee's work began to focus on shaping the party message and helping members to communicate it.

### Partisan Communication and the Policy Committee Chair

In the Policy Committee's communications role, we can see particularly clearly the influence the elected chair of a party leadership organization can exert in its direction. Over several decades, the committee mixed coordination and communication. Chapter 4 discusses the importance of coordination in the 1980s and the decline of that role in the 1990s. This dynamic, I argue, is consistent with strengthening party government demands in the 1980s, followed by majority control and very high levels of polarization in the 1990s. At the same time, some variation in the Policy Committee's communications focus appears to correspond to the goals of the elected Republican Policy Committee chair. Connelly (1988) noted in his research on the 1980s Policy Committee that its activity shifted according to the goals of the chair, and that trend seems particularly pronounced in the committee's communications emphasis and in the content of the communications.

As early as the 1970s, the chair's influence was notable. Bud Shuster (R-PA), committee chair in the 96th Congress, engaged the committee in regular deliberations over issues that were immediately before the House and systematically publicized the Conference's position on these issues to highlight the contrast with the Democratic majority. Shuster was aiming to rise in the ranks of the Republican leadership, and he drew on this record in his bid for the minority whip post in the 97th Congress.[21] And, as noted above, the Edwards-led Policy Committee of the late 1980s was similarly engaged in linking substance and external communication. Edwards' focus apparently followed from both Policy Committee member expectations and Edwards' motivation to become a more visible figure within the leadership. His own goals as a leader reinforced his vision of an active committee that promoted and publicized cohesive positions within and beyond the Conference.[22]

The changing leadership approach of the new Republican majority left the continuing Policy Committee as a kind of blank slate for an ambitious elected Policy chair. As chair from 1995 until 2005, Christopher Cox strongly influenced the committee's direction, and the committee's message-oriented policy activity followed his concerns and policy expertise. Cox's personal policy goals included a major emphasis on foreign affairs, particularly the economic, military, and human rights policies of China and Russia—he gained a good deal of attention in the late 1990s as the chair of a House select committee that produced a controversial report on military and trade issues with China (Doherty 1999; McCutcheon 1999). Cox devoted a considerable amount of the Policy Committee's attention to controversies over China, and Russia to a lesser extent, during his chairmanship. The Policy Committee was particularly involved in the debate over most-favored-nation trading status for China in the 105th Congress (Schlesinger 1997), and it produced an extensive 1997 report on China, offering 11 pieces of legislation and a "comprehensive initiative on U.S.-China relations that moves beyond the current policy stalemate in Washington and provides creative responses to every facet of our complex relationship."[23] The 27 major Policy Committee public statements issued in the 105th Congress include positions on China's environmental record, Bill Clinton's visit to Tiananmen Square, Chinese tobacco, missile defense, and human rights and trade in China.[24] The committee addressed the party's long-term positions on other issues as well, particularly on domestic economic policy, another area of expertise for Cox.[25] At times, the strong emphasis on the Policy Committee chair's own policy concerns led to controversy among House Republicans (Crabtree 2000; Fonder 2001), but Cox's direction seems to have maintained a distinct communications role for the committee in the Republican Conference at a time when its fate was uncertain.

A set of contested races for Policy Committee chair in 2006 illustrated very clearly the leader-driven character of the committee and the continuing debate over the role for a Republican Policy Committee in the majority.[26] Tellingly, Thaddeus McCotter (R-MI), who was elected chair after Adam Putnam's (R-FL) very brief tenure in 2006, argued the Policy Committee should be "reformed" to "focus less on specific 'policies' and more on core principles," envisioning a "more philosophical entity" that would "cease messaging pending and passed legislation" and "cease attempting to influence specific legislation" (*Roll Call* 2006). When McCotter took control, the committee followed this blueprint, and during the Republicans' return to minority status from 2007–11, the Policy Committee did not take on a renewed role in helping to coordinate short-term minority positions as it had in the late 1980s and early 1990s. Instead, the committee continued with a communications focus, but the content of the external message was much broader. The Policy Committee routinely issued sweeping—and somewhat eccentric—documents on ideological underpinnings for conservative views, promoted with what *Roll Call* called "oddball marketing tactics" (Heil 2007). McCotter conflicted with Republican leaders over the Policy Committee's role and other issues (Whittington 2007; Hooper 2011), and, although he was able to shift the committee in his preferred communications direction during his chairmanship,[27] the committee did not occupy an important place in the Conference's messaging. By the end of his tenure, McCotter even made a surprising effort, opposed by other Republican leaders, to eliminate the Policy Committee entirely (Kucinich 2010).

In the most recent GOP-majority Congresses, the Policy Committee's chair has been a visible part of the majority's communications efforts, although available public reporting does not reveal much evidence of the full committee engaging in regular work as it had under Christopher Cox. The post-2010 Policy Committee's first chair, Tom Price (R-GA), was a conservative Tea Party Caucus member and former chair of the Republican Study Committee (RSC). Price took an active role in GOP messaging, particularly on budget and health care issues, and he was frequently quoted in the press as a Conference leadership voice (e.g., Brady 2012). Like many of his predecessors, Price seemed to use the Policy Committee position as a stepping stone for his leadership goals (Newhauser 2012), and he took an active campaigning role in the 2012 elections (Haberkorn 2012), publicly describing his most important job in the leadership as an electoral one: maintaining a GOP House and flipping the Senate to Republican control.[28] When Price unsuccessfully pursued a step up the leadership ladder, losing a bid for Conference chair in the 113th Congress, his successor at the Policy Committee, James Lankford (R-OK), continued the pattern of using the committee as a platform to offer a public leadership voice.

Overall, the Republican Policy Committee illustrates the impact of individual leaders on party organizations: throughout its history, the committee has responded not only just to the goals of top elected leadership and the participatory expectations of members but also to the goals of individuals elected to chair the committee. The communications activity of the committee and the content of those communications have varied with the policy and career goals of the chair. In addition, the succession of elected Policy Committee chairs tracks the committee's narrowing communications focus and decline in policy-making relevance. Active Policy Committee chairs in the 1970s and 1980s, when the coordination function remained important, were successful in linking substantive policy activity to public position-taking. In the 1990s and 2000s, committee chairs worked on developing public party positions according to their interests and expertise, while the Policy Committee in the last few Congresses appears to have been largely a megaphone for its chair as part of the elected GOP leadership team.

### Republican Research Committee

For about three decades, the Republican Research Committee was responsible for long-range policy development, often through member task forces. Although the Research Committee was sometimes described— both approvingly and critically—as a "think tank,"[29] its processes and its products played a more political role in bolstering the minority's efforts at communicating Republican alternatives during the long Democratic majority period. Some of the committee's products provided the sort of staff research to support public positions that was in short supply for a minority party. Without a significant voice in foreign and defense policy during the Carter Administration, for example, the Republicans used the Research Committee to produce position papers on big-picture defense policy issues, including the long-term role of NATO and U.S. ground forces in Europe.[30] But other Research Committee work was more directly linked to the Conference's message-communication attempts through member involvement. According to a report from the Research Committee's chair in the 98th Congress, James Martin (R-NC), the committee linked its long-term research to the Republican minority's strategy in floor debates. In doing so, it offered a platform for minority party members:

> [The Republican Research Committee] has reached out to more junior members with high levels of interest in particular subject matters, brought them together, and provided the support needed to spring them as a potent force in support of the party position in House debate. Following the longer-than-expected floor debate on the [nuclear] "Freeze" a wag on the other side described the process as "taking some nice puppies and unleashing them as dogs of war."[31]

The Republican Research Committee, in other words, not only served the party by offering substantive background material, but it also linked that goal to the party's efforts at conveying a focused legislative alternative to the majority. In another example from the same time period, the Committee created a in-depth publication (*Ideas for Tomorrow, Choices for Today*) on the House Republicans' plans for the first 100 days of a second Reagan term, and two years later, it published a follow-up piece assessing the party's progress on the issue items.[32] Like other elements of the extended Republican party organization, the Research Committee produced communication-oriented materials designed to assist members with constituency and electoral activity. These included election-year issue guides for members, as well as speechwriting materials.[33]

Detailed records of the Republican Research Committee from Mickey Edwards' tenure as chair illustrate the committee's task force activity and its communications function. Edwards expanded the roster of task forces (see table 5.2), in some cases responding to requests from Research Committee members to chair task forces on particular issues, and he sought to connect the existing task force model with more publicly salient issues, such as education reform.[34] Some of the task forces were well established and had a long-standing routine for developing and distributing policy information. The Task Force on International Trade, chaired by Don Sundquist (R-TN), included nine members and was directed by two staffers from Sundquist's office. The task force regularly produced trade policy information, bill analyses, and op-eds for Republican members and staff with trade-related policy interests, and it held formal events and briefings on trade policy.[35] The Task Force on Regulatory Reform, chaired by Dick Armey (R-TX), was similarly productive.[36] Other task forces, to Edwards' frustration, rarely met or failed to respond to the direction of the Research Committee, so some of the Research Committee's product was staff- rather than member-driven.[37]

At times, the Research Committee overlapped with or duplicated the Policy Committee's communications on short-term issues. The committee's chair in the 101st Congress, Duncan Hunter (R–CA), greatly expanded the range of issues on which the committee acted. The 101st Congress Research Committee listed 31 task forces, including those addressing very narrow legislative topics such as acid rain and the Social Security earnings test.[38] This expansion of the Research Committee's role continued to the committee's end after the 103rd Congress (see table 5.2).[39] In the early 1990s, congressional Republicans framed public responses to major Clinton administration initiatives through Research Committee hearings, including its effort to modify policy on gays in the military and its health care reform proposal.[40]

TABLE 5.2. Task Forces of the Republican Research Committee

| 98th Congress | 100th Congress | 103rd Congress |
|---|---|---|
| Agriculture | Budget Reform | Crime |
| Congressional and Regulatory | Defense | Drugs |
|   Reform | Education | American Air Power |
| Crime | Energy | Military Personnel |
| Economic Policy | Family Values | Military Relief Missions |
| Energy and Natural Resources | Federal Accounting | Nuclear Proliferation |
| Foreign Policy | High Technology | SDI |
| Health and Environment | International Trade | Terrorism/Unconventional |
| High Technology | Regulatory Reform |   Warfare |
| Income Maintenance | Rural Communities | Veterans Health Care |
| National Defense | Women's Issues | Budget Reform |
| | | Competitiveness |
| | | Corporate Accountability |
| | | Energy |
| | | Financial Industry Reform |
| | | Tax Reform and Job Creation |
| | | Social Security |
| | | Clean Oceans |
| | | Environmental Balance |
| | | Project 103: Environmental |
| | |   Leadership for the 103rd |
| | |   Congress |

*Source:* House Republican Research Committee, Robert Michel Papers, Leadership Series, Box 6, Folder: 98th Congress: Republican Research Committee; Task Force Membership list, 1987, Mickey Edwards Collection, Legislative Series, Box 81, Folder 30; Committee on Research, Armey Collection, Legislative Series, Box 56, Folder 22.

The Research Committee housed resources to produce substantive issue materials with a Republican emphasis at a time when Republicans lacked the institutional resources that come with majority control of the standing committees. It did so by involving interested members who wished to participate in publicizing Republican alternatives. At its best, the task force system of the Research Committee functioned as a kind of shadow committee system for the minority's messages, affording a legitimate venue for hearings on Republican priorities, much as the DSPC has for Democrats in the 2010s.

### Republican Whip Organization

The minority Republican whip system, in its day-to-day work, served the party's communication efforts as early as the 1960s and 1970s. Where the party had identified a clear alternative to the Democratic majority's position, the whip system was typically unable to thwart the Democrats, but the whip system helped Republicans send a clear message through their legislative strategy, particularly when the party controlled neither the White House nor the House of Representatives (see chap. 6 for examples).

As the whip system gradually strengthened over time, Republican leaders made more deliberate attempts to link external communications and whip activity. In a relatively early example, Deputy Whip John Myers (R-IN) and the four regional Republican whips initiated the Whips' Fund for a Republican Majority to raise money to support Republican challengers in the 1980 elections. The whips linked their effort to build support on rollcalls to the larger effort to build a GOP majority in the House.[41]

With the election of Newt Gingrich as minority whip in 1989, the whip organization took a turn toward a more aggressive legislative strategy. Gingrich's whip system changes included a newly assertive public communications component. Starting in the 101st Congress, Gingrich assembled a "Strategy Whip" team. The Strategy Whip innovation was Gingrich's attempt to build a new leadership structure to develop and execute public communication and legislative strategies (Harris 2010). Gingrich added to the conventional whip structure five designated Strategy Whips, and he placed moderate Steve Gunderson (R-WI) in charge of this "strategy development arm of the Republican Whip organization." Among the members' tasks was "professional development": improving the ability of individual Republican members to communicate leadership themes.[42]

Recruiting members from in and outside of the whip organization, Gingrich held weekly Strategy Whip meetings of about 25 members.[43] The group discussed communications on both immediate legislative issues and Gingrichian long-range concepts. At a July 1990 meeting, for example, the strategy whip meeting attendees encountered two agenda items: reviewing strategies and tactics for communicating on the campaign finance reform issue (e.g., "Contact outside groups encouraging them to issue press releases and newsletters to their members on the need for prompt action on campaign reform") and discussing the GOP political implications of Kevin Phillips' book *The Politics of the Rich and Poor* (Phillips 1991).[44] The strategy whip effort, which did not survive into the Republican majority as part of the whip organization, appears to have duplicated the contemporaneous efforts of the Republican Policy Committee and, to a lesser extent, the Republican Research Committee. That Gingrich chose to create his own policy communication entity within the minority whip organization illustrates the use of extended leadership structures to serve individual leader goals, and it demonstrates the adaptation of the extended leadership to a changing electoral environment.

Some of the Republican leadership's adaptation in the early 1990s involved some ad hoc participatory communications centers outside of the existing party organizational framework. In the 103rd Congress, the whip and the minority leader had assembled a "Communications Advisory Group" of eight members "tapped for their communications experience, creativity, eye for image, and knowledge of media venues." The group met weekly and worked with existing elements of the organizational structure to transmit party messages.[45] Republicans had also established a "Theme Team" to work on strategic messaging, with a particular emphasis on one-minutes and special orders. In the early 1990s, the Team had 20 Republican members who were significantly more junior, more conservative, and more party-loyal than the rest of the Conference. In the 103rd Congress, the Theme Team was responsible for coordinating, on average "over 30 one-minutes 'on theme' each week."[46] The Republican Theme Team— which was matched by a similar Democratic group—continued through the 1990s and beyond (Harris 2013; Malecha and Reagan 2012, 78–79; Schneider 2007).

## Communication and the Expanded Party Network

Although scholarly attention to expanded party networks is a relatively recent development, the efforts of House party organizations to build connections with elements of these networks date to the 1970s or earlier. In its early post-reform iteration, the Democratic Steering and Policy Committee served as a link between the Democratic leadership, the membership, and important outside actors. Key interest group leaders, important Democratic-affiliated analysts, and (in the late 1970s) figures from the Democratic White House all occupied time on the DSPC's formal meeting schedule during the O'Neill speakership. The committee held lengthy meetings on both strategy and substance with outside advisors on economics, energy, and politics. Party-connected pollsters like Richard Scammon advised the committee both before and after the important 1974 elections. Throughout this time period, a range of Democratic-linked economists like Walter Heller, Leon Keyserling, Otto Eckstein, and Alice Rivlin met with the committee to discuss economic policy and legislative initiatives. The committee also conferred with representatives of core constituencies of the Democratic Party, such as George Meany and other AFL/CIO leaders. In one example, a September 1977 DSPC meeting brought together labor, liberal, religious, and minority group leaders to confer with Democratic members on unemployment. A series of meetings with the Business Roundtable during the Carter era illustrates that the committee also worked to neutralize or co-opt groups outside of the party network on occasion. Finally, the DSPC provided a center for formal interaction between the Democratic leadership and the Carter Administration, particularly during the administration's first year. Vice President Mondale, National Security Advisor Zbigniew Brzezinski, Energy Secretary James Schlesinger, and Carter advisor Hamilton Jordan were among the figures that conferred with DSPC members in 1977, sometimes to share messages from the administration but in other cases to address challenges in coordinating congressional and administration priorities.[47]

The Republican Party, too, has used its organizations actively to foster connections between its membership and the larger party system. As a minority party, the party used the Republican Policy Committee to facilitate meetings between Republican members and important outside actors. The Policy Committee's regularly scheduled forum meetings in the early 1990s, under committee chair Henry Hyde (R-IL), involved regular discussions with GOP policy figures including Bob Gates, Elliot Abrams, and Richard Perle.[48] Under the Republican majority, particularly during Christopher Cox's chairmanship (1995–2005), the Policy Committee made communication with party figures outside of Congress a main emphasis. In the late 1990s, Cox created a "Congressional Policy Advisory Board" (CPAB) to work in conjunction with the committee. A 2001 document describes the CPAB as having been a "government-in-waiting" during the second Clinton term (with board members including Cheney, Rumsfeld, and Rice).[49] After the Republicans took the White House, the Policy Committee developed a set of issue-focused subcommittees, and between 2001 and 2003, the Republican Policy Committee met either as a full committee or in issue-focused subcommittees approximately 40 times per session.[50] These meetings frequently involved conversations with outside figures. Table 5.3 illustrates the range of party actors in and out of government who met with the committee during the second session of the 107th Congress (2002).[51] The list represents the majority of the Policy Committee's formal meeting activity during the session, and it includes high-level and more obscure Republican appointees, GOP party leaders, and party-connected actors from think-tanks and academia. Around this time, the committee's

TABLE 5.3. Party-Connected Visitors to the Republican Policy Committee, 2002

| Guest | Title |
| --- | --- |
| Paul O'Neill (3 visits) | Secretary of the Treasury |
| Patricia Sheikh | USDA Deputy Administrator for International Trade Policy |
| Roger Noriega | Ambassador to Organization of American States |
| Otto Reich (2 visits) | Assistant Secretary of State |
| Henry Kissinger | Former Secretary of State |
| Jean Marie Peltier | EPA Agricultural Liaison |
| Mitch Daniels | OMB Director |
| Bobby Jindal | Assistant HHS Secretary for Planning and Evaluation |
| Frank Miller | Special Assistant to the President, Senior Director for Defense Policy and Arms Control |
| Loren B. Thompson, Jr. | COO, Lexington Institute |
| J. D. Crouch II | Assistant Secretary of Defense for International Security Policy |
| Marc Racicot | RNC Chair |
| Jack Oliver | RNC Deputy Chair |
| William J. Haynes II | General Counsel, Department of Defense |
| Norman Lorentz | U.S. Chief Technology Officer |
| R. Glenn Hubbard (2 visits) | Chair, Council of Economic Advisors |
| Janet Hale | Assistant HHS Secretary for Budget, Technology, and Finance |
| Gaddi H. Vasquez | Peace Corps Director |
| John Engler | Republican Governor of Michigan |
| Arthur Laffer | Economist |
| Vice Adm. Stanley Szemborski | Deputy Director of Program Analysis and Evaluation, Dept. of Defense |
| John B. Taylor | Undersecretary of the Treasury for International Affairs |

*Source:* House Policy Committee meetings list, 25 Nov 2002. At http://policy.house.gov/html/meetings.cfm, viewed via http://wayback.archive.org.

executive director, Paul Wilkinson, summarized the Policy Committee's network role by noting that the committee "bridge[s] the gap between the wonks and the pols" (*National Journal* 2003).

As these examples from the 1970s through the 2000s show, leaders in both caucuses recognized value in organized external communication between their members and the expanded party. These connections do not serve merely as opportunities for exchanging policy information and building members' linkages with the party. Rather, the leadership has made use of the expanded party in some instances to affect coordination and persuasion on specific choices. This practice dates at least to the 1970s, when the DSPC coordinated with outside interests on some legislation,[52] but it seems to have become much more commonplace in the 1990s and after. In 1993, the House pushed to build a bipartisan coalition in support of North American Free Trade Agreement (NAFTA) legislation, and strong constituency pressures made the issue a tough vote for many members in both parties (Box-Steffensmeier, Arnold, and Zorn 1997). Republican leaders and the whip system worked with supportive Democrats to whip the bill (*CQ Weekly* 1993), and the Republican leadership deployed outside groups to whip the membership. Staff in Bob Michel's office ran a working group that coordinated with lobbyists and corporate figures to make contact with both Democratic and Republican members as the vote approached.[53]

The leadership's instrumental use of broader party networks was perhaps best illustrated by GOP whip Tom DeLay (R-TX) and his "Mirror Whip Operation."[54] As majority whip, DeLay developed a public reputation as "The Hammer" for his effectiveness; inside the Conference, he was known for developing power by distributing rewards, ranging from Texas barbecue to plum committee assignments (Cohen 2002; Martinez and Koszczuk 1999; Mitchell and Lacey 1999). DeLay's influence on Republican leadership, though, goes beyond his reputation as a heavy-hitter. DeLay sought to advance not just party unity but also the linkages between the congressional party and a GOP-aligned business and lobbying community in service of a durable Republican majority. The K-Street Project, which worked to build Republican influence within Washington, D.C. lobbying firms, also extended to DeLay's systematic use of business lobbyists as part of the whip process. According to a 1999 *CQ* report (Martinez and Koszczuk 1999), the whip organization regularly farmed out assignments to sympathetic lobbyists, relying on their influence both to gather intelligence and to pick up votes. Responsibility for outside connections to the whip operation often fell to the chief deputy whip, who spearheaded the use of business coalitions for whipping. In explaining the pervasiveness of lobbyists functioning as whips, Chief Deputy Whip Roy Blunt (R-MO) cited the narrow margin of Republican control in the 107th Congress: "With a six-vote margin, we realized we needed all the outside help we could get, just to get our job done" (Jacobson 2001). Although the DeLay whip organization made outside network lobbying a core part of its operation, the activity was neither a Republican innovation nor entirely new in the 1990s. According to Barry's contemporary account, the Democratic whip system under Coelho made effective use of external interests to lobby members. Barry quotes an aide to the Democratic leadership observing "if you want to control votes, you have to manage the outside groups" (1989, 189).

## Conclusion

The Republican and Democratic party organizations from the post-reform era to the present have taken on a portion of the caucuses' growing concern with external communication. This chapter has reviewed examples of communication activities in five House party organizations, and the overall picture shows the extended leadership structures facilitate communication through a few key activities. Party organizations have taken responsibility for publicizing party policy agendas, particularly during election cycles. In earlier decades, it was more common for organizations like the Democratic Steering and Policy Committee and Republican Policy Committee to house substantive deliberations over agenda content and transmission of that content; the communication itself is the focus more recently. In both parties, partisan committees have been important for publicly framing the minority party's short-term response to the majority's agenda—a particular focus for the 1970s and 1980s Republican Policy Committee. In a related way, these organizations have offered the minority party resources and a veneer of legitimacy for organized public efforts to discuss minority criticisms and priorities. The post-2010 Democratic Steering and Policy Committee here has followed a pattern established in earlier Congresses by the (now-defunct) Republican Research Committee. The whip organizations, sometimes joined by more informal groups like the Republican Theme Team, have taken responsibility for organizing floor activity and other legislative action, such as discharge petitions, that convey messages on the party's priorities. These communications-directed whip actions seem particularly important to both parties in the minority.

Party organizations have connected the goals of individual members and the collective party by assisting members in communicating party messages. The party committees and whip systems have a long-standing practice of providing communications materials, talking points, and even prewritten speeches that assist overworked members during district visits while transmitting the caucuses' electoral messages. By the 1980s, as illustrated by Gingrich's "Strategy Whip," the party organizations had adopted more elaborate mechanisms for teaching members to communicate party messages more effectively.

Both parties, meanwhile, have used their committees and whip systems to link the congressional party with elements of the expanded party network. Formal briefings and meetings have helped to connect party leaders and the rank-and-file with influential party actors. Leaders of party organizations have become increasingly adept at developing these external connections and deploying them strategically to influence legislative decision making.

Although congressional literature has emphasized the relatively recent strengthening of communications expectations and strategies, this look at communications in the party organizations reveals that the parties' twenty-first century practices have considerable commonality with party activities in the post-reform era. The minority Democratic Steering and Policy hearings in the 112th Congress are similar to the hearings of the Republican Research Committee in earlier decades, and the majority Republican Policy Committee's regular meetings with external party actors in the 2000s looks a lot like the practice of the majority Democratic Steering and Policy Committee in the 1970s. At the same time, communications has become more central to the work of party organizations as party government and electoral competition have strengthened, particularly when the party has backed away from using some of its organizations for other functions like coordination.

# SIX

# The Process of Persuasion in
# Party Leadership Organizations

Partisan persuasion in Congress conjures particular images and anecdotes: Lyndon Johnson cornering other legislators with the "Treatment" (Caro 2002); Tom DeLay playing hardball with reluctant Republican members on the Medicare prescription drug vote (Hulse 2004); members regretfully voting against their electoral interests under party pressure, as Marjorie Margolies-Mezvinsky (D-PA) infamously did on a 1994 budget bill (Woodward 1994). This sort of persuasion emphasizes arm-twisting by individual, powerful party leaders, particularly at the last minute. And while the hard sell is sometimes an element of the party's struggle to pass or defeat legislation, these images distort the more typical *process* of party persuasion in the House. In working to build party loyalty in the long run and the short run, the party's top leaders do more than corner, cajole, and threaten. The modern party leadership in the House relies heavily on party organizations to build specific support and to distribute benefits that reward and encourage long-term support. It is a process that involves large segments of the caucus in both parties and provides legitimacy to the task of encouraging party loyalty.

I define *persuasion* broadly for purposes of this chapter. Persuasion includes the party's attempts to solidify and expand support for leadership-identified positions on process and policy; it also includes the long-term work to build and reward loyalty to the party leadership among the caucus rank-and-file. Persuasion certainly includes the difficult task of convincing House members to support the party position when their ideological and/or constituency-induced preferences dictate a different position (see, e.g., Kre-hbiel 1998 and Smith 2007), but the party's persuasive role does not hinge solely on whether it regularly moves members to vote against other interests. As Lee argues, much party conflict derives from "partisans' widespread and willing cooperation in pursuit of collective goals and on the inherent zero-sum conflicts between the two parties' political interests" (2009, 18). In my view, a crucial part of the party leadership's task is to help to strengthen members' connections to the party's political interests and to remind members of those interests—persuasion, in this sense, is about strengthening the party as a "team" in the near term and over the long term.

Partisan persuasion in the House is a participatory process, and it is an offshoot of internal party coordination. As a result, it grows out of other functions of the party leadership organizations and is another identifiable purpose for the modern party committees and whip systems. If congressional partisanship is in significant part "teamsmanship," as Lee (2009) argues in the Senate context, then party persuasion will involve participation by members of the party (and their staff). Short-term persuasion, broadly speaking, is a participatory process that conveys information and arguments through the caucus to build support for a party position. Long-term persuasion is a participatory process in which members make decisions about whether and how to allocate party benefits to encourage party support.

As the conditions for party government in Congress have changed since the 1970s, the process of persuasion has changed as well. The parties began to institutionalize their processes, particularly in the growing whip organizations, in the post-reform era. The changes unfolded differently in the two parties. Democrats in the majority greatly expanded the scope of involvement in an increasingly complex and routinized whip process, and they adapted the process to the particular needs of an electorally competitive minority party in the 1990s and 2000s. Republicans used a less institutionalized whip process in the 1970s and 1980s but still relied on participation to build support; the majority Republican Conference of the 1990s rapidly expanded involvement in the process while simultaneously placing the persuasive role of the party under tighter control. At the same time, in both caucuses, the party steering committees have changed their role in long-term persuasion. Committee assignment decisions have been and remain a participatory process, but the use of the process to reward and reinforce party support—both in voting and in financial backing—has greatly strengthened.

This chapter first examines the activity of the House whip organizations from the 1970s through the 2000s, demonstrating how their persuasive process involving a large number of members served the party's collective interest and how that process changed under shifting political circumstances. Where chapter 4 views the whip system as a tool for internal information flow, this chapter considers how the whip organizations use that process to build support. I then consider the place of the Democratic Steering and Policy Committee and the Republican Steering Committee in collective decision making about a central party selective benefit: standing committee assignments. Throughout the chapter, my objective is to assess the role of the party organizations and their members and changes to their persuasive processes over time. I discuss examples of the outcomes of these processes—whip counts and committee assignment decisions—but readers interested specifically in empirical analysis of these outcomes will find recent work by Larry Evans (Evans et al. 2003; Evans and Grandy 2009) and Frisch and Kelly (2006) an important accompaniment to the material in the chapter.

## Party Whip Organizations: The Process of Persuasion

JERRY: *Hey, do you know what the Whip does?*
KRAMER: *What whip?*
JERRY: *The Whip. In the Senate, in the House.*
KRAMER: *Well, you know in the old days, when the senators didn't vote the way that the party leaders wanted 'em to . . . they whipped them. [Holds imaginary whip.] You better vote the way we want you to, or there's gonna be big trouble. [Cracks invisible whip and makes sound effect.]*
                                                            —*Seinfeld* 1995

In both the Democratic and the Republican Parties in the House, whips have been a part of the legislative process since about the beginning of the 20th century. The whip organizations were relatively weak through the 1960s and served mostly a coordinating role. The process of developing accurate intelligence and deploying the whip system to solidify and build member support began to strengthen in the 1970s and 1980s, particularly in the Democratic caucus, followed by rapid changes to the Republican process after the GOP gained majority control. However, the kind of brute force that some observers, including *Seinfeld*'s Kramer, might expect is not the primary persuasive approach of even the strong-party-government whip systems.

*Democratic Whips*

In the early 1970s, the Democratic whip organization had begun to formalize its processes under Tip O'Neill as whip. Burden and Frisby (2004) show that the process at this time was reasonably effective, but it saw more significant changes after O'Neill replaced Speaker Carl Albert and the Class of 1974 demanded both participation and a more effective central whipping process. The sheer number of whip polls grew, with 26 in the 92nd Congress, 53 in the 93rd Congress, and about 80 by the 96th Congress (Burden and Frisby 2004; Dodd 1979; Sinclair 1995, 129). The count routine at the start of the reform era involved the leadership formulating a question, submitting it to the elected zone whips for polling by a set deadline, collecting zone reports, and initiating leadership lobbying of opponents and/or undecideds.[1] In addition to using the growing number of appointed whips to refine and grow initial whip counts, the leadership in the late 1970s regularly used short-term task forces to follow up on initial regional counts for major legislation. This system, which has been evaluated in some detail elsewhere (Garand 1988; Garand and Clayton 1986; Sinclair 1983, 138–46), served general participatory goals at the same time as it built support for party priorities. DSPC staff director Irv Sprague observed that task forces gave members "an awareness of the problems of leadership and a feeling of meaningful participation that paid dividends on later legislation, as they felt some obligation to cooperate with other task forces."[2] The participatory task forces provided a mechanism by which the leadership could strengthen the information-gathering and vote-pressuring functions of the whip system by co-opting, rather than alienating, the diverse components of the caucus. Members would be more accepting of party direction if they had a hand in its execution and could help to hold the leadership accountable. Participation in the task force system was extensive: Democrats used task forces to whip major legislation 15 times in the 95th Congress (the first under O'Neill's speakership), drawing on 116 members in total.[3] The problematic zone whip system (see chap. 4) was never completely dismantled, but instead it was counterbalanced with the growing appointive whip system, the use of task forces, and closer leadership monitoring of the whip process.

The Humphrey-Hawkins example in chapter 1 provides a good illustration of the Democratic majority whip-plus-task-force system in operation. In that instance, broad participation in both information gathering and targeted persuasion helped to move a major party priority past big obstacles and through the chamber. Another example from the same time period, the battle over the Clinch River Breeder Reactor, shows the process was sometimes deployed aggressively even in the face of apparent lost causes in the House. President Carter had pressed Congress to end funding for the reactor in the 1978 energy research authorization bill; the reactor was intended as a demonstration project for the breeder reactor concept, but Carter opposed the costly project because of nuclear proliferation concerns (*Congress and the Nation* 1981a). When the energy authorization bill reached the House floor, the Democratic leadership planned a vote on an amendment to limit the breeder reactor funding to wind down costs, in keeping with Carter's demand. This important vote in support of the Democratic administration received a full-court press from the participatory leadership system. A 17-member task force met daily in the days before the vote and assigned members so "the entire House [was] covered and cross-checked at least three times." Members who "would be receptive to an Administration call [were] funneled daily to the White House," and the leadership worked with a number of interest groups to pressure members, including labor unions, environmental groups, and the National Taxpayers Union. Yet in the end, the staff reported to Speaker O'Neill on the day before the vote that the Democrats had nowhere near enough votes to "win on the president's position," and that task-force whip count proved to be an overestimate, presumably as wavering members peeled off when the amendment's failure was in sight.[4] Table 6.1 compares the whip positions reported on the day before the vote with members' final vote positions. The leadership lost half of the yes-leaners as well as 13 members who had committed as yeas while gaining only a handful of members who had expressed opposition in the count and splitting undecideds evenly. The whip system and the committed task force members made an aggressive effort to bring the majority party in support of the president but, in the end, could barely muster a majority of the majority for a relatively unpopular position—not nearly enough to sustain the amendment with only 22 Republicans on board.

TABLE 6.1. Democratic Whip-Count Data, Clinch River Reactor, September 1977

| | *Whip Count* | | | | | | |
|---|---|---|---|---|---|---|---|
| *Roll Call* | No | Yes | Lean Yes | Lean No | Undecided | Absent | Total |
| **No** | 84 | 13 | 10 | 13 | 13 | 0 | 133 |
| **Yes** | 4 | 111 | 9 | 2 | 13 | 1 | 140 |
| **Absent** | 3 | 4 | 1 | 0 | 0 | 6 | 14 |
| **Total** | 91 | 128 | 20 | 15 | 26 | 7 | 287 |

*Note:* Whip totals calculated from archived whip lists in O'Neill Papers, Series III, Box 70, Folder 2. Roll call final totals exclude one Democrat unlisted in the archived count data.

The changes that brought about this more participatory whip process in the 1970s reflect the balance of collective goals as well as the objectives of individual leaders. Changes began during O'Neill's brief tenure as Democratic whip and continued through the first several years of his speakership. The whip process corresponded to his preferences for collegial coalition building. The whip system, though, also bore the imprint of the conflicting pressures at work at this time. Strong demands for participation by key caucus groups and for central leadership by some groups helped fuel a newly capable and flexible whip system that finally began to overcome the constraints of the regional whip structure. At the same time, the combination of the broad participatory expectations and the limited overall party government conditions meant the whip system was set up to provide good information and access for the leadership even though that meant some trade-off with the absolute loyalty of the whips and power of the whip system to reward and punish, to the continuing dissatisfaction of some members (Rosenbaum 1975).

In the early 1980s, the whip system's counting process became more institutionalized, and the expanding system of appointive whips increased both the scope of participation and the predictability of the process. As Sinclair has described in detail (1983, 133–46) and as numerous count records in the Foley papers document, the whip process began with a substantive memo to the whips offering background, signaling the leadership's position, and outlining the precise questions for the whip count. Initial zone counts were refined by extensive follow-up by appointed whips, often through the formal mechanism of the task force. Task forces usually included appointed members of the whip system, key committee members, and other members.[5] Through this process, Democratic whip counts in the 1980s were typically subject to several rounds of refinement by leadership-selected teams that centered on appointed members of the whip organization. The result of the iterative whip counting (and persuasion) process was gradually increasing coverage, accuracy, and persuasion to the leadership position as a count unfolded (Evans et al. 2003; Evans and Grandy 2009). By the mid-1980s, the whip system, through its large appointive membership and associated task force system, had been developed into a complex informational and persuasive tool that could process a weak initial zone whip count into a more precise instrument for building support in a short time. However, the fairly heterogeneous party of the early 1980s remained somewhat unpredictable, and the diverse whip system was less than a perfect tool of persuasion.

An Illustration of Persuasion: The Whips and the DSPC

One example—the Health Care for the Unemployed Act of 1983—provides a case study in how the participatory extended whip system worked in conjunction with the Democratic Steering and Policy Committee and the rest of the leadership, yielding changing and nuanced, though far from perfect, information and persuasive communication on a difficult set of votes in the 1980s.

In the context of extended high unemployment in the early 1980s and after the successful midterms of 1982, Democrats in Congress pushed forward a multifaceted plan to address the jobs crisis. The second phase of the Democratic plan targeted middle class Americans who had suffered the effects of extended unemployment,[6] and a centerpiece was a program of government-supported health insurance for workers who had been laid off and lost group health insurance. Democrats conflicted with Republicans over the program's funding and scope, and when the committee bill approached the floor, the leadership offered a restrictive rule and faced opposition from Republicans and some Democrats over the process, as well as on the bill's merits (*Congress and the Nation* 1985; Lardner and Rich 1983).[7] The efforts to move the bill in late July and early August of 1983 involved the full extended leadership. The DSPC considered and unanimously endorsed (and the top leadership publicized) a resolution declaring votes for the rule, against the motion to recommit, and for final passage all to be matters of party policy.[8]

Simultaneously, the whip system was activated to conduct separate counts on each of the three votes, and a task force consisting of appointed whips and a number of key subcommittee members refined the count numerous times.[9] Data on the three whip counts shows the initial counts were quite limited, with more than 30 members failing to report a position on each vote and a similar number reporting "undecided" (see table 6.2). On each of the three questions, the initial poll yielded insufficient yes or "leaning yes" votes for the leadership position to hold on a party-line vote; by the final count, the "yes" tallies had grown substantially, particularly on the procedural questions. None of the polls predicted the final votes perfectly, with the final rule count overestimating and the final recommittal count underestimating support for the leadership.

The 1983 health care polls reveal considerable fluidity in individual member positions, suggesting the whips were dealing with much member uncertainty in the face of Republican attacks against both the process and the substance of the bill. On all three questions—rule, motion to recommit, and passage—the whip system's refinement efforts yielded a substantially more complete count *and* significant increases in support for the leadership position. For each question, the leadership picked up the majority of the initially undecided or unresponsive members and converted some members initially reporting as no or "leaning no." However, comparing the final positions with the roll-call positions reveals that, on both the rule and final passage, the leadership lost more yes and "leaning yes" members than they gained from the members who polled no/leaning no. The bill passed 252–174, with 45 Democratic defectors and 37 Republican yes votes.

The 1983 health care case represents one of 32 issues on which the leadership deployed the whip system in the 98th Congress, and not all were as challenging for the leadership as the health care case.[10] The Foley files contain at least one example of a 1983 count that corresponded perfectly to the final results.[11] Still, the "tough case" of the health care bill shows both the comprehensiveness of the extended leadership's efforts—involving the elected leadership, the DSPC, and the whip organization—and the fact that the elaborate leadership organization system in place in the 1980s was an imperfect but vital tool for gathering information and building support.

TABLE 6.2. Democratic Whip-Count Data, H.R. 3021, August 1983

*A. Rule*

|  | Yes/Leaning Yes | Undecided | No/Leaning No | No Response/Vote |
|---|---|---|---|---|
| First Count | 189 | 35 | 11 | 31 |
| Final Count | 238 | 13 | 14 | 2 |
| Roll Call | 227 |  | 31 | 8 |

*B. Motion to Recommit*

|  | Yes/Leaning Yes | Undecided | No/Leaning No | No Response/Vote |
|---|---|---|---|---|
| First Count | 179 | 37 | 19 | 31 |
| Final Count | 229 | 14 | 21 | 2 |
| Roll Call | 243 |  | 18 | 5 |

*C. Final Passage*

|  | Yes/Leaning Yes | Undecided | No/Leaning No | No Response/Vote |
|---|---|---|---|---|
| First Count | 187 | 33 | 16 | 30 |
| Final Count | 216 | 20 | 28 | 2 |
| Roll Call | 215 |  | 45 | 6 |

*Note:* Data reflects earliest and latest whip counts on three polls for H.R. 3021 and is drawn from the leadership's Whip Count Analysis in the Foley Papers, Box 166, Folder 4800. "Yes" is the leadership position: for the rule, against recommittal, for passage.

## Democratic Whips in a Partisan Era

At the start of the 100th Congress, Jim Wright and Tom Foley moved up the leadership ladder and opened up the (now-elective) majority whip post, which Tony Coelho won after several terms as DCCC chair. Coelho—a "brash, hustling, wily partisan who ha[d] carved out a role as a key Democratic tactician and Republican-basher," according to a contemporary *Los Angeles Times* account (Secter 1987)—together with Wright brought more tightly controlled use of the whip system. The changes were evolutionary, but with a more partisan and assertive leadership and with the much-strengthened party government conditions of the late 1980s, the modern whip count process that had begun in the 1970s was now institutionalized (Rohde 1991, 88). The expansive appointive whip system was at the center of task-force-based counting efforts for nearly all whipped legislation (Sinclair 2006, 100). During the 100th Congress alone, the leadership operated 53 task forces.[12] The institutionalization of the task forces illustrates the complex, persuasive task of the whip system at this point. The task forces reflected a significant degree of centralized party direction, but effective persuasion required broad-based task forces in order to incorporate key committee players and others who could affect the leadership's efforts. The appointive whip system reached its modern peak in size around this time, and as chapter 3 shows, began to take on a much more party-loyal character. Coelho was willing to use even lower-level appointed whip positions as a cudgel: in one instance, he threatened Tim Penny (D-MN) with removal from the whip system if Penny voted no on a close and critical budget bill (Barry 1989, 467–68).

The leadership's close control of the whip process—as well as the scope of that process—in the Wright-Coelho period is revealed by an extensive internal report on the operation and effectiveness of the 100th Congress whip system. Coelho's view was that "if you're in the whip organization, you're supposed to work" (Barry 1989, 455), and the whip report establishes the leadership's concern with the whips' involvement. The report summarizes the whips' refinement work on counts, noting that whips returned over 6,000 reports (i.e., information on individual voting intentions or persuasion efforts) in the Congress, with an error rate of less than one percent on 1988 votes covered in the study. Participation in the system was uneven, with just 25 whips completing more than 65 percent of the reports, but major and difficult bills could see very widespread whip participation. On a late 1987 welfare reform vote, for instance, 50 whips returned reports on 152 members.[13]

The 1988 whip study provided the leadership with very fine-grained information on the performance of each appointed and elected (zone) whip in the Congress. Drawing on the 1988 votes covered by the whip system, the report ranks all whips and other task force participants according to a score reflecting "how much work each whip did, the percentage of assignments returned for each whip, how many issues each whip made an impact on, how accurate the whip's reports were, and how many times each whip failed to return any of their assignments."[14] The archived report preserves only the whip rankings, not the original scores (or the ranks for most non-whip task force participants), but it is still possible to conduct some basic analysis to see who was active within the whip system. By dividing the whips into two categories—high participation and low participation—based on their rank among the 160 members studied, we can compare the characteristics of the more active and reliable whips with those who were less so. Specifically, we should expect that, under the strengthened partisan environment of the late 1980s, the top members within the system should be those who are more partisan and more ideological. Table 6.3 shows the more effective whips were indeed more loyal to the party ($p < .10$) and significantly more liberal than their lower-ranked counterparts ($p < .05$).

As the whip system in the Wright-Coelho period became more centrally controlled, the leaders preserved the basic structure while expanding it rapidly. As noted in earlier chapters, the appointive system continued to grow at a faster rate than in the "inclusive" O'Neill period, adding dozens of new whips in the 100th and 101st Congresses. But the strategy for constituting the organization in the late 1980s was complex. On one hand, the leadership maintained a broad-based system that included members of virtually all stripes, recognizing the value of connections with all parts of the caucus. Existing appointed whips who were less effective in the 1988 analysis were, with a few exceptions, *not* excluded from the system in the following Congress. However, even as the leadership continued elements of inclusion in the whip system, it began to increase the homogeneity of the whips overall to emphasize those who would most effectively serve strong-party-government leadership objectives and carry the party message faithfully. The large classes of new appointed whips in the 100th and 101st

TABLE 6.3. Democratic Whip Effectiveness Ranking Comparisons, 100th Congress

|  | Mean, High-Ranked | Mean, Low-Ranked | $t$ |
| --- | --- | --- | --- |
| DW-Nominate (1st Dim.) | −0.353 | −0.293 | 1.999** |
| Party Unity | 90.90 | 88.28 | −1.423* |

$*p < .10, **p < .05$, one-tailed tests, df = 84.

Congresses were significantly more loyal than their counterparts outside the system. The late majority-period Democratic whip process helped to advance party loyalty within the caucus by building upon an increasingly loyal team of members in the extended whip system.

Majority whip David Bonior inherited a large and routinized whip system in the early 1990s, and he continued the procedures from the Coelho era.[15] When House Democrats went into the minority in 1995, this persuasive process remained important. David Price (D-NC), a member of the appointive whip system, observed "the whip's vote-gathering operation, in the minority as in the majority, remain[ed] an essential component of the strengthened party operations . . . This machinery . . . helped strengthen and solidify an increase in partisan voting" (Price 2004, 195). Several examples illustrate the whip system's work during the 1990s, when the minority Democrats used the whip process extensively to build support both for major issues at the center of party disagreement and for more minor issues, particularly in support of the Democratic president's position.

The 2000 census produced intense partisan conflict in the late 1990s, and as part of the tug-of-war over census procedures, Republicans proposed expanded local review of census housing units. Minority whip David Bonior described this legislation in his instructions to regional whips as an effort to "slow down and delay an accurate count" in order to "doom the use of modern statistical methods." A regional whip count and a whip task force whipped against passage of the Republican bill and for a Democratic substitute that accounted for local involvement.[16] Only four Democrats supported the census measure on final passage, and all but six Democrats voted in favor of the substitute. On another common late-90s issue, Democrats whipped against the spending-cut-laden GOP budget resolution for fiscal year 1999. The Democratic whip organization used the whip question to transmit the reason for party opposition: "Will you OPPOSE final passage of the Republican's [*sic*] Budget Resolution (H.Con.Res. 284) which cuts domestic spending by $101 billion over the next five years?"[17] On this highly partisan question, the Republicans passed the budget with all but three Democrats voting against. In other instances, the whip process was insufficient to persuade enough Democrats even on sharply partisan issues. In February 2000, Bonior's organization whipped against the Small Business Liability Reform Act (H.R. 2366), a bill that would preempt more rigorous liability standards in most states and cap punitive damage awards.[18] Although the whips were whipping against an important GOP position and in support of Clinton veto threat, the bill passed the House with enough Democratic votes to offset 17 Republican defections.

On several much narrower issues, the whip organization used a task-force-based count to whip against Republican initiatives in part to prepare for a Clinton administration veto. House Democratic leaders opposed the Senate version of a Y2K liability bill, which they believed would be pushed through to final passage for a blame-game veto. Prior to the completion of a conference report, a whip task force was used to assess and rally opposition to a final report that included Senate amendments to the original House bill.[19] The House ultimately passed a compromise conference bill, 404–24.

A final example involves a GOP measure to restrict a UNESCO program of designating world natural and cultural sites by "requir[ing] congressional approval before any area within the United States was included in an international land reserve" (*Congress and The Nation* 2002). A Democratic whip task force whipped in opposition to final passage of the American Land Sovereignty Act, anticipating a need to build opposition to sustain a presidential veto.[20] In the end, though the bill passed the House, it never reached the Senate floor. In sum, the minority whip organization in the closely divided House of the late 1990s used the whip process to effect party unity against the majority on both high-profile party conflicts and on smaller issues, with attention to providing legislative support for the president's position.

### Procedural Evolution in the Democratic Whip Organization

*"In whipping PERSISTENCE is key . . . You are doing a necessary task and represent the Leadership on this matter. Do not let people blow you off."*

—Instructional materials for Regional Whips, 1999[21]

These 1990s whip actions continued to follow the established persuasive process involving a regional count, followed by task force and appointed whip work to refine and persuade.[22] Task forces remained commonplace and could also be quite large: more than 100 members participated in the task force on campaign finance in early 2002.[23] Staff work in member offices had become important to bringing about effective early counts; the initial regional count was "primarily a staff to staff level whipping operation," according to a Bonior memo.[24] Each regional whip had a staffer designated to whip work, and the regular member meetings of the whip organization were supplemented by weekly meetings of staffers to whip system members. Regional whip staff, in initiating the whip count process, relied on the whip telephone system, which distributed whip questions to all Democratic member offices prior to the contact from the whip staffer.[25]

But Democrats also made important evolutionary changes to their persuasive process in the minority whip organization, changes that continued the two-decade trend toward a more centrally controlled process that maintained extensive member involvement. In the 106th Congress, the minority whip's office used a large team of floor whips to respond to both minority status and the close margins dividing the minority and majority parties. Democrats anticipated that "the closeness of [their] margin" in 1999 would create "more opportunities than ever to defeat rules and legislation" on "short notice." A whip office memo outlined talking points for explaining the system to floor whip recruits:

> To deal with these special situations, [the minority whip office] would like to set up a new "rapid response team" within the whip organization to almost immediately count our votes. . . . We alert your office to be ready to go to work on the next vote. When you get to the floor, we'll give you a card with a whip question, and a couple of bullets about why the vote is important. You then whip your group of 5 or 6 members, and immediately report back. To make it easy, we'll ask you to pick who you'd like to whip and then keep those names for the entire Congress. . . . We will still use the regular whip organization for most whipping, but this additional structure will enhance our efforts.[26]

The whip office created a roster of 33 appointed floor whips in the 106th Congress. About half of the designated floor whips were already involved in the traditional whip system in some capacity, but the other half were chosen from outside the appointed and regional whip rosters.[27] Members of the floor whip team were both more loyal than the average member and more junior, compared to other members not in the top Democratic leadership, as table 6.4 shows. The floor whip innovation was an effort to

TABLE 6.4. Party Unity and Tenure of Democratic Floor Whips, 106th Congress

|  | Mean, Floor Whips | Mean, Other Members | $t$ |
| --- | --- | --- | --- |
| Party Unity | 89.21 | 85.42 | $-1.62^*$ |
| Tenure | 3.91 | 5.55 | $2.15^{**}$ |

$^*p < .10$, $^{**}p < .05$, one-tailed tests, df = 203.

create a broadly inclusive *and* loyal group that could assist the party in the short-term, reactive floor activity that came with minority status.

The idea behind the floor whips became part of significant changes to the Democratic whip process in the 108th Congress. Steny Hoyer's election as whip in 2003 (after Nancy Pelosi's single term) brought the first major changes to the persuasive process since the 1980s. The large appointive and smaller zone systems were maintained. But task forces were no longer the go-to mechanism for working toward a final count on major votes—for the first time since O'Neill established them in the 1970s. The Democratic leadership instead created new specializations within the appointed whip membership, dividing what had been dozens of at-large whips into a set of senior whips (28) and assistant whips (38). Senior whips were given primary responsibility for weekly short-term strategy meetings, which also served a consensus-building coordination role. Assistant whips had defined responsibilities for each whip count—each assistant was charged with reporting on the voting positions of a few rank-and-file members. David Price, an assistant whip in the 108th Congress, notes he "had a list of five members with whom it was [his] responsibility to check on every major bill" as the whips refined the initial zone count (Billings 2003b; Billings 2004a; Price 2004, 195; Remini 2006, 534; Wallison 2003). This shift away from the more inclusive, task-force-based system marked a further step toward centralization of the whip organization, even as it remained expansive in membership. This approach continued under James Clyburn as majority whip in the 110th and 111th Congresses (Evans and Grandy 2009, 205), and Clyburn maintained Hoyer's revised division of labor (Yachnin 2006).

### Republican Whips

Archival evidence of Republican whip activity suggests the process was slower to institutionalize in the GOP minority than in the Democratic caucus, but the party did rely on a whip process with some participation fairly regularly by the 1970s. Republican persuasion in the whip organization in the 1970s and 1980s was heavily centered on the presidential agenda. The minority whip system advanced GOP presidential priorities, supported presidential veto strategies, and in the late 1970s worked to hold off Carter priorities.

When Bob Michel was elected Republican whip for the 94th Congress, the whip organization's structure had been in place for many years, and the whip office had a significant budget (equivalent to the Democratic whip's budget), including two statutory positions. At the same time, the system remained flexible and responsive to individual leadership choices: a staff memo to Michel from the end of 1974 reported the conclusion that he could "just about run things any way you choose."[28] Michel would maintain the small, decades-old structure of the system (see table 3.6) in the 94th Congress and its regional counting process. Whip polls in the Michel-led whip organization began with distribution of the whip question to four regional whips, who communicated questions and deadlines to assistant regional whips. The assistants, assigned to members from one or more states, polled members and returned information to the regional whip, who communicated tallies to Michel's office.[29] Extensive records of whip polling from the 94th Congress reveal the Republican whip system conducted at least 29 full counts in calendar year 1975, often refining initial counts over a short time frame.[30]

Several specific examples from the 1970s illustrate the concerted effort to build congressional minority party support for the president's veto power. In early 1975, President Ford announced a plan to use executive authority to increase fees gradually on crude oil imports as part of a larger effort to limit imports of foreign energy. Congressional opposition to the fee hike was strong, and the House passed a bill (H.R. 1767) suspending presidential authority to impose the fees for 90 days. (Initially, the bill attached the routine debt-limit increase to the fee suspension, but this provision was removed under the rule for the bill.) Despite overwhelming support for House passage on February 5 (309–114), Ford vetoed the bill when it reached him on March 4. House Republican whips were at work on the initial House passage and then, even before passage, began counting on the veto override question. With 42 Republicans joining the nearly unanimous Democrats on passage, sustaining the veto could not have been a foregone conclusion, and constituency pressure on the salient question of energy prices appears to have made this a particularly difficult issue. William Goodling (R-PA) wrote to his region's assistant regional whip and to Michel: ". . . I indicated that I would hope I could find some way to vote to sustain the veto. . . . After spending a week in the District, I am going to find voting to sustain the veto a very, very difficult thing to do. My constituents feel exactly as I do."[31] Despite these pressures, Republicans were successful in preparing to sustain the veto; by mid-February, the whips had developed a list of 20 GOP members who were "promised" or "possible" switches to the president's position, and by the time of the president's veto in early March, the whip count identified 115 Republicans who planned to support the president.[32] With strong Republican support combined with some Democrats' willingness to sustain the veto, the majority leadership eventually scuttled a scheduled override vote entirely (Lyons 1975a). The whip system in the minority supported a White House-led veto strategy, providing strategic information and building support as the issue unfolded over many weeks.

The first actual override vote in the 94th Congress was on an "emergency" farm bill in May.[33] The House-Senate compromise bill, which passed in the House on April 22 (248–166), set increased price supports for important crops, including corn, cotton, and wheat. President Ford, joined by about two-thirds of the Republican Conference, opposed the bill because of its deficit-funded costs and potential effects on consumer food prices. Ford vetoed the bill on May 1. The whip tally sheets show an ongoing and successful effort to increase Republican votes even before the House passage vote and Ford veto. By April 21, the whips had counted 109 Republican votes to sustain the veto (compared to 92 votes against passage) and had identified 8 additional targets, several of whom joined the total of 112 Republicans voting against override.[34] Contemporary accounts emphasized the importance of lobbying not only from the administration but also from outside groups on both sides of the issue. Because of strong Republican efforts to sustain the veto and urban Democratic unease over consequences for food prices, the House produced fewer total votes for the veto override (245–182) than it had for final passage.

In May 1975, the Democratic Congress passed legislation (H.R. 25), with the support of a majority of House Republicans, to regulate coal strip mining. The bill created environmental standards for reclaiming strip-mined land and taxed coal production to fund the clean-up of abandoned strip mines. President Ford, who had already pocket-vetoed a strip mining bill at the end of the 93rd Congress, vetoed the new bill on May 20. Democrats and Republicans in the House were quite divided over the issue, and Democrats put off an override vote until June 10 after their own count showed insufficient majority-party support for the override.[35] The Republican whips conducted a count in mid-May and a second count just before the override vote in June.[36] The first count (see table 6.5) revealed a substantial increase in support for the administration's position over the House final passage vote. Interestingly, in addition to the 89 reported votes to sustain Ford's veto, the whips recorded 7 "if you need me" pledges (see King and Zeckhouser 2003), noted on the whip tally as "if needed" or "if difference." In the second count, numerous Republicans moved positions, with some switching to the administration's side, some switching away or to "undecided." The Republican leadership netted two votes to sustain the veto on this second count. On the override vote, the leadership lost most of the undecided votes and also lost four Republicans who switched to the override position. However, House Republicans gained a net 23 GOP votes for the administration over the May passage vote, with 25 supporters of the regulatory bill voting to sustain the veto (two opponents voted to override). Floor manager Morris Udall (D-AZ) blamed "arm twisting by the administration" for the shifts, and the fluid votes in the whip counts suggest some uncertainty on an issue with partisan pressure as well as constituency implications (Franklin 1975). The May whip count includes the notation "President" next to the name of one Republican override supporter, James Martin (R-NC), who joined the White House position on the second count and the final vote, possibly indicating specific White

TABLE 6.5. Republican Voting and Whip Counts on Strip Mining Regulation, May–June 1975

*A. Passage Vote and Override Vote*

| | House Conference Report Vote, 5/7/75 | | | |
| | Nay | Yea | Absent | Total |
|---|---|---|---|---|
| *Veto Override Vote, 6/10/75* | | | | |
| Sustain | 55 | 25 | 6 | 86 |
| Override | 2 | 50 | 4 | 56 |
| Absent | 2 | 1 | 0 | 3 |
| *Total* | 59 | 76 | 10 | 145 |

*B. First Whip Count and Second Whip Count*

| | First Override Whip Count | | | | | |
| | Sustain | Override | Undecided | Pocket | Absent | Total |
|---|---|---|---|---|---|---|
| *Second Override Whip Count* | | | | | | |
| Sustain | 84 | 2 | 2 | 3 | 0 | 91 |
| Override | 3 | 35 | 0 | 4 | 1 | 43 |
| Undecided | 2 | 6 | 3 | 0 | 0 | 11 |
| *Total* | 89 | 43 | 5 | 7 | 1 | 145 |

*C. Second Whip Count and Override Vote*

| | Second Override Whip Count | | | |
| | Sustain | Override | Undecided | Total |
|---|---|---|---|---|
| *Veto Override Vote, 6/10/75* | | | | |
| Sustain | 85 | 0 | 1 | 86 |
| Override | 4 | 43 | 9 | 56 |
| Absent | 2 | 0 | 1 | 3 |
| *Total* | 91 | 43 | 11 | 145 |

*Note:* First whip count data from whip poll dated 5/15/75; second whip count data from whip poll dated 6/6/75, Michel Papers, Leadership Series, Box 1, Folder: 94th Congress 1975–76 Whip Polls. Pocket votes on first count indicate "if needed" or "if difference" notations. Roll-call results are author's calculations from raw roll-call data; absences include paired and announced votes.

House coordination in lobbying this member. The mining issue, overall, reveals a minority whip system working with a Republican administration to facilitate a veto-based strategy, and it highlights the importance of the whip system's members in providing information to the leadership and persuasion on a very close victory—the House sustained Ford's veto by only three votes. The activity of the minority whips in the 94th Congress illustrates how party leaders use congressional party organizations to support collective party goals and White House leadership even under conditions of political weakness.

The systematic, oppositional whip activity of the 94th Congress continued in the Republican Conference after Gerald Ford's defeat in 1976. The Republicans whipped 36 questions in the first Carter Congress (95th), focusing now on opposition to Carter proposals and on Republican alternatives.[37] Question wording was more neutral than the pointed, information-conveying House Democratic whip questions, but the Republican whip did pose complex queries to gather intelligence to support persuasive efforts. In September 1977, for instance, the Republicans polled on a minimum wage revision with the following question about Republican amendments:

How will you vote on the following amendments to the minimum wage bill, HR 3744?

(1) The Cornell/Simon/Erlenborn amendment establishing a "youth differential"?
(2) The Quie amendment providing for "tip" credits?
(3) The Erlenborn substitute for indexing providing for a minimum wage of 2.65 in '78, 2.85 in '79, and 3.05 in '80?[38]

On the last question, the final GOP whip count identified 84 yes votes, 18 no votes, and a relatively high number of undecided members—37. By the time of the floor vote on the amendment a week later, the Republican leadership enjoyed the support of most of the undecideds, with the Conference voting 126–15 for the indexing amendment, which passed in the House. The amendment had the effect of watering down a more aggressive indexing plan adopted in committee. With a small party and a lack of majority agenda control or White House support, the House Republicans were able to make use of the extended leadership system to build support for minority party alternatives.

In the 1980s, the whip system, led by Trent Lott, adapted to minority party support of a politically stronger White House with mixed results.

The Republican whip, as we would expect, was active in building support for the core elements of the early Reagan economic agenda and on other contentious, close issues like the MX missile (Fuerbringer 1985; Roberts 1982). Tony Coelho observed after the first year of the 97th Congress that Lott "runs the most effective whip system I've ever seen" (quoted in Roberts 1982). However, the whip and other Republican leaders also conflicted with the Reagan White House over agendas and process, particularly in the second-term, tax-reform process. The minority whip's office led a successful effort to defeat the rule on the administration-backed tax reform bill after closing off the White House's access to crucial whip count information.[39]

By the end of Lott's tenure as minority whip, the whip system's activity had increased markedly over its levels a decade earlier, and the technology for communicating and analyzing whip information had improved.[40] In the first session of the 100th Congress (1987), the House GOP whips conducted 35 whip checks, compared to 36 whip counts in both sessions of the 96th Congress. Of the 177 Conference members in 1987, 68 supported the party position on more than 90 percent of the whip votes (attendance-adjusted), and only 25 failed to support the party at least 80 percent of the time.[41] Although its basic structure and operation remained similar through the 1970s and 1980s, the strengthening party conflict of the 1980s led the GOP to deploy its whip organization for counting and persuasion more routinely.

Chapter 5 discusses Newt Gingrich's innovations in the whip organization in the late 1980s when he expanded its role to encompass message communication activities. In its more conventional whip work, the Gingrich minority whip system sustained the much higher level of whip count activity from Lott's tenure (Evans and Grandy 2009, 196). Primary source records provide little basis for analysis of the Gingrich whip organization's processes,[42] but contemporary reports suggest the whips were effective in supporting early Bush administration priorities, although Gingrich also led GOP opposition to Michel's approach to campaign finance and to the 1990 budget deal. Gingrich's leadership of the whip organization, as a result, remained controversial among House Republicans (Hook 1989a; Hook 1990).

As previous chapters have described, the Republican whip organization was entirely overhauled in the 1990s Republican majority. The number of GOP whips roughly doubled between the 103rd and 105th Congresses (see fig. 3.4). As the Democrats had done in the 1980s and 1990s, the Republican Conference in the majority relied on a broad-based but decentralized counting system involving the participation of a large number of members.[43] The example of the 1996 Right to Know Act, discussed in chapter 4, illustrates the count process in the GOP majority. The process centered on regional contacts but was controlled by appointed whips. All GOP members were categorized in one of four regions and then subdivided into 39 groups that correspond to the assistant whips.[44] Through the process of contacts by appointed whips, aided by the increasingly regular use of outside actors to pressure members (see chapter 5 and Evans and Grandy 2009, 204), Republicans now had an elaborate but centrally controlled whip process that built on the changes pioneered by Democrats in the 1980s.

Republicans effectively used the whip organization not just to build short-term support on votes; the GOP majority whip organization was a tool for encouraging member support of the party's broader electoral goals. Through the "mirror whip" operation, the majority was already connecting its external constituencies to its persuasive processes; now the whip organization became a direct tool for building external support. Heberlig and Larson (2012, 3) demonstrate that the congressional parties "have increasingly used their control over the institutional structures of Congress, particularly prestigious party and committee positions, to motivate members to support the parties' fundraising goals" (see also Currinder 2008; Heberlig, Hetherington, and Larson 2006; Larson 2004). Although it has long been the case that top figures in the party were expected to make sizeable donations to the party and to candidates in key races,[45] the parties now place fundraising at the center of their majority-keeping or majority-making efforts, and they marshal considerable resources through pressure placed on their own members.[46] In the DeLay whip organization, this pressure reached to the individual whips in the extended whip network, who were expected to make substantial contributions to vulnerable incumbent Republicans through DeLay's Retain Our Majority Program (ROMP) (Eilperin 1999; Mitchell 1999; Mitchell and Lacey 1999). DeLay's use of his own whips to build party resources and his use of outside lobbyists to build support for legislation can be seen as two components of his broader goal of building a strong Republican majority through close connections with powerful business interests. DeLay maintained—and strengthened—the House Republican whip system's core structure and its vote-counting and persuasive functions, but he bent the organization to his own power goals and to the collective electoral goals of a very narrow majority party in a highly partisan era.

The narrow GOP majority and high polarization and cohesion continued in the 108th Congress when Roy Blunt became majority whip. Although Blunt faced some criticism for a faltering whip system on a few early votes (Cohen 2004), Blunt appears to have run a tightly controlled organization that expanded leadership control over the whip process. Under Blunt, the whip system developed a set of formal rules for the whip organization, rules that mandated party loyalty from all whips on procedural votes (Bolton 2003). Following these procedures, Blunt ejected at least four whips from the organization for their failure to support the party on key votes in the 108th Congress (Cohen 2004; Pershing 2003).

The new Republican majority in 2011 brought a lower-intensity style in Majority Whip Kevin McCarthy (R-CA), whose organization whipped somewhat fewer votes than its recent majority predecessors and held "listening sessions" with the large freshman class on key issues (Stanton 2011; Stanton and Palmer 2011). Although coordination seemed to be particularly important to McCarthy, the whip organization's iterative persuasive process did not change substantially (Kane 2013), even though its persuasive task in the 112th and 113th Congresses was particularly challenging. Despite the high overall loyalty of the membership and the huge distance between the caucuses, the whip organization failed on several occasions to build bare majority support for key GOP bills (Drucker 2013). The Republican majority was larger than that of the 1990s and early 2000s, but the small group of Tea Party-influenced members helped to make the vote-building task nearly impossible in some instances. McCarthy worked to instill a sense of teamsmanship and loyalty through the more informal activity of the whip organization, but short-term persuasion remained a weakness for the post-2010 Republican whip system (Draper 2012, esp. chap. 14).

### Beyond the Whip: Persuasion in the Distribution of Party Benefits

The whip organizations in both caucuses have matured into institutionalized tools for building member support on process and policy. They are far from foolproof in gathering intelligence and using it for targeted persuasion, but the changes in the processes since the 1970s have made the systems more efficient and effective mechanisms, now combining both central control and extensive member participation. Republicans and Democrats have each used other elements of the extended party leadership system— particularly the steering committees—to persuade rank-and-file members to support the party over the long run by distributing (and occasionally revoking) benefits. Party-organization participation in these processes dates to the 1970s or earlier, but as with the whip process, polarization and electoral competition have channeled participation in committee selection more toward central party goals, and these shifts are a main focus of the discussion that follows.

### Democrats

The Democratic Steering and Policy Committee has served, to varying degrees since the 1970s, as a mechanism for encouraging long-term support of the party among rank-and-file members. In the 1970s, reform-era Democrats overhauled the weak Steering Committee[47] in two stages. First, in the 93rd Congress (1973), the caucus established the Democratic Steering and Policy Committee as a center for developing recommendations on policy and procedural directions.[48] For the next Congress, Democrats transferred committee assignment authority from Ways and Means Democrats to the new DSPC.[49] The decision to grant this authority again reflected multiple motivations. The shift advanced the movement to erode the power of senior conservatives, a movement that was gaining strength with the liberal class of 1974, and it similarly served the participatory goals of members, broadening the authority of the enlarged committee (Frisch and Kelly 2006, 57). But the committee assignment reform also shifted the authority to a body more controlled by the central party leadership (Rohde 1991, 24). The voting structure of the DSPC from the 94th Congress to the present has given a major stake to the elected leadership, although the leadership's actual use of that committee-assignment control has increased since the 1970s (Frisch and Kelly 2006, 62–63, 201–03, 212–13). The DSPC, on one hand, would give to the Democratic leadership greater ability to reward members and shape party support, but it would do so through the involvement of a substantial group of caucus members who could bring accountability and credibility to the gradually increasing power of the party.

As chapter 4 discusses, the DSPC in the 1970s and 1980s regularly considered policy questions, and, at the leadership's direction, it considered and approved resolutions on Democratic Party policy; DSPC resolutions seem to have been given some weight by members (Sinclair 1995, 101). In one illustrative example from 1983, the DSPC approved a resolution on the first fiscal year 1984 budget resolution. The DSPC vote resolved that:

> [A]ll votes during House consideration of the first concurrent resolution on the budget for fiscal year 1984 and the rule governing consideration of such resolution are matters of Democratic Party

Policy and Democratic members are expected to vote as follows: (1) In favor of the previous question on the rule governing consideration of the budget resolution. (2) In favor of the rule governing consideration of the resolution. (3) Against the Republican substitute to the resolution reported by the Committee on the Budget. (4) In favor of final passage of the budget resolution reported by the Budget Committee.[50]

In addition to serving a coordination purpose, these resolutions were calls for party loyalty. As such, DSPC resolutions signaled votes that would receive scrutiny when the DSPC considered committee assignments (Frisch and Kelly 2006, 258).

Evidence on both process and outcomes indicates that DSPC choices rewarded party loyalty. In the process and the results, other factors such as seniority certainly are relevant, but most analyses find voting loyalty to the Democratic party has increased both request success (Frisch and Kelly 2006, 284; Maltzman 2007) and transfer success (Cox and McCubbins 2007; Heberlig 2003).[51] Coker and Crain (1994) find that, in general, more prestigious committees in the 1980s had higher loyalty to the party as measured by correlation with DSPC members' own roll-call votes. Moreover, members who were loyal to the leadership's preferred positions when their own preferences were out of the party mainstream seem to have enjoyed particular rewards (Asmussen and Ramey 2014). Some of these analyses show that loyalty's effect predates the Democrats' 1970s reforms and the DSPC (but see Kanthak 2004), but process evidence indicates the relevance of loyalty to the DSPC's decision-making process in particular. The DSPC scrutinized members' support for party positions: starting in the late 1970s, the Democratic leadership used the electronic voting system to maintain fairly elaborate individual voting statistics based on leadership-identified key votes.[52] The DSPC then employed voting scores to assess member loyalty to the party when deliberating on committee assignments (Meinke 2013; Sinclair 1995, 93). Records from the O'Neill-era DSPC show that the party calculated support scores for each session. Until the early 1980s, the DSPC employed two sets of scores—one drew on a large set of "Speaker preference" votes (anywhere from about 20 to about 70 roll-calls, depending on the session) and another was based on a subset of "key votes" (fewer than 10 to several dozen roll-calls). In later years, the leadership assembled only a key vote list and voting scores. Leaders and other DSPC decision makers appeared to have a good deal of data from these scores at their disposal, with charts displaying members with very high and low support scores as well as support levels within committees and state delegations. By the mid-1980s, data sheets on individual members displayed not only the latest leadership support scores for the member but also their history of past support and their record of electoral challenges.[53] Archived committee assignment records also show the leadership studied support records on particularly contentious issues, such as a series of five difficult debt-ceiling votes in the 95th Congress, and the leadership sometimes systematically examined party support on whipped roll-calls as well as on DSPC-endorsed positions.[54]

In an interview with Frisch and Kelly (2006, 213), Jim Wright elaborated on the role loyalty records played in transfer requests by the late 1980s:

> A sitting member who wanted another committee assignment would be graded [on party support], yes. Within the [DSPC] there were a good many people who were interested in party loyalty. . . . Now, on how many of these [party votes] was he with us? And look at how many times he was against us. And if he was against you more than he was with you, well, that old boy is lucky [to have the] assignment that he has.

Records of the DSPC's committee-assignment discussions in the 101st Congress provide further illustration. While the committee discussed electoral considerations, endorsements, and other issues, party loyalty enters into the conversation overtly as well. Considering Ben Cardin (D-MD) as a nominee to Ways and Means, DSPC member David Bonior cited procedural voting loyalty as a reason to prefer Cardin, initiating a debate with John Murtha (D-PA) over the importance of voting loyalty.[55] While the use of committee assignments as a reward and incentive for loyalty remained somewhat controversial as late as 1989, it is clear the DSPC membership gave close attention to loyalty in evaluating individual nominees.

Through the 1990s and 2000s, the DSPC received additional assignment power, and the elected party leadership exerted greater control over the committee's decision making. Tom Foley increased the size and leadership footprint on the committee such that leaders and Speaker appointees could control the committee-assignment function, and he used this control with an increasing emphasis on loyalty as his tenure progressed (Frisch and Kelly 2006, 214–15). In 2004, the DSPC's committee assignment role was strengthened when it gained the power to select subcommittee chairs (or ranking members) for exclusive committees (Billings

2004b; Sinclair 2006, 139), following defections on the Medicare Part D vote in 2003. Even as greater assignment power flowed toward the DSPC, Nancy Pelosi as leader gained more control over the DSPC's choices. By the 110th Congress, the Speaker would "make all Democratic committee assignment nominations, subject to the ratification of the [DSPC] and the Democratic Caucus" (Peters and Rosenthal 2010, 69), solidifying a change that had begun in the minority-party period under Gephardt (Frisch and Kelly 2006, 65).[56] In keeping with these changes, the top leadership and the DSPC in this time period emphasized loyalty, not only in the form of party voting but also in financial contributions, demonstrating an increasing use of the party's leadership organization to pursue collective electoral goals (Billings 2004c; Heberlig 2003). And although the DSPC under Pelosi did not put fundraising at the center of committee chair selection as the contemporary Republican Steering Committee did (see below and Cann 2008a), the Democrats did expect substantial dues from chairs of committees and subcommittees (Peters and Rosenthal 2010, 115–16).

The Pelosi DSPC illustrates the patterns that emerge from the three decades since the modern committee was formed. The committee was structured to simultaneously shift more control over committee assignment to the top leadership while allowing meaningful participation in this process by the rank-and-file. The DSPC has long used its authority to advance long-term persuasion by distributing committee benefits with an eye to party support. Over time, top party leaders have bent the institution to use it more overtly to achieve party goals, taking more control over decision making and adding new financial loyalty considerations to the continuing importance of party voting.

### Republicans

House Republicans have never made the same organizational attempt to link party positions and distribution of benefits that the Democrats advanced with the DSPC in the 1970s. The Republican Policy Committee has largely served communication and coordination functions without much direct role in persuasion. The GOP party organizations empowered with the committee assignment role—the Committee on Committees and, later, the Republican Steering Committee—wielded control over benefits that could be used for reward and punishment, although the consistent use of the committee for long-term persuasion did not emerge until the Republican majorities of the 1990s.

From the early 20th century[57] until the late 1980s, the House Republican Committee on Committees selected Republican committee members. The committee gave votes to state Republican delegations according to their size, and therefore skewed committee assignment decision making toward large, heavily Republican states (Frisch and Kelly 2006, 35; Peters 1997, 99–102; Remini 2006, 287–88). The Committee on Committees was, at least from the 1960s through the 1980s, effectively a rubber stamp for the Executive Committee on Committees, which considered committee assignment requests and submitted a slate to the full Committee on Committees. The Executive Committee on Committees distributed voting power in ways that avoided central party control of the committee-assignment selective benefit.

Table 3.5 depicts the complex structure of the Executive Committee in the 99th Congress. Within this Executive Committee, the assignment process in the 1980s began with requests from the individual members to the minority leader. The Executive Committee considered the committee assignments one at a time, casting ballots on each. Decisions on key committees—Ways and Means, and Appropriations—were reached first, and then the committee moved through the other standing and joint committees. After several weeks of Executive Committee action produced a slate of recommendations for committee assignments and ranking member designations, the Committee on Committees unanimously voted to approve the Executive Committee's action before the Republican assignments moved to the Conference and the House for ratification.[58] In order to manage the initial assignment process in each Congress and ongoing changes to the committee rosters, the Executive Committee met frequently—23 times in the 99th Congress and 21 times in the 100th.[59]

Committee assignments, of course, can be a source of significant power, both for the recipient and for the assigners. As others have documented in detail, the Executive Committee received requests from members, accompanied by frank statements of the reasons why they had earned the assignment, needed the committee post, or both. Completing his required committee assignment sheet for the 99th Congress, Sherwood Boehlert (R-NY) requested a seat on Ways and Means and wrote that he was "told to win and win big if I wanted a major assignment . . . [I] earned 72% in a three-way race. I'm ready!" Rod Chandler (R-WA) implied a constituency goal in his request, noting "the press has commented on my poor assignments." And Dan Burton (R-IN) pleaded with the committee: "Because I enjoyed a large plurality in 1982, I was passed over for every committee assignment I requested—PLEASE I need help this time!!"[60] The committee's votes on these requests were sometimes quite close. John Napier (R-

SC), for example, won a Veterans Affairs seat in 1981 in an 87–84 vote, and voting for an Energy and Commerce seat in the same year ran to nine ballots.[61] In short, the Executive Committee on Committees was a home for participatory decisions about distributing limited minority party benefits. Although power was not distributed equally within the committee, it did not centralize power with the top Conference leadership. Party loyalty was one factor in the outcomes, but the Executive Committee process involved a good deal of less-programmatic "political deal making" (Frisch and Kelly 2006, 238, 286).

The imbalances in the committee selection process led to conflict and some minor changes to the participatory process in the late 1980s.[62] The House Republican Conference adopted a set of reforms to the Committee on Committees in December 1988, but the new committee for the 101st Congress was, in practice, quite similar to the one it replaced. The rubber-stamp full committee was dissolved; the "Committee on Committees" was now the former Executive Committee. More notably, key leaders were now voting members on the committee—the minority leader with 12 votes and the whip with 6 votes (Mills 1988). Otherwise, the Committee on Committees that determined committee assignments in 1989 was essentially the same as the committee from the 99th Congress.[63] The 18 votes held by Bob Michel and Newt Gingrich represented a strengthening of the leadership's position—a modest centralization of power in a time of rising party government conditions that accompanied other contemporaneous changes, particularly the minority leader's new control over minority members of the Rules Committee (Rohde 1991, 137). But these changes alone would have little effect on voting outcomes in the newly named Committee on Committees in the last few GOP-minority Congresses (Frisch and Kelly 2006, 51).

### The GOP Majority and the Republican Steering Committee

*"There is no secret behind it all, it was control. We decided to take it away from the . . . regions, away from others' ability to manipulate it and have us [the leadership] manipulate it. Plain and simple."*

—Leonard Swinehart, Gingrich Senior Floor Assistant
(quoted in Strahan 2007, 150)

In the majority after 1994, Republicans entirely restructured the old Committee on Committees, now retitled as the Republican Steering Committee, to reshape participation in committee assignment decisions. The changes for the 104th Congress were the first of several changes over the next decade that would make this party organization more responsive to central leadership control under strong party government conditions and small majority margins. The Steering Committee would be less of an independently deliberative body and less representative of the Conference in some ways (see chap. 3), but these changes also addressed the collective goals of the majority and the demands of the younger, activist members who had been dissatisfied with the Committee on Committees in the minority era.

The Steering Committee was a Gingrich "organizational innovation." Formed within Gingrich's office, the Steering Committee mirrored the Democrats' contemporary committee-selection structure in its emphasis on top leadership involvement. Although it was developed with little rank-and-file involvement, the Conference approved the overhaul nearly unanimously (Strahan 2007, 148–51). Under the new system, the leadership took the lion's share of the votes—the Speaker cast three votes and named two additional appointees with one vote each, the majority leader cast two votes, and five other top leaders and four committee chairs were each given a vote.[64] The committee was filled out by 10 regional representatives and several freshman and sophomore representatives, all with one vote each.[65] The new committee's size increased over its predecessor's, but this increase maintained the committee's scope as a proportion of the Conference. (Table 3.5 details the committee's structure in the 105th Congress.) The new Steering Committee structure joined other centralizing changes to standing committee procedures, including term limits for committee and subcommittee chairs and Gingrich's decision to assert control over committee chair appointments (Aldrich and Rohde 2000b, 7; Evans and Oleszek 1997, 92; Sinclair 2006, 124–25; Strahan 2007, 149).

In its committee-selection tasks, the Steering Committee generally has followed a similar procedure to its predecessor, voting rules notwithstanding. The leadership solicits assignment requests via member-completed forms in advance of the election for a new Congress, and the committee submits slates of nominees to be ratified by the Conference.[66] Within this process, though—as the Gingrich design anticipated—the top leadership and committee chairs control about half of the total votes (16 of 29 in the 105th Congress). In addition, the regional advantage in the committee's voting shifted toward the growing southern and western portions of the Conference, reversing the trend under the old committee (Frisch and Kelly 2006, 53–54). The elected leadership did not use the Steering Committee entirely as a rubber stamp, and deal making remained part of the participatory process (Frisch and Kelly 2006, 192), but the Steering Committee in the mid-1990s represented a clear departure toward leadership control.

The Steering Committee's role expanded during the 106th and 107th Congresses. Although Hastert brought a lower-key approach to his speakership in general and to his own role in committee assignments in particular (Cohen 2001; Smith and Gamm 2009), the Republican leadership during his tenure used the Steering Committee to further increase the accountability of the standing committees to the central party leadership. First, when term limits on committee chairs began to kick in, Hastert implemented a process of vetting committee chair candidates in the Steering Committee (Cohen 2001; Cohen 2005; Foerstel 2000; Hastert 2004, 182–84; Sinclair 2006, 136–37). Under this procedure, campaign contributions became the primary predictors of the Steering Committee's chair selections (Cann 2008a). Then, for the 108th Congress, the Conference approved an expansion of the committee's jurisdiction, assigning to it the power to choose the Appropriations Committee's 13 powerful subcommittee chairs (the "cardinals"). Moving subcommittee chair selection from the Appropriations chair and to the Steering Committee afforded the leadership greater leverage in budget process, especially after a struggle over spending cuts in the 107th Congress (Cohen 2002; Sinclair 2006, 138). Both of these changes had the added benefit of allowing the leadership to push these key figures to raise more party money (Willis 2002; Heberlig and Larson 2012, 160).

Evidence of the Steering Committee's actions in the last decade show that it was assertive in exercising these powers to effect long-term persuasion, denying requests and favoring candidates on the basis of overall loyalty, specific party-defying choices, and fundraising (or the lack thereof). As with the Democrats, outcome evidence suggests that Republicans have rewarded loyalty to the party in committee assignments, but campaign money now seems to outweigh votes as indicators of party loyalty in the Republican assignment process (Heberlig 2003).

Recent examples of the Steering Committee's willingness to reward and punish in the interest of long-term persuasion are particularly striking. In 2003, Conference Chair Deborah Pryce (R-OH) told *The Hill* that the Steering Committee was taking into account "procedural betrayals" from the previous Congress in making its committee assignments. In particular, the committee denied bids for key committee seats by moderate Republicans who had signed a discharge petition on campaign finance legislation—Todd Platts (R-PA), Charlie Bass (R-NH), and Rob Simmons (R-CT) (Bolton 2003; Sinclair 2006, 136). In 2005, the committee ousted

Chris Smith (R-NJ) from his chairmanship of Veterans Affairs, following several years of warnings over his loyalty to the leadership, particularly on budget issues (Pershing 2004, 2005).

The Steering Committee has placed an emphasis on members' financial contributions to the party and to competitive races in keeping with the broad trends within the parties that Heberlig and Larson (2012) have documented. For example, with term limits driving out Appropriations Chair Bill Young (R-FL) in 2005, Republican cardinals on the Appropriations committee began to compete with one another via large donations to the NRCC and to candidates with an eye toward the chairmanship, donations that exceeded their already sizable required contributions (Bolton 2004).[67] A similar dynamic was at play in the following Congress when the prospect of open chairs on as many as 10 committees drove competition over fundraising (Kaplan 2005).

Returning to the majority after the 2010 elections, the Steering Committee continued to grill candidates for key committees, and the leadership surveyed prospective chairs on their compliance with expected changes in the 112th Congress and warned of likely Steering Committee monitoring of "Member performance in committees" (Kucinich and Palmer 2010; see also Goode 2010; Sherman and Aujla 2010). In the 112th Congress, the Steering Committee placed a number of freshmen on "A" committees (Isenstadt 2011), returning to a practice that Gingrich had controversially used in the 1990s but that had become less common under Hastert (Frisch and Kelly 2006, 192–93). The Steering Committee's willingness to promote junior members to top positions in the 112th Congress further illustrates the continued strength of party priorities over seniority norms; it also reflects the leadership's decision to accommodate, and perhaps work to co-opt, the very large class of freshmen.

A final example from the start of the 113th Congress highlights the Committee's aggressive use of committee posts as selective benefits. In this instance, the Steering Committee revoked desirable committee posts from four Republicans: Justin Amash (R-MI) lost his Budget Committee assignment and both David Schweikert (R-AZ) and Walter Jones (R-NC) were relieved of their positions on Financial Services. Tea Party-aligned sophomore Tim Huelskamp (R-KS) took an even bigger hit, losing seats on the Budget and Agriculture committees (Schroeder 2012). A key factor in the decision was the review of a "spreadsheet listing each GOP lawmaker and how often he or she had voted with the leadership" (Strong 2012a). Although Steering Committee members provided somewhat different accounts of the decision process, reporting suggests the decisions did not reflect a general ideological (i.e., anti-conservative) house cleaning (Hooper 2012; Newhauser and Strong 2012). Instead, the leadership sent the message that the party was punishing members who had failed to cooperate with the party on key issues. According to *Roll Call*, the Republican whip organization had pushed for this kind of party discipline—Majority Whip Kevin McCarthy (R-CA) prepared the voting scorecard and was a "driving force behind the purge" (Strong 2012b). The four demoted members had cast major votes against the leadership on key party-defining issues. Both Amash and Huelskamp, for instance, had opposed the Ryan budget in the 112th Congress (Strong 2012a).[68] In a Conference meeting shortly after the Steering Committee decisions, Speaker John Boehner (R-OH) clarified the message by reminding Republican House members that the leadership follows their choices on key votes (Hooper 2012).

## Conclusion: Participation in Persuasion

The discussion in this chapter demonstrates that party persuasion is more than just buttonholing members, applying pressure to tally up votes. Persuasion is, in a larger sense, a process by which members of Congress are reminded of their interests in connection with the party and members' sense of team play is reinforced. From this perspective, member participation in the persuasive process is fundamental. Participation brings legitimacy to the task of persuasion, showing the party's position to be more than the diktat of the Speaker or minority leader and demonstrating the collective nature of the party. More tangibly, the persuasive process, especially in short-term whip persuasion, is made more effective by the personal connections between the large number of extended leadership members and the rank-and-file who are contacted.

The short-term whip process in both parties has grown to involve about a third of each caucus, even as it has become more systematic and efficient. The process conveys important coordinating information, as chapter 4 discusses, but archival evidence shows that it also serves to solidify support and move votes in both parties. The examples here from the 1970s Republicans and the 1990s Democrats also reveal that the whip process is as crucial for House minority parties as it is for majorities. The whip organization provided particularly important support for the minority party when its president was in the White House, as the whip system could persuade members to defend presidential opposition to (and vetoes of) majority-passed legislation.

Republicans and Democrats both have a long tradition of involving members in the decision to allocate benefits in the form of committee positions. Prior to the 1974 Democratic changes and the 1994 Republican changes, however, the party organizations decentralized this decision. Loyalty to the party was related to assignment outcomes prior to the reforms in each party, but the restructuring set up a process in which participating members could make more effective use of committee seats as a selective benefit for party support. In this sense, the DSPC and the Republican Steering Committee became important elements of the parties' attempts at long-term persuasion. Participation by a large number of members, particularly in the Democratic caucus, where the size of the DSPC grew noticeably, remained essential to both parties, providing legitimacy to committee assignment.

The shift over time in the caucuses' approach to their leadership organizations is very visible in the persuasive function. Both parties' whip organizations have moved toward greater control by top party leaders since the 1970s; at the same time, both have expanded rapidly to incorporate a substantial part of the membership. For Democrats, the early expansion of the persuasive process allowed more members to be involved at a time when the caucus was diverse but demands for more assertive policy and process leadership were increasing. As party government conditions strengthened, the process became more routinized, was used more often, and involved a large but select group of more loyal party members. By the 2000s, Democrats had largely left aside the more open task force model of whip persuasion and kept persuasion within the large appointive whip organization. Republicans changed their procedures more suddenly in the 104th Congress, favoring a similarly large but closely controlled process. In a similar way, both parties' steering committees have taken a more assertive role in distributing committee seats as well as chair/ranking positions. For Republicans as well as Democrats, steering committee members now account for loyalty to the party on key votes as well as financial support for the party's electoral efforts.

# SEVEN

# Conclusion

Participation matters. Without it, the parties in the modern House would find it difficult to function. Leaders would be constrained in their ability to guide the caucus in everyday functions and in major policy and electoral initiatives. Members, for their part, would be both less willing to delegate authority and less responsive to the top leadership's calls for action and support. In considering party leadership, the scholarly and media focus is overwhelmingly on the power possessed by a few key figures, but the organizations that structure interactions between party leaders and the membership have played more than a minor, supporting role in the work of House Republicans and Democrats. Participation's importance is not confined to a particular era or style of leadership. The most fundamental aspects of party power over time—majority control over the House agenda, the ability of majority and minority party leaders to build member support for strategic choices—rely on the active participation of many caucus members on a regular basis. The party organizations are where the collective party goals of leaders and individual goals of rank-and-file members meet for the benefit of both.

In what follows, I summarize the key findings of the book, emphasizing the connections between the theoretical framework and the range of evidence presented in the previous chapters. I then discuss some directions for future research on party organizations and the contribution of this book's methodological approach. Finally, I consider some possible implications of the changes in party organizations since the 1970s on the ability of the House and its political parties to govern and the future prospects for participatory parties.

## Participation in Party Organizations Serves Multiple Goals
## of Rank-and-File Party Members

From the perspective of the membership, participation is a crucial element of the delegation that empowers the party. Members cede some of
the authority they possess as they create an effective elected leadership, but
when they have given the leadership meaningful authority, they also seek
to maintain the leadership's accountability and shape its direction. Participants in Democratic Steering and Policy Committee meetings in the 1970s
regularly communicated to the party leadership and committee chairs
about problems with the leadership's planned legislation. In the same way,
minority Republicans shaped party positions that might have threatened
their individual interests through Republican Policy Committee deliberations, and GOP whip meetings in recent Congresses have allowed the
membership to exercise a similar privilege. But participation for members
is about more than keeping a watchful eye on an empowered party leadership. Members who participate in the leadership process, at least when the
party is relatively strong, get the opportunity to advance their individual
goals through the power and resources of the party. We know that members with strong policy interests work to affect outcomes on legislation
through their leadership roles; this fact is well illustrated by Democratic
members participating in the vital whip task forces of the 1970s and 1980s
majority and by junior Republican activists in the 1990s flooding the larger
and very active GOP whip system. The quantitative evidence presented in
chapter 3 demonstrates that members benefit personally from participation as they strive for power within the House. Members tend to enter
their party's leadership structure early in their House careers, and their
participation in party activity gives them an advantage over other members
as they seek prestige committee assignments, even when other important
factors are accounted for. And most members who advance to an elected
post within the Republican or Democratic parties launch their bid from a
post in the party organization system. More generally, members involved
in the extended leadership have been able to build connections not only
with other party members and the top leadership but also with key figures
in the expanded party through organization activity. Finally, while power
and policy goals seem the most naturally linked to party service, we can
see that some members also connect their constituency goals to their participation in the party. Many members eschew public presentation of their
party activity, but a sizable minority presents and explains party involvement to the constituency. When they do, their explanations link party par-

ticipation with the constituencies' interests or simply allow members from very homogenous districts to show that they are faithful partisan soldiers.

## Participatory Party Organizations Facilitate Core Leadership Tasks in Pursuit of Collective Policy and Electoral Goals

The other side of this participatory view of party government is the ability of the top party leadership to pursue collective party objectives. Through the party organizations, the leadership is able to coordinate with the diverse segments of the caucus on policy objectives and on strategy. Information flows two ways through networks that require broad participation by members. By building either representative or loyalist systems of members, as conditions demand, the Republican and Democratic whip organizations have been able to gather strategic information to support leadership decision making, and they disperse critical information about leadership plans and the justifications for them. We have also seen that the DSPC and the Republican Policy Committee coordinated between the party leadership, committee chairs, and rank-and-file members on difficult issues, allowing the leadership to identify positions that could hold broad support in the caucus and to make strategic decisions about pursuing those positions. Coordination in the party organizations, in turn, provides the backdrop for party persuasion in both parties. The examples in chapter 6 show the whip organizations relying on an extensive participatory process to "grow" short-term support. The party's large network of members with close contacts throughout the caucus now allow it to quickly gather good information and then pursue targeted persuasion. The long-standing institution of committees on committees, meanwhile, shows that what had been a participatory organization for distributing selective benefits in a decentralized fashion has, over time, become a way for the leadership to distribute those benefits to strengthen long-term support with the legitimacy of a participatory decision-making framework. And, while coordination and persuasion serve primarily the party's collective policy goals, the importance of leadership organizations for communication activity reveals that participation advances the electoral goals of the party, too. The DSPC, the Republican Policy Committee, and the Republican Research Committee have all been stages for members to conduct public hearings or transmit messages for electoral consumption, and the whip organizations have used their networks of members to coordinate to use the floor and the legislative process for communicating messages.

Taken together, the qualitative and quantitative evidence offers a picture of the modern Republican and Democratic parties in the House as institutions whose ability to act relies on organized member involvement. Neither party, even when party conditions have been very strong, has been led exclusively by the exercise of power in the hands of a few leaders. Member participation in the work of the party happens because the membership needs to be involved for its own purposes and because the coordination, communication, and persuasion needed for the party's policy and election goals requires involvement of many members.

### High Polarization, Cohesion, and Electoral Competition Reshaped But Did Not Eliminate the Need for Participatory Organizations

I have argued that parties modify their organizations with the dynamics of party government, and the narrative evidence in this book highlights many important changes in the organizational roles and the scope of participation between the 1970s and the present. Under weaker but strengthening party government conditions, participation facilitates the complicated task of leading a party of diverse interests, and it brings in members who wish to shape the growing power of the leadership or to benefit from it. Organizational participation in the Democratic majority leadership became important during the post-reform era, helping to balance expanding party roles with the remaining strength of the decentralized "textbook" Congress. The Steering and Policy Committee allowed Democrats to coordinate with and monitor the important standing committees while maintaining open lines of communication among elements of the caucus. By expanding the appointed ranks of the whip organization, the party could better connect with different types of members to gather information and persuade, particularly with an appointed whip system that was representative of the large Democratic caucus; the task force model for major bills further extended this approach. In the GOP minority, participation in party government had a more established history prior to the 1970s (I discuss this further below), but strengthening party government conditions and subsequent pressure from activists in the Conference brought a greater use of the leadership organizations for party coordination in the 1980s. The whip system changed little in form, but the party increased its use sharply through the 1980s; the Republican Policy Committee did substantive coordination work, housing intraparty deliberation and communicating strategic information on party positions.

As polarization and cohesion increased, the Democratic majority made significant modifications to the participatory structure of its organizations and, eventually, to their roles. After a period of rapid growth and increasing use in the 1980s, the appointive whip system also became less representative and more loyal to the party. The whip organization was more tightly controlled and emerged as the center for both coordination and persuasion in the strong-party period of the 1990s and after. The Steering and Policy Committee lost much of its regular coordination responsibilities by the late 1980s as the strong whip system took on these roles. The DSPC served the party's interest in long-run persuasion by exercising its committee assignment responsibility with increasing focus on party support, but it no longer served as a hub for leaders, committee chairs, and the rank-and-file on policy and strategy. Something similar was unfolding in the GOP in the same period. With strong party government conditions and newly won majority control, the Republican leadership eliminated the Research Committee and essentially relieved the Policy Committee of its short-term coordination function. A decentralized process of ratifying party positions on bills and coordinating among diverse members was unnecessary with a very unified Conference and with the policy focus moving away from standing committees (Aldrich and Rohde 2000b; Aldrich, Perry, and Rohde 2013; Stewart 2012). These changes did not mean that participation was unimportant, however. As the Democrats had done a few years earlier, the House GOP greatly expanded its appointed whip system, stocking it with loyalists and using it assertively for internal communication and persuasion. By restructuring the Steering Committee at the same time, Republicans also realigned that organization to serve the goals of an increasingly strong party, maintaining a participatory process but reserving that participation for party loyalists.

When electoral competition reached very high levels following the 1994 election, both parties' organizations began to place greater emphasis on collective electoral goals. Its role in coordination diminishing, the Republican Policy Committee became a vehicle for party messaging, as well as a place for loyal GOP members to connect with party figures outside of Congress, especially during the George W. Bush administration. The DSPC, similarly, reoriented for a more public role in the 1990s. The Republican whip organization increasingly linked its internal communication and persuasion with party electoral interests, and members of both the DSPC and the Republican Steering Committee began to integrate electoral support for the party into their scrutiny of standing committee candidates.

## Individual Leaders Have Affected the "When" and "How" of Key Leadership Organization Changes

In the context of these larger party-government trends that shape the roles of leadership organizations, individual leaders still possess some agency, and the trajectory of the Republican and Democratic organizations shows that moments of leadership turnover punctuated some of the important changes in their roles. The process evidence in the preceding chapters also points to connections between individual leaders' initiatives and their personal goals. The changes to the majority Democratic whip system and DSPC in the late 1980s are consistent with the rising party government conditions of the period, but several of them also coincide with important changes in leadership. Speaker Jim Wright modified the roles of the DSPC substantially in the 100th Congress, and Majority Whip Tony Coelho worked quickly toward a more unified whip structure; each had a more centralized vision of House leadership than their predecessors. Newt Gingrich's ascent to the Speaker's chair reveals the role of individual leader goals even more clearly (Strahan 2007; Strahan and Palazzolo 2004). The change to the GOP's leadership structures in 1995 was quite significant, and the changes there are not entirely attributable to Gingrich's individual leadership; however, we do have evidence that the changes to the Republican Steering Committee were largely on Gingrich's initiative. In addition, the changes Gingrich made to the Republican whip organization in the years before majority control demonstrate Gingrich's use of the extended leadership to achieve his own objectives, and the overhaul of the party organizations to become more leader-centered and linked to the junior classes of Gingrich loyalists in 1995 bears the same marks.

Other developments in the party committees and whip systems further illustrate the role of individual leader goals. Tom DeLay's extensive efforts to link the Republican Conference with outside lobbyists and businesses—and to use those ties for both whipping the membership and fundraising—are part of the larger partisan trend toward an intensified electoral focus, but DeLay had pursued this approach even before the Republican majority and his election as majority whip.[1] Mickey Edwards, as the leader of the Republican Research Committee and the Republican Policy Committee in the 1980s, brought new focus to those organizations, helping them to serve coordination and communication needs of the minority, and the direction he chose reflected in part his own objectives as a rising figure in Republican politics.

Of course, the approach I have taken in this book—a combination of primary-source-based narrative evidence and quantitative analysis—does not allow precise statements about the weight of the multiple explanatory factors in every situation. It is clear, for instance, that DeLay's changes to the Republican whip organization in the 1990s, as well as the narrowing role of the DSPC in the 1980s, were in keeping with broader trends of polarization and electoral competition, and the overall power of the leaders who implemented these changes derived from the partisan situation. "Institutional context," Cooper and Brady warned three decades ago, "rather than personal skill is the primary determinant of leadership power in the House" (1981, 423). But the mixed evidence presented here also shows the ways in which individual leaders' own goals shape some of the when and the how of the bigger contextually driven trends in party organization.

### Parties Use Participatory Organizations for the Challenges of Minority Status as Well as Majority Control

The framework in chapter 2 made no detailed claims about majority control—or the lack of it—and the roles of party leadership organizations. The evidence in the subsequent chapters, however, allows some tentative conclusions about how majority control and minority status affect party organizations and how the leadership makes use of participation. Overall, it is quite clear that the majority and the minority leadership both need party organizations and that members in the minority and in the majority both have personal incentives to participate. Some aspects of the parties' organizational activity are similar in the majority and in the minority. In particular, Republicans and Democrats have both used the whip system assertively for coordination and persuasion in and out of the majority. Whip activity has grown substantially over time in both parties; these changes do not correspond closely to majority status. In the same way, both parties diminished the role of less centralized organizations (the DSPC and the Republican Policy Committee) in active coordination and increased the whip organizations' responsibility for this kind of internal communication. In these shifts, the Republican Conference lagged the Democratic caucus by several years, and the exigencies of majority control eventually pushed the GOP to speed up the changes in its participatory organizations, but we have not seen the parties reverse the direction of these shifts as they have traded majority control.

Despite these similarities, we can also see that House minority parties use the leadership organizations to deal with the particular challenges of minority status. The GOP's long stint in the minority led to some early organizational innovations in the 1960s in response to the party's electoral frustration (Jones 1964; Jones 1970), and party organizations provided an important outlet for member participation when Republicans lacked the majority party's standing-committee opportunities (Connelly and Pitney 1994). Minority Republicans used the Republican Policy Committee and the Republican Research Committee to consider alternatives to majority policy and to communicate messages about those positions outside the chamber. In the external, electoral communications emphasis, the Democrats in the minority have done something similar, using the DSPC to allow members to participate in official public messaging activities for their own benefit and the party's. The sharp upswing in the DSPC's membership after 1994 is also an indication of how the leadership uses party posts to provide opportunity to members in the minority. Note also the available staff resources for the two caucuses move roughly in tandem over time (see fig. 4.1) such that participants in minority party organizations continue to have access to resources that help to offset the lost advantages in standing committees.

The archival evidence also points to the important role House minority party whip organizations play when their party is in control of the White House. Regardless of White House control, minority whip systems coordinate and persuade on the party's votes against the majority, for alternatives, and even on maneuvers such as discharge petitions. When the House minority controls the White House, though, the whip organization helps to coordinate strategy between the president and his partisans in the House, and House minority whip systems have been especially active in building support to sustain presidential vetoes, actual and threatened, to help support the president's position. During the Ford Administration, the GOP minority whip organization was particularly effective in keeping a very small Conference together to sustain Ford's frequent vetoes, and Clinton-era Democrats used their much more elaborate whip system to support the president's combat with House Republicans on even minor issues. In sum, the evidence has shown that both parties make use of participatory organizations for the tasks of majority governance, but Republicans and Democrats have both found that the organizations provide participatory opportunities and leadership resources that support the more constrained House minority.

## Future Research Directions

This research represents the first focused look at the House party organizations over a long period of time, and it has provided strong evidence that these structures play a key role in the careers of many members and in the work of the party. In doing so, it points to several avenues of inquiry that should be part of the future agenda of congressional scholars. Party participation should become part of how we think about member success and the distribution of benefits in the House. For instance, since members in the extended leadership have an opportunity to gain information and advance their own policy goals, it is likely that party participation is a component of legislative success for policy-oriented members. On the electoral side, as the flow of money through the party increases, we should investigate whether members who actively participate are financially rewarded, as some research has found is the case for party-voting loyalty. Since some members participate for constituency-related goals, the distribution of earmarks or other benefits to party-participants' constituencies is also a potentially fruitful area of research. House organizations are also ripe for the kind of network analysis of information flows, for member and leader objectives, that has been productive in other areas of congressional research (e.g., Ringe and Victor 2013; Victor, Haptonstahl, and Ringe 2014).

On the party leadership's side of the equation, there is more to know about the processes within the leadership organizations and the details of their use, particularly in the last decade or so where archival evidence is not yet available. More broadly, because the roles of party organizations vary with polarization, cohesion, and electoral competition, we might also learn more by turning to earlier eras of congressional history. The parties began to develop some participatory leadership in the early decades of the 20th century, though some of it fell into disuse, and the roles and fates of these structures might allow more generalization about party participation if archival work could reveal more of their details.

Most obviously, this work also points toward the need for comparisons with the Senate. The upper chamber has a structure of party leadership organizations that roughly parallels that of the House. The two Senate parties have had whip structures in place for much of the last century (Gamm and Smith 2002; Oleszek 1985). Although those organizations have been quite small and even dormant during some periods (Canon 1989), the modern Senate whip systems "resemble scaled-down versions of their House counterparts" and serve similar functions (Evans and Grandy

2009; also Bradbury, Davidson, and Evans 2008). While the Senate whip organizations have been somewhat less active than those in the House, the Senate Republican Policy Committee and Democratic Policy Committee each have a long history and have served important communication and coordination functions (Crespin et al. 2014; Jones 1970; Kelly 1995; Peterson 2009; Ritchie 1997). Senate Democrats in recent Congresses have created specialized party committees for communications and technology (Schneider 2003), and both Senate parties also operate steering committees with responsibility for standing-committee assignments and sometimes other tasks. Although the Senate organizations share a similar structure with the House, the greater individualism, weaker parties, and different party-power dynamics (Smith 2007, 214) suggest the role of participation should be different, and organizational changes over time may not follow the same patterns.

Finally, the research in this book joins a set of recent projects that demonstrate the added value archival evidence brings to congressional scholarship. This methodological approach is uniquely suited to the objectives of this book—in order to understand *how* the party does what it does under different conditions, process evidence is a fundamental piece of the scholarly story. The uneven archival record of the party leadership means the researcher must deal with fragments and try to fill gaps with secondary sources,[2] but the fact remains that archives offer great potential for interpretive and quantitative research on congressional parties. The evidence marshaled in this book sheds new light on recent directions in the congressional literature and points toward the value of archival work in several areas. For instance, the examples from Republican and Democratic archives show the mechanics of how members of congressional parties interact in ways that enhance the sense of "team" that underpins Frances Lee's arguments on partisanship (2009). The archival evidence in these chapters provides tangible support for the important theoretical claim that House parties actively pursue both policy and electoral goals and that the balance between those goals is variable over time (Smith and Gamm 2009). Evidence on the parties' activities, similarly, reveals the regular interactions between House members and their extended party network (e.g. Koger, Masket, and Noel 2010), interactions that have increased over time but have a long history. And examining the organizational work of party leaders—including not only top figures but also lower-level leaders like the Republican Policy Committee chair—illustrates the consequential actions individual leaders take within the broader contextual determinants of party power and outcomes (Strahan 2007).

## Prospects and Normative Consequences

From the mid-1990s to the present, House party organizations have remained fairly constant in size, representativeness, and roles. After several decades of change, this period of stasis is consistent with the strong and fairly stable party government context, particularly with its routinely high levels of electoral competition. As long as these conditions continue, the House is unlikely to see a real return to a less centralized approach to participation and party organizations, and the parties will continue to place an emphasis on electoral communications while keeping coordination and persuasion controlled in the whip organizations. House Republicans and Democrats obviously find these organizations well-suited to the priorities of a strong-party, high-competition Congress. Yet there is some important value in the earlier forms of the participatory party that is lost in the 21st-century version of these organizations. In particular, the Republican Policy Committee, the Republican Research Committee, and the Democratic Steering and Policy Committee of the 1970s and 1980s held some party capacity for policy development, consensus building, and strategy development. As these organizations showed, electoral communications, policy considerations, and strategic coordination can coexist and even reinforce one another within party organizations. What is especially important here is that the capacity for work on policy and on strategy—but especially policy—existed *within* the congressional parties. Since the mid-1990s, and particularly in the last decade, the parties have no longer had a robust set of organizations that were equipped to do this work well. Party leadership organizations could still coordinate and persuade as the top leadership required on votes, and they grew in their capacity to shape external messaging; but it is now hard to find much evidence of broad-based participation in policy debate and development. The Republican Policy Committee provides a clear example. Its regular, active role in coordinating on important short-term policy matters faded by the early 1990s; a big-picture policy coordination function remained for another decade, but by the mid-2000s, even that work was no longer visible.

To be clear, the decline of these organizations and their integration of these roles is not necessarily a cause of congressional dysfunction; the argument of this book has been, instead, that these changes followed from broader changes in House partisanship. A somewhat perverse consequence, though, is that just as the party leadership has taken on a much bigger role in driving the congressional policy process, the parties have also outsourced some of the capacity they held, particularly for policy development. This change is part of a bigger trend toward reduction in congressional capacity (Glastris and Edwards 2014; Mann and Ornstein 2012; Stewart 2012). If the parties are to be the engines of policy making in the House, as they are under strong party government, then the interests of good policy, as well as the party brand, could be served by *internal* capacity to coordinate around strategy and policy items rather than leaving these choices to be driven by outside interests. And it may be that at least some internal policy focus and strategic autonomy could be restored within the current, centralized organizations, possibly through more effective use of the existing participatory whip systems. The lesson of the last four decades of House party organizations, at least, is that the participatory framework of the parties can be adapted to the shifting collective goals of the party and the needs of individual members.

# Appendix A

## Membership Data Sources

For this research, I have created new data sets on the membership of the extended leadership organizations from the 94th through 110th Congresses. No single source has compiled complete and continuous lists of leaders from across this time period, and sources that have reported on leadership organization rosters have not consistently drawn distinctions between members according to their selection (i.e., leadership appointed, ex officio, or elected by a region or caucus subgroup). I have drawn on multiple reference and primary sources, as a result, to assemble data sets that are as close to comprehensive as possible. Available primary source documents have also allowed me to confirm, generally, the accuracy of the reference-source lists.

*CQ Almanac* and CQ's *Politics in America* have provided lists in many Congresses. The CQ membership lists are generally complete in the late 1970s and 1980s but sometimes do not break down party committee members by appointment type. When possible, I have found lists of appointees in the archived leadership papers to supplement the CQ lists. Starting in the 1990s, the CQ lists are more often truncated or, in some cases, missing entirely. In addition to primary source lists, various editions of the *Congressional Yellow Book* and the *Congressional Staff Directory* have sometimes included complete lists in the 1990s and 2000s (see Hammond 1998 for a similar approach).

For some analyses, my data has gaps in which I have not been able to locate accurate lists. For Democratic whips, no source provides a reliable list of appointed whips below the deputy whip level after the 106th Congress, and no source fully documents the Republican whip system after

179

the 106th. (The Republican whip roster in CQ for the 107th Congress is missing the lowest-level whips; thereafter, none of the appointees are publicly listed. Democrats generally have listed their deputy whips and regionally elected whips, but the large group of lower-level appointees is not released. The missing whip data over the last decade follows from a deliberate strategy to keep whip operations more secretive.) Republican Policy Committee data is not available broken down by selection type for the 94th–95th and 99th–100th Congresses, and the Democratic Steering and Policy Committee membership similarly is not available by type for the 95th–96th and 104th–105th Congresses. Republican Committee on Committees executive committee membership is not available prior to the 97th Congress. The analyses in chapter 3 exclude these Congresses from the relevant models.

The leadership organization data sets themselves, as well as a complete list of data sources by organization type and Congress, are available from the author upon request.

## Other Quantitative Data

Other quantitative data analyzed in chapters 4 through 6, including whip count data and measurements of Democratic whip effectiveness, is coded directly from primary sources, which are documented as footnotes in the chapters.

Data for independent variables in the chapter 3 multivariate models includes party-loyalty data, which is CQ's attendance-adjusted party unity scores (averaged across the two sessions of each Congress), drawn from ICPSR study 7645 before the 98th Congress and coded directly from the annual *CQ Weekly* tables thereafter. DW-Nominate data used to construct the indicator of ideological centrism in the party were made available by Keith Poole at Voteview.com.

In several places, I present descriptive data on staffing levels for the partisan leadership organizations between the early 1980s and 2008. Total staff counts, along with salary expenditures attached to each organization, were coded from House of Representatives publications recording official disbursements. Through 1994, this information was obtained in the *Report of the Clerk of the House*; after 1994, the data comes from the *Statement of Disbursements of the House*. For staff counts, I tallied all individual staff members who appeared by name in the salary listing for each party leadership organization. (Whip organization totals for each party include both the majority or minority whip office and the separately funded chief deputy majority or minority whip office.) The totals include both statutory and lump-sum staff.

In collecting staff data, I sampled House disbursement reports annually, coding data from the last regular report available from each year. Sampling annually from the same time period allows for general comparability across Congresses, and drawing on the last report from each year avoids the instability that may be associated with leadership staff rosters at the start of a new Congress. Still, it is important to keep in mind that staff listings are subject to short-term fluctuations, and some volatility in the staffing findings I report may reflect this kind of noise in the data. As Glassman notes in his recent report on leadership staffing, "counting leadership staff is a tricky endeavor, and almost any methodology needs to be taken as an estimate, especially methodologies seeking temporal consistency" (2012, 22).

# Appendix B

## Congressional Archives Consulted

Carl Albert Papers, Carl Albert Center, University of Oklahoma

Richard K. Armey Papers, Carl Albert Center, University of Oklahoma

David Bonior Papers, Walter P. Reuther Library, Wayne State University

Mickey Edwards Papers, Carl Albert Center, University of Oklahoma

Congressional Papers of Thomas S. Foley, Manuscripts, Archives, and Special Collections, Holland and Terrell Libraries, Washington State University

Richard A. Gephardt Collection, Missouri History Museum, St. Louis, MO*

Robert Michel Papers, Dirksen Congressional Center, Pekin, IL

Thomas P. O'Neill Congressional Papers, Burns Library, Boston College

Bud Shuster Papers, Pasquerilla Library, Saint Francis University

Speaker Jim Wright Collection, Special Collections, Texas Christian University*

Bob Wise Collection, West Virginia Archives and History Library, Charleston, WV*

*Note:* Collections marked with an asterisk (*) were not visited in person but provided primary documents used in the research.

# Notes

*Note:* The notes below include documentation of the archived primary sources used in the research. In some cases, letters or other original documents did not include complete information about authorship, recipients, or dates. Where these details were unspecified in a document but fairly clear from the document's content or the content of the file in which it was located, I have noted my assumptions about authorship, recipients, or dates in brackets.

## CHAPTER I

1. Committee membership totals reflect the 109th and 110th Congresses, from recent editions of *Politics in America* and *Congressional Yellow Book*; whip totals reflect the full counts obtained by Remini (2006, 534) for the 108th Congress. Staff estimates are based on author calculations from the December 2007 release of the *Statement of Disbursements of the House*.

2. Irv Sprague, file memo "Anatomy of a Victory," 20 Mar 1978, Thomas P. O'Neill, Jr. Papers, Burns Library, Boston College. Series V, Box 20, Folder 2.

3. Minutes of DSPC, 8 Sep 1977, O'Neill Papers, Series III, Box 61, Folder 5.

4. Speaker's Humphrey-Hawkins Task Force agenda, 6 Mar [1978], O'Neill Papers, Series III, Box 69, Folder 5.

5. Humphrey Hawkins Targeting Chart, 7 Dec 1977, O'Neill Papers, Series III, Box 69, Folder 5; Untitled chart displaying task force member assignments, O'Neill Papers, Series III, Box 69, Folder 6.

6. "Several Important Aspects of Humphrey-Hawkins Victory," handwritten notes, O'Neill Papers, Series III, Box 69, Folder 6.

7. Minutes of DSPC, 2 Mar 1978, O'Neill Papers, Series III, Box 61, Folder 5.

8. Billie [Billie Gay Larson] to the Speaker, 2 Mar 1978, O'Neill Papers, Series III, Box 61, Folder 5.

9. Billie [Billie Gay Larson] to the Speaker, 7 Mar 1978, O'Neill Papers, Series V, Box 20, Folder 2.

10. Irv Sprague, file memo "Anatomy of a Victory," 20 Mar 1978, O'Neill Papers, Series V, Box 20, Folder 2; Steve Bourke and Spencer Smith to the Speaker, 14 Mar 1978, O'Neill Papers, Series III, Box 69, Folder 5.

11. Whip Count—H.R. 50. O'Neill Papers. Series V, Box 20, Folder 2.

12. Staff memo to Bud Shuster ("Ken" to "Congressman"), 21 Feb 1978, Bud Shuster Papers, Pasquerilla Library, Saint Francis University, Series I: Congressional Papers, Sub-Series A: United States, Box 35A, Folder 1. See also Peters (1997, 222).

13. Republican Policy Committee Statement No. 7, 7 Mar 1978, Shuster Papers, Series I: Congressional, Sub-Series A: United States, Box 35A, Folder 1.

14. Republican Whips Tally Sheets, 7 Mar 1978, Robert H. Michel Papers, Dirksen Congressional Center, Leadership Series, Box 2, Folder: 95th Congress: Whip Polls-3/7/78. Unlike some Republican whip questions in the 1960s and 1970s, the H.R. 50 poll question prompted the membership to consider the party position: "Will you join the Republican Leadership and oppose H.R. 50, the Humphrey-Hawkins bill?" Five members voted for the bill after committing to the GOP leadership's "nay" position; 9 undecideds voted with the leadership and 11 voted against. The leadership failed to anticipate three abstainers and seven who paired or announced, although all but one of the pair/announce members took the position they had recorded in the whip poll.

15. This discussion of House campaign finance reform efforts draws generally on *Congress and the Nation, 1989–1992* (1993) for background.

16. Republican Policy Committee records, 20 Jul 1989, Mickey Edwards Papers, Carl Albert Center, University of Oklahoma, Legislative Series, Box 81, Folder 22; Michel to Mickey Edwards, 19 Jul 1989, Robert Michel Papers, Dirksen Congressional Center, Staff Series, Van Der Meid Files, Box 6: Campaign Reform: Policy Committee Consideration.

17. Edwards to Michel, 7 Aug 1989, Edwards Papers, Legislative Series, Box 80, Folder 14; Handwritten notes on 20 Jul 1989 Policy Committee meeting, Michel Papers, Staff Series, Van Der Meid Files, Box 6: Campaign Reform: Policy Committee Consideration.

18. Dave to Mickey [Edwards], 7 Aug 1989, Edwards Papers, Legislative Series, Box 80, Folder 14. See also Alston (1990).

19. File on Republican Conference Consideration, Michel Papers, Staff Series, Van Der Meid Files, Box 6. See also Alston (1989).

20. "Pelosi Announces Hearing with Americans Set to Lose Patients' Rights Under GOP Repeal Plan," Press Release, 16 Jan 2011, http://pelosi.house.gov/news/press-releases/2011/01/pelosi-announces-hearing-with-americans-set-to-lose-patients-rights-under-gop-repeal-plan.shtml (Accessed 17 Jul 2012). See Millman (2011).

21. "Pelosi Announces Hearing on Risks of Default to the U.S. Economy and Jobs," Press Release, 6 Jul 2011, http://pelosi.house.gov/news/press-releases/2011/07/pelosi-announces-hearing-on-risks-of-default-to-the-us-economy-and-jobs.shtml (Accessed 17 Jul 2012).

22. "Pelosi Opening Remarks at Steering and Policy Committee Hearing on Gas Prices and Excessive Oil Speculation," Press Release, 4 Apr 2012, http://pelosi.

house.gov/news/press-releases/2012/04/pelosi-opening-remarks-at-steering-and-policy-committee-hearing-on-gas-prices-and-excessive-oil-spec.shtml (Accessed 17 Jul 2012); "Pelosi Opening Remarks at Steering and Policy Committee Hearing—'Paycheck Fairness Act: Responding to Financial Pressures on Women by Closing the Gender Wage Gap,'" Press Release, 30 May 2012, http://pelosi.house.gov/news/press-releases/2012/05/pelosi-opening-remarks-at-steering-and-policy-committee-hearing-paycheck-fairness-act-responding-to.shtml (Accessed 17 Jul 2012).

23. Both parties had used extended leadership organizations in the past to send messages for public consumption. Democrats, in particular, had held several hearings in the Democratic-led 110th Congress, including one on health care reform at the height of the public debate in September 2009. "Pelosi Remarks at Democratic Steering and Policy Committee Forum on Health Insurance Reform," Press Release, 15 Sep 2009, http://pelosi.house.gov/news/press-releases/2009/09/releases-Sept09-steer.shtml (Accessed 17 Jul 2012).

24. "Pelosi, House Democratic Steering and Policy Committee Hearing on Women's Health," Press Release, 23 Feb 2012, http://pelosi.house.gov/news/press-releases/2012/02/pelosi-house-democratic-steering-and-policy-committee-hearing-on-womens-health.shtml (Accessed 17 May 2012).

25. The need for more assertive treatment of disloyal members became an issue in the 2014 race to replace McCarthy when Peter Roskam (R-IL) claimed he would do more to punish those who strayed (Newhauser 2014).

26. When I am referring to the parties generally, I use the term "caucus" to describe the full assembly of all members of a House party. The Republican Party in the House technically refers to itself as the Republican Conference while the Democratic Party uses the caucus label.

CHAPTER 2

1. A good illustration is the party leadership chapter in a standard, high-quality Congress text (Davidson et al. 2014). The bulk of the chapter considers party power through the lens of the top party leadership; only a few paragraphs each are devoted to the House whip system and to the set of other caucus organizations, which seem like an afterthought in the account.

2. Larry Evans' forthcoming whip-count research promises an exhaustive study of whip counts and vote fluidity in both parties across both chambers (see Evans and Grandy 2009 for a sample). As Evans' work is considering the count results in detail, my focus is on the whip organizations' development as part of the larger system of party leadership organizations; I draw on whip counts primarily as illustrations of the changing coordination and persuasion roles of the whip system.

3. I use conditional party government as the starting point for the argument rather than cartel theory (Cox and McCubbins 1993, 2007). With refinements discussed by later authors, CPG offers a much better framework for interpreting the change that I observe in party leadership organizations. In viewing the power delegated to party leadership as less variable over time, cartel theory offers little leverage over the considerable change in these organizations across the four decades in this study.

4. On the risk members face in delegating authority to party leaders, see Sinclair (1995, 13–14).

5. It is not universally the case that members who seek extended party leadership positions—even higher ranking posts—are using the positions as stepping stones. The policy or electoral goals are primary for some members in this choice. A good example is Barber Conable (R-NY), chair of the Republican Policy Committee in the mid-1970s. Elected chair in the Watergate-era leadership shuffle, Conable apparently felt conflicted about the party leadership role as well as frustrated by the trade-off it posed for his policy work in the Ways and Means Committee (Fleming 2004, 165, 173).

6. Paul Wilkinson, interview with the author, 19 Jan 2015.

7. For an excellent treatment of individual goals, collective party and policy goals, and the interrelated nature of these goals, see Smith (2007, 25–43). Smith's focus is on the party's influence in voting and outcomes, but his argument applies to an understanding of how the party organizes its internal structure as well.

8. My argument that the organizations' roles can be best understood in these categories is based on my overall observations from archival research on their actions. It has some parallels, though, with a 1993 article by Little and Patterson, which has been virtually (and unfortunately) ignored. Little and Patterson outlined the "distinct organizational life" of the parties in both chambers at the time. Their taxonomy of the party organizations' roles is more fragmented than mine, but Little and Patterson similarly stress the importance of party coordination and the effect party participation can have on members' own electoral and career goals.

9. DW-Nominate scores are a commonly used indicator of members' voting positions in ideological space, with the first dimension representing the typical liberal-conservative dimension underlying modern American politics (Poole and Rosenthal 2007).

10. Following the procedure outlined in Aldrich, Berger, and Rohde (2002), the median scores in figure 2.1 were standardized for comparison by dividing each party median by twice the chamber standard deviation for each Congress. The party cohesion measure is standardized by finding the ratio of the majority standard deviation to the full chamber's standard deviation and subtracting from 1.

11. For the three archives I did not visit in person (see appendix B), my approach was necessarily more selective; I requested documents from files that appeared most directly relevant to party organization operations based on the finding aids.

## CHAPTER 3

1. Individual data on membership rosters is not available for all Republican leadership organizations prior to 1981, but the structure of the party committees and whip system had remained essentially stable since the 1960s, so the figures for the early 1980s are a good approximation of the leadership size since that time.

2. Member requests for DSPC appointment: Austin Murphy to Tip O'Neill, 8 Nov 1976, O'Neill Papers, Series V, Box 11, Folder 10; James Weaver to O'Neill, 14 Nov [1976], O'Neill Papers, Series V, Box 11, Folder 10; Tom Bevill to O'Neill, 17 Sept 1976, O'Neill Papers, Series V, Box 11, Folder 10; Barbara Jordan to O'Neill, 7 Dec 1976, O'Neill Papers, Series V, Box 11, Folder 10; William Brodhead to O'Neill, 9 Nov 1976, O'Neill Papers, Series V, Box 11, Folder 10; Shirley Chisholm to O'Neill, 29 Nov 1978, O'Neill Papers, Series V, Box 12, Folder 1. In declining

Brodhead's request, O'Neill wrote that DSPC appointments were "a particularly difficult choice . . . since so many 'quality members' expressed an interest in serving on the committee." O'Neill to Brodhead, 13 Dec 1976, O'Neill Papers, Series V, Box 11, Folder 10.

3. John Jenrette to O'Neill, 7 Dec 1976, O'Neill Papers, Series V, Box 1, Folder 4.

4. The leadership-controlled committee remained a coveted appointment for members through the majority period—the Foley papers contain letters from members soliciting DSPC appointments, continuing the practice from the O'Neill era. Eckart to Foley, 14 Nov 1990 and McCloskey to Foley, 20 Nov 1990, Foley Papers, Box 170, Folder 4964.

5. Interestingly, the 98th Congress is the first in which the caucus codified any portion of the extended whip system in the rules, and the rules discuss only the zone system, leaving the appointive system subject entirely under leadership prerogative. 98th Congress Caucus Rules, Foley Papers, Box 165, Folder 4775.

6. GK [George Kundanis] to Foley, 16 Jan 1985 and 22 Jan 1985, Foley Papers, Box 133, Folder 3834.

7. Boucher to Wright, 12 Dec 1986, Foley Papers, Box 168, Folder 4844; Wise to Foley, 22 Jan 1991 and Kildee to Foley, 23 Jan 1991, Foley Papers, Box 170, Folder 4957. In support of his request for reappointment as at-large whip, Kildee cites his participation record, as well as his *CQ* rating: "among the top five Democrats in terms of voting with [the] party caucus on crucial floor votes."

8. Kundanis to Foley, 16 Jan 1985, Foley Papers, Box 133, Folder 3834.

9. "The Whips of the 100th Congress," Foley Papers, Box 168, Folder 4846.

10. On communications: "Steve" to BA [Bill Alexander], 30 Nov 1983, David E. Bonior Papers, Walter P. Reuther Library, Wayne State University, Box 134 (loose material). For an example of important policy actions driven by a Chief Deputy, see Bonior to Wright, 23 Jul 1987, Bonior Papers, Box 148, Folder 2. Bonior's office oversaw a *contra*-related taskforce, counting and persuasion of majority and minority "swing Members," and developing support from outside groups and leaders.

11. Coelho's relatively brief tenure as majority whip was followed by William H. Gray's (D-PA) even shorter tenure prior to Bonior's election in 1991.

12. Evidence from the late Democratic-majority period for whip appointments is in: Wise to Foley, 22 Jan 1991 and Kildee to Foley, 23 Jan 1991, Foley Papers, Box 170, Folder 4957; Mineta to Foley, 21 Dec 1988, Foley Papers, Box 170, Folder 4960; Engel to Foley, 14 Jul 1989, Foley Papers, Box 170, Folder 4961; Coleman to Foley, 26 Jun 1989, Foley Papers, Box 170, Folder 4962; Vento to Foley, 15 Nov 1990, Foley Papers, Box 170, Folder 4964. (Vento offered an idiosyncratic promise in exchange for the whip appointment, vowing "not to tell jokes at the weekly meetings and sit on [Chuck] Schumer whenever necessary!") Evidence on DSPC appointment solicitations is in: Eckart to Foley, 14 Nov 1990 and McCloskey to Foley, 20 Nov 1990, Foley Papers, Box 170, Folder 4964. (McCloskey promised Foley he "would back you and your concerns in every way possible" if appointed to the committee.)

13. E.g., Harley Staggers to Bonior, 11 Jul 1991, Bonior Papers, Box 2, Folder 4; Michael McNulty to Bonior, undated [1991], Bonior Papers, Box 2, Folder 4; Jose Serrano to Bonior, 31 Mar 1994, Bonior Papers, Box 135, Folder 32.

14. Lynn Woolsey to Bonior, 15 Dec 1994, Bonior Papers, Box 135, Folder 89.

15. Members Requesting Appointments as Whips, undated [1999], Bonior Papers, Box 4, Folder 37. Although member letters and a few memos provide extensive documentation to support the fact that extended leadership posts were desirable and actively sought, there are no available complete lists of requests from any Congress in either caucus, with the possible exception of this 1999 list. As a result, it is not feasible to perform a quantitative analysis of who requests and who succeeds in their requests to parallel the standard analysis in the standing-committee-assignment literature.

16. Bonior to Buddy Darden, 11 Jun 1989; Bonior to Roy Dyson, 11 Jun 1989; Bonior to Claude Harris, 9 Jun 1989; Bonior to Lindsay Thomas, 11 Jun 1989; Bonior to Billy Tauzin, 11 Jun 1989; Bonior to Richard Ray, 11 Jun 1989, all in Bonior Papers, Box 78, Folder 2.

17. "Hoyer Announces Whip Team for 113th Congress," 4 Jan 2013, http://www.democraticwhip.gov/content/hoyer-announces-whip-team-113th-congress (Accessed 22 Jul 2013).

18. Preamble and Rules of the Democratic Caucus, 104th Congress, 10 Oct 1996, Bob Wise Collection, West Virginia Archives and History Library, Box 3, Folder: Democratic Caucus 1996 Forward.

19. Richard Gephardt to Bonior, undated [1996?], Bonior Papers, Box 51, Folder 37. Although it is not addressed as a Dear Democratic Colleague letter, it appears to be a general solicitation of support for reelection as minority leader after the 1996 election.

20. The models in table 3.2 are similar to those presented in Meinke (2008), but they are based on updated data and slightly different specification.

21. Information on the identity of leadership-appointed DSPC members is available for the 94th, 97th–103rd, 106th, and 108th–110th Congresses. A separate analysis of the DSPC's leadership-appointed membership in the Congresses for which data is available (not shown) reveals no generally clear patterns in the selection of DSPC appointees, although the $n$ of appointees is quite small, especially in the earlier period. In several Congresses, notably in both the 109th and 110th, the Democratic leadership did choose appointees who were significantly more electorally secure than their counterparts, possibly suggesting an effort to create a diverse but politically well-situated coalition on the committee.

22. Linda to Michel, 24 Mar 1983, Michel Papers, Leadership Series, Box 6, Folder: 98th Republican Policy Committee.

23. Letters and lists in Michel Papers, Leadership Series, Box 4, Folder: 97th Congress Republican Policy Committee and Box 6, Folder: 98th Republican Policy Committee.

24. Moore to Michel, 19 Dec 1980, Michel Papers, Leadership Series, Box 4, Folder: 97th Republican Policy Committee. Moore received his appointment and served on the committee through the 99th Congress when he left the House to run for the Senate.

25. House Republican Research Committee [98th Congress], Michel Papers, Leadership Series, Box 6, Folder: 98th Congress: Republican Research Committee; Committee on Research [103rd Congress], Richard K. Armey Collection, Carl Albert Center, University of Oklahoma, Legislative Series, Box 56, Folder 22; Edwards to Republican Colleague, undated draft [1987], Edwards Collection, Leg-

islative Series, Box 81, Folder 30. Analysis of the Research Committee's executive membership (not shown) reveals no clear patterns of significant biases in loyalty, seniority, electoral security, or region from the 97th Congress through the 103rd Congress.

26. Kathy to Steve Hofman, 8 Oct 1987, Edwards Collection, Legislative Series, Box 81, Folder 35; Edwards to Steve Hofman, 8 Oct 1987, Edwards Collection, Legislative Series, Box 81, Folder 35; Hofman to Edwards, 12 Oct 1987, Edwards Collection, Legislative Series, Box 81, Folder 35; Hofman to Edwards, 17 Nov 1987, Edwards Collection, Legislative Series, Box 82, Folder 3. See also Connelly and Pitney (1994, 44).

27. Task Force Membership list, 1987, Mickey Edwards Collection, Legislative Series, Box 81, Folder 30.

28. Memo from Gingrich and Gunderson, 26 May 1989, Armey Collection, Legislative Series, Box 64, Folder 1; Laurie James to Vicky Grant, 7 Jul 1989, Armey Collection, Legislative Series, Box 64, Folder 1; Invitees to Strategy Whip Meetings, undated, Michel Papers, Staff Series, Van Der Meid Files, Box 6, Folder: Campaign Reform: Whip Strategy.

29. In later years, representatives of recently elected classes also held seats on the committee, casting one vote each. See Republican Committee on Committees, January 1983, Michel Papers, Leadership Series, Box 5, Folder: 98th Congress: Committee on Committees.

30. Republican Conference Rules excerpt, Committee on Committees, undated [97th Congress], Michel Papers, Leadership Series, Box 5, Folder: Committee on Committees.; Michel to Republican Colleagues, 2 Dec 1982, Michel Papers, Leadership Series, Box 6, Folder: 98th Congress: Dear Colleague 12/2/82.

31. Resolution on the Committee on Committees for the 99th Congress, undated, Michel Papers, Leadership Series, Box 7, Folder: 99th Congress: Committee on Committees, Executive Committee.

32. Appointment information from 108th Congress Policy Committee document provided by Paul Wilkinson, interview with the author, 19 Jan 2015.

33. Majority Whip Organization, undated, Armey Collection, Legislative Series, Box 56, Folder 23.

34. The best available whip rosters for the 101st and 102nd Congresses are missing several Assistant Regional Whips, so the results here should be interpreted with caution relative to the surrounding Congresses.

35. Republican Policy Committee Members—97th Congress, Michel Papers, Leadership Series, Box 4, Folder: 97th Congress Republican Policy Committee.

36. Republican Policy Committee appointee data is missing for the 94th–95th and 99th–100th Congresses; the described analysis excludes those Congresses. Because the appointees themselves generally do not differ significantly from other regular Republican members, the biases in representation on the committee must have resulted from changes in the committee's structure or the selection of regional representatives on the committee—which, in turn, may reflect perceptions of the committee's role—rather than solely from biased leadership selection of appointees.

37. The effect is statistically significant in all Congresses except the 101st, where it falls just short of $p = .10$, two-tailed.

38. The Republican "Theme Team" has been an informal organization of the Conference focused on carrying out party messaging on the House floor.

39. For Republicans, this pattern was complicated by both the growth in the extended leadership in 1995 and the new majority's preference for very junior members in the leadership. As a result, a cohort analysis for GOP members like the one displayed above for Democrats would show that few GOP members from the early 1980s were still in the leadership after 1994.

40. These models exclude Republicans prior to the 97th Congress because of incomplete membership data on some party organizations.

41. The assignment data was collected (and later updated) by Nelson and Stewart (Swift et al. 2000).

42. Although the status of some of these committees, particularly Rules, in very recent Congresses might be questionable, Edwards and Stewart (2006, 37) find they rank as the top four most valued committees (based on transfers).

43. I define "top party leadership" to include the Speaker, majority/minority leader, majority/minority whip, caucus/conference chair, and the chairs of party committees. Most of these positions are elected posts during the time period of this study, but some were appointed positions.

44. Press release on Baird (19 Nov 1998) and others from 1996–98, Bonior Papers, Box 51, Folder 37.

45. E.g., "Swalwell Chosen as Democratic Assistant Whip," 7 Jan 2013, http://swalwell.house.gov/press-releases/swalwell-chosen-as-a-democratic-assistant-whip/ (Accessed 3 Jan 2014).

46. E.g., "U.S. Rep. Dan Kildee Appointed Assistant Democratic Whip," 8 Jan 2013, http://www.mlive.com/news/flint/index.ssf/2013/01/us_rep_dan_kildee_appointed.html (Accessed 3 Jan 2014).

47. The CQ lists for the 111th and 112th Congresses are limited, with most whips and some other positions omitted. I rely on these lists for this analysis because I seek to analyze the presentation and explanation decisions of those members for whom participation was already a matter of public record.

48. For the 112th Congress, data was collected during early 2012 while the 112th Congress websites were active. For the 111th Congress, the internet archiving site www.archive.org was used to reconstruct member websites from early 2010 during the 111th Congress.

49. Some members even blur the distinction between standing and party committees on their websites. Henry Cuellar (D-TX), for example, listed two memberships on his committee service page in the 113th Congress: the Appropriations Committee and the "House Steering and Policy Committee" (i.e., DSPC). In the 109th Congress, Lincoln Diaz-Balart (R-FL) listed (and described at some length) his role on the "House Policy Committee" (i.e., Republican Policy Committee) in between his explanations of his Rules Committee and International Relations Committee positions.

## CHAPTER 4

1. Brodhead memo to DSPC, 18 Jun 1975, Albert Collection, Legislative Series, Box 220, Folder 14.

2. "Whip Polls," O'Neill Papers, Series V, Box 1, Folder 1.

3. Whip count for H.R. 5376, 4/20/71 and whip count for H.R. 3313, 5/13/71, O'Neill Papers, Series V, Box 2, Folder 1. Some southern whips were reporting totals and withholding names as late as the 93rd Congress. Whip counts for H.R. 1107 and H.R. 8480, Albert Collection, Legislative Series, Box 192, Folder 5.

4. "Notes on Whip Coffee," 8 Jul 1971 and "Agenda for Whip Coffee," 15 Oct 1971, O'Neill Papers, Series V, Box 1, Folder 14.

5. Unsigned staff memo to O'Neill, O'Neill Papers, Series V, Box 2, Folder 1.

6. E.g., "Whip Count Information June 1, 1971" and "Results of Whip Call, June 24, 1971" in O'Neill Papers, Series V, Box 2, Folder 1. Systematic tracking of voting records begins in the 95th Congress (O'Neill Papers, Series V, Box 6, Folder 13) and continues thereafter.

7. Olin Teague to O'Neill, 25 Mar 1971, O'Neill Papers, Series V, Box 1, Folder 13; Speech cards, 15 Nov 1973, O'Neill Papers, Series V, Box 4, Folder 14.

8. Whip Notice Information, 7 Apr 1971, O'Neill Papers, Series V, Box 2, Folder 4.

9. O'Neill Papers, Series V, Box 2, Folders 9–11, and Box 3, Folders 1–2.

10. The Boggs-era meetings were informal conversations between the zone whips, the majority leader, and some staff, fueled by coffee and homemade baked goods. O'Neill Papers, Series V, Box 1, Folder 14; also Farrell (2001, 296).

11. Minutes and notes for whip coffees, 8 Jul 1971, 29 Jul 1971, 16 Sep 1971, 16 Mar 1972, O'Neill Papers, Series V, Box 1, Folder 14.

12. Minutes and notes for whip coffees, 20 May 1971, 8 Jul 1971, 15 Oct 1971, 28 Oct 1971, 4 Nov 1971, O'Neill Papers, Series V, Box 1, Folders 13 and 14.

13. Irv Sprague to Pat Clancy, 3 Oct 1978, Foley Papers, Box 190, Folder 5618; "Democratic Steering and Policy Committee Meetings—1973" and "Democratic Steering and Policy Committee Meetings—1974," Foley Papers, Box 192, Folder 5669; DSPC minutes, 27 Jun 1974, Foley Papers, Box 192, Folder 5692; DSPC minutes, 24 Sep 1974, Foley Papers, Box 192, Folder 5711.

14. Irv Sprague to Pat Clancy, 3 Oct 1978, Foley Papers, Box 190, Folder 5618; "Democratic Steering and Policy and Committee on Committee Meetings—1975," Foley Papers, Box 192, Folder 5669.

15. John Barriere to Albert, 7 Oct 1975, Foley Papers, Box 192, Folder 5669.

16. "Announcement of Democratic Program on the Economy," 13 Jan 1975, Foley Papers, Box 192, Folder 5728.

17. DSPC minutes, 24 Jan 1975, Foley Papers, Box 193, Folder 5737; Barriere to Albert, 7 Oct 1975, Foley Papers, Box 192, Folder 5669.

18. William Brodhead to Albert, 6 Jun 1975 and Brodhead memo to DSPC, 18 Jun 1975, Albert Collection, Legislative Series, Box 220, Folder 14. See also Rosenbaum (1975).

19. O'Neill to Carl Albert, 29 Mar 1973, Foley Papers, Box 192, Folder 5692.

20. Bolling to Albert, 2 Apr 1973 and Barriere to Albert, 2 Apr 1973, Foley Papers, Box 192, Folder 5692.

21. Paraphrase of Carl Albert remarks in minutes of the Organizational Meeting of the Democratic Steering and Policy Committee, 5 Apr 1973. Foley Papers, Box 192, Folder 5692.

22. Albert and the early DSPC staff apparently warded off other efforts to

broaden the committee's role and, as a result, draw power away from the Speaker and limit House Democrats' autonomy. In late 1974, Sen. Mike Mansfield's office suggested implementing the long-dormant 1946 recommendation for congressional policy committees by joining the Senate Democratic Policy Committee and the DSPC into a "Legislative-Executive Council" to work with President Ford. In an internal staff memo, Barriere strongly rejected this "fanciful concept" on general separation-of-powers grounds and because of inherent policy differences between the Democratic Congress and the Ford Administration. Charles Ferris to Mike Mansfield, 4 Dec 1974 and John Barriere to Mike Reed, 28 Jan 1975, Albert Collection, Legislative Series, Box 238, Folder 15.

23. "Democratic Steering and Policy Committee Proposed Rules and Procedures, 95th Congress," 25 Jan 1977, O'Neill Papers, Series V, Box 11, Folder 8; Irv Sprague to Pat Clancy, 3 Oct 1978, Foley Papers, Box 190, Folder 5618.

24. Billie [Billie Gay Larson] to O'Neill, 5 Jun 1979, O'Neill Papers, Series III, Box 61, Folder 6.

25. "Legislative Resolutions Passed in the Steering and Policy Committee," 1977–78, Foley Papers, Box 192, Folder 5669. Sinclair depicts the DSPC's resolution activity as a "new function . . . under O'Neill" (1983, 74), although the evidence above shows that the reconstituted DSPC of the 93rd and 94th Congresses had considered and approved resolutions in a similar fashion.

26. Democratic Steering and Policy Committee minutes, 8 Feb 1977, 9 Mar 1977, 30 Mar 1977, 20 Apr 1977, 26 Apr 1977, 7 Jun 1977, 18 Jul 1977, 26 Sep 1978, O'Neill Papers, Series III, Box 61, Folders 4 and 5.

27. Billie [Billie Gay Larson] to O'Neill, 5 Jun 1979, O'Neill Papers, Series III, Box 61, Folder 6.

28. Democratic Caucus minutes of 8 Apr 1981, 5 May 1981, 20 May 1981, 28 May 1981, Foley Papers, Box 185, Folder 5539.

29. See, e.g., DSPC minutes, 4 Jun 1985, Foley Papers, Box 195, Folder 5947.

30. "Democratic Steering and Policy Journal 101st Congress," Foley Papers, Box 193, Folder 5955.

31. Examples of "Legislative Status Briefing Book" from 1990 and "Democratic Steering and Policy Committee Issues Update" from 1991 in Foley Papers, Box 168, Folders 4854 and 4874.

32. See examples in George Kundanis files, e.g., John Dingell to Tom Foley, 14 Jan 1991, Foley Papers, Box 170, Folder 4957. Reformers in the Democratic caucus made an effort in the early 1990s to strengthen the central policy planning power of the leadership vis-à-vis committees. The result, the Democratic Policy Council in the 103rd Congress "quickly faded into obscurity," according to Evans and Oleszek. Although the Council was formed in response to pressures for stronger central party leadership, Evans and Oleszek suggest the party was too divided at this time to sustain these further centralizing efforts (1997, 52–55; also Price 2004, 306–7). The Democrats' return to the White House at the time of the Council's formation likely also diminished the need for central coordination in the House party.

33. David Bonior's daily schedules from the first half of 1993 (the start of the 103rd Congress) provide detail on leadership meetings at this time. From January through May 1993, Bonior's schedules note eight DSPC meetings, but the schedules record the purpose as committee assignment business on most of those dates.

1993 Daily Schedules, David E. Bonior Papers, Walter P. Reuther Library, Wayne State University, Box 144, Folder 1.

34. Sinclair's account of the 1980s whip meetings does not draw out this change, but her earlier narrative of weekly whip meetings in the late 1970s places much more emphasis on information exchange and less emphasis on the role of the top leadership (Sinclair 1983, 58–62).

35. 1993 Daily Schedules, Bonior Papers, Box 144, Folder 1. Between January and May 1993, Bonior attended 14 full whip meetings and more than 20 formal whip task force meetings on a range of issues.

36. Galloway similarly characterized the early 1960s Republican Policy Committee as "an active branch of the House Republican leadership" (1962, 150).

37. The committee also issued 19 press releases. Summary of Activities: House Republican Policy Committee, 96th Congress—2nd Session, undated, Bud Shuster Papers, Pasquerilla Library, Saint Francis University, Series I: Congressional Papers, Sub-Series A: United States, Box 36A, Folder 18.

38. Reply card examples from 95th Congress in Shuster Papers, Congressional Papers, United States, Box 35A, Folder 1.

39. Republican Policy Committee Endorses Regulatory Reform of Trucking Industry, 10 Jun 1980, Statement No. II-10, Shuster Papers, Congressional Papers, United States, Box 36A, Folder 18.

40. Republican Whip chart, 88th Congress, January 1963, Michel Papers, Leadership Series, Box 1, Folder: 88th Congress 1963–64 Whip; Republican Whip chart, 89th Congress, January 1965, Michel Papers, Leadership Series, Box 1, Folder: 89th Congress 1965–66 Whip.

41. Whip poll sheet on increasing House size, 1 Mar 1962, Michel Papers, Leadership Series, Box 1, Folder: 88th Congress 1963–64 Whip.

42. Whip poll sheet on urban affairs department, 30 Jan 1962, Michel Papers, Leadership Series, Box 1, Folder: 88th Congress 1963–64 Whip; Whip poll sheets on oil tax deferral, 27 Jan 1975, Michel Papers, Leadership Series, Box 1, Folder: 94th Congress: 1975–76 Whip Polls.

43. Connelly was an APSA Congressional Fellow with Dick Cheney during Cheney's leadership of the Policy Committee in the 99th Congress (1985–87), and he conducted interviews with members and staff during that time period (Connelly 1988).

44. A Profile: The Republican Policy Committee, Robert Michel Papers, Dirksen Congressional Center, Leadership Series, Box 11, Folder: Republican Conference Leadership Responsibilities. The Committee's official role is described similarly in the 103rd Congress in: A Blueprint for Leadership, Office of the Republican Leader, Michel Papers, Leadership Series, Box 16, Folder: 103rd A Blueprint for Leadership.

45. Mickey Edwards to Gordon Jones and Vicki Martyak, 21 Mar 1989, Edwards Papers, Legislative Series, Box 81, Folder 19.

46. Edwards to Duncan Hunter, 2 Mar 1989, Edwards Papers, Legislative Series, Box 44, Folder 1.

47. Republican Policy Committee Forum announcement, 30 Jan 1990, Armey Papers, Legislative Series, Box 58, Folder 14; Republican Leaders to Republican Colleague, 1990, "House Republican Leaders' Legislative Agenda for the Second

Session of the 101st Congress," Michel Papers, Staff Series, Van Der Meid Files, Box 20, Folder: Republican Leaders' Agenda 1990; Forum announcement, 9 Aug 1994, Armey Papers, Legislative Series, Box 58, Folder 14.

48. Mickey Edwards, invitation to Republican Policy Committee meetings, 3 Feb 1989, Richard K. Armey Papers, Carl Albert Center, University of Oklahoma, Legislative Series, Box 58, Folder 14.

49. GSJ [Gordon Jones] to Mickey [Edwards] and Vicki [Martyak], 29 Mar 1989, Mickey Edwards Papers, Carl Albert Center, University of Oklahoma, Legislative Series, Box 81, Folder 19; Tracy Grant letter, 9 Jun 1989, Edwards Papers, Legislative Series, Box 81, Folder 19.

50. Policy Meetings and Statements, 1990, Edwards Papers, Legislative Series, Box 81, Folder 26.

51. Minutes of Republican Policy Forum Meeting, 9 Feb 1989, Edwards Papers, Legislative Series, Box 81, Folder 19.

52. Republican Policy Committee forum announcements, 25 Sep 1990, 7 Dec 1987, 2 Jun 1988, 16 Jun 1988, Armey Papers, Legislative Series, Box 58, Folder 14.

53. Gingrich succeeded Dick Cheney, who served for only a few months as Republican whip before joining the Bush Administration as Defense Secretary.

54. House Republican Policy Committee, Resolutions and Statements, 1990–1992, Edwards Papers, Legislative Series, Box 81, Folders 26–28.

55. There does not appear to be an important distinction between the committee's resolutions and statements in this period, although the resolution wording was usually used for specific pending legislation.

56. Bob Michel, Newt Gingrich, and Mickey Edwards voted with the party majority on each of the issues on which they cast a vote. Gingrich, it should be noted, was elected to fill the vacant whip post at the end of March 1989; he was not yet an elected leader for the first two roll-calls in the table.

57. Kathy to Steve Hofman, 8 Oct 1987, Edwards Collection, Legislative Series, Box 81, Folder 35; Edwards to Steve Hofman, 8 Oct 1987, Edwards Collection, Legislative Series, Box 81, Folder 35; Hofman to Edwards, 12 Oct 1987, Edwards Collection, Legislative Series, Box 81, Folder 35; Hofman to Edwards, 17 Nov 1987, Edwards Collection, Legislative Series, Box 82, Folder 3.

58. Conference publications in the 1990s, in addition to the *Legislative Digest*, included *Boarding Pass, The Cutting Edge, Floor Prep,* and *Radar Screen.* Examples in Armey Collection, Legislative Series, Box 55, Folders 21 and 22; Box 56, Folders 8, 12, 14; Box 57, Folders 19 and 20. See also Little and Patterson (1993, 58).

59. E.g., Special Whip Notice: H.R. 6—Elementary & Secondary Education Reauthorization, 23 Feb 1994, Armey Collection, Legislative Series, Box 51, Folder 7. The Republican whip in the 1990s provided other services as well—including a "job bank" of resumes for members to use in staff searches. "Hitting the Ground Running," 6 Nov 1996, p. 17, Armey Collection, Legislative Series, Box 55, Folder 3.

60. Within a few weeks of the 1994 midterm election victory, the Republican House leadership reached a "consensus" that the Republican Research Committee should be terminated, a decision that was announced around the same time as the Gingrich restructuring of the Committee on Committees (see chap. 7) and the realignment of the standing committee system (Burger 1994a; Camia 1994).

There is little direct evidence to explain the choice, but the decision to eliminate the Research Committee is consistent with Newt Gingrich's decisions to centralize committee assignments and House legislative processes and with the early tendency of other leaders and the rest of the Conference to support these dramatic changes. The Research Committee represented a relatively open, decentralized view of coordination on policy development that we would expect to see deemphasized in a majority party under strong party government and a leader with strong ideological and electoral goals. Gingrich's own preference in the 104th Congress for leadership task forces on legislation joined with a trend from the last several Congresses of the minority period toward more leadership-directed task forces. From the perspective of the top Republican leadership, it is likely that the wide range of task forces from the 103rd Congress (see table 5.2) would seem redundant, risky, or both. Finally, the rise to majority status, with its attendant institutional resources, meant the party's own organizations were less important as a venue for participation and general policy development. It bears mentioning that the majority Republican Policy Committee has been mentioned occasionally as a candidate for the same fate as the Research Committee since 1995 (Bresnahan 2001; Burger 1996).

61. Republican Policy Committee forum and executive session announcements, 13 Feb 1995 through 10 Sep 2001, Richard Armey Collection, Legislative Series, Box 58, Folders 14 and 15. House Policy Committee [*sic*] Meetings page, 24 Apr 2003, http://www.policy.house.gov/ html/meetings.cfm, viewed via http://wayback. archive.org.

62. Paul Wilkinson, interview with the author, 19 Jan 2015.

63. The ethics issue divided members of the leadership, including key figures in the Republican whip organization (Eilperin 1997b).

64. Whip Summary Report #167, 8 Jul 1996, Armey Collection, Legislative Series, Box 47, Folder 25. Issue details from Cassata (1996).

65. Various memos from Ari Weiss to Tip O'Neill, O'Neill Papers, Series III, Box 50, Folder 1; various memos from Jack Lew to Ari Weiss or Tip O'Neill, O'Neill Papers, Series III, Box 53, Folder 1; various memos from Tod O'Connor to Ari Weiss, O'Neill Papers, Series III, Box 53, Folder 2. Also see O'Neill Papers, Series III, Box 3, Folder 9 and Series III, Box 53, Folder 2; Foley Papers, Box 133, Folders 3834–3835. On DSPC staff communication with committee chairs, see 1977 Irv Sprague letters in O'Neill Papers, Box 70, Folder 12.

66. In one example, DSPC staffer Spencer Smith weighed the political challenge of the Democrats' position on tax cuts in terms of both policy outcomes and Republican electoral arguments. Spencer Smith to the Speaker, 23 Jul 1979, O'Neill Papers, Series II, Box 53, Folder 4.

67. During late 1978 and early 1979, for instance, the DSPC conducted a review of the congressional budget process at the direction of the caucus (*National Journal* 1978). DSPC staff would continue to be important in the 1980s for research on issues, process, and even member voting behavior. O'Neill Papers, Series III, Box 3, Folder 9 and Series III, Box 53, Folder 2; Foley Papers, Box 133, Folders 3834–3835.

68. Ben Procter staff reports, 19 Feb 1987, 27 Feb 1987, and 6 Mar 1987, Speaker Jim Wright Collection, Texas Christian University, Box 1026, Folder: Steering and

Policy; Steering and Policy Committee Staff Assignments, undated, Wright Collection, Box 939, Folder: Steering and Policy Staff Assignments.

69. See discussion in the "Coordination in the Democratic Caucus" section of this chapter.

## CHAPTER 5

1. Task Force on Information materials, 1975, O'Neill Papers, Series V, Box 19, Folder 21.

2. To "report resolutions regarding party policy, legislative priorities, scheduling of matters for House or Caucus action, and other matters as appropriate to further Democratic programs and policies," in addition to the committee-on-committees role. 1981 Caucus rules, O'Neill Papers, Series V, Box 19, Folder 17.

3. Caucus Task Forces, 11 Dec 1981, O'Neill Papers, Series III, Box 36, Folder 4. See also Kathy Tuttle to Al From, 24 Feb 1982, O'Neill Papers, Series III, Box 36, Folder 4; Al Gore to Environmental Task Force, 13 Jan 1982, O'Neill Papers, Series III, Box 36, Folder 11; "Draft Policy Position Paper, Democratic Caucus' Task Force on Small Business," O'Neill Papers, Series III, Box 57, Folder 7.

4. "Policy and Research Staff, Democratic Policy Committee," Richard A. Gephardt Collection, Missouri History Museum, Congressional Papers, Series 7, Subseries 29, Box 842, Folder 13.

5. "Pelosi, House Democratic Steering and Policy Committee Hearing on Women's Health," Press Release, 23 Feb 2012, http://pelosi.house.gov/news/press-releases/2012/02/pelosi-house-democratic-steering-and-policy-committee-hearing-on-womens-health.shtml (Accessed 17 May 2012).

6. On one occasion in spring 2014, the DSPC's public hearings led to conflict with the Republican majority. The GOP denied the committee access to a room for a hearing on unemployment benefits after a technical problem with the room request, leading to accusations that the majority was trying to silence the minority (Bellantoni and Fuller 2014).

7. "Steve" to BA [Bill Alexander], 30 Nov 1983, Bonior Papers, Box 134 (loose material). This memo, which summarizes the activities of the chief deputy whip's office in late 1983, illustrates the broader communications role of the chief deputy whip. In addition to the work on study and coordination of one-minutes, the staff were attempting to build links between the leadership and external constituency groups ("an area where there is currently no effort being made by the party leadership in either House except by the campaign committees") and between the leadership and 1984 congressional candidates ("to help them feel they have a contact point within the party leadership outside the campaign committee").

8. E.g., Speech Cards, 15 Nov 1973, O'Neill Papers, Series V, Box 4, Folder 14.

9. HMO Whip Task Force notes, undated, Bonior Papers, Box 35, Folder 31.

10. Jerry [Hartz] and Erich [Pfuelher] to Bonior, 16 Apr 1999, Bonior Papers, Box 101, Folder 25. See also Nitschke (1999).

11. Republican Policy Committee Policy Statements, various dates, 95th Congress, Shuster Papers, Congressional Papers, United States, Box 35A, Folder 1.

12. Republican Policy Committee Statement #10, Revisiting the Hatch Act, 10

May 1977; Republican Policy Committee Statement #4, The Tax Reduction and Simplification Act of 1977, 1 Mar 1977; Republican Policy Committee Statement #12, Clean Air Act Amendments of 1977, 23 May 1977, Shuster Papers, Congressional Papers, United States, Box 35A, Folder 1.

13. Republican Policy Committee Agenda, 9 Sep 1980; Policy Committee Statement, "Jimmy Carter: Builder of Potemkin Villages," 9 Sep 1980; Press Release, "(GOP Congressional Nominee) Blasts Carter Stealth Leak, Accuses Him of Building 'Potemkin Villages,'" undated, Shuster Papers, Congressional Papers, United States, Box 36A, Folder 8.

14. Connelly (1988, 13) also discusses the political nature of Policy Committee products, noting that "Policy Committee staff research, rather than provide a pale reflection of minority staff work on the standing committees, has generally taken the form of more overtly political, partisan propaganda for purposes of press releases and speeches."

15. A Profile: The Republican Policy Committee, Michel Papers, Leadership Series, Box 11, Folder: Republican Conference Leadership Responsibilities. The Committee's official role is described similarly in the 103rd Congress in: A Blueprint for Leadership, Office of the Republican Leader, Michel Papers, Leadership Series, Box 16, Folder: 103rd A Blueprint for Leadership.

16. "Op-ed, Press Release, and Radio talk-show Strategy," undated, Mickey Edwards Collection, Legislative Series, Box 81, Folder 19.

17. Republican Policy Committee publications, Michel Papers, Legislative Series, Box 79, Folder: 103rd Republican Policy Committee.

18. Rules of Procedure, Committee on Policy, U.S. House of Representatives, 107th Congress. 2 Feb 2003, http://policy.house.gov/assets/rules.pdf, viewed via http://wayback.archive.org.

19. The Clinton-Gephardt Abandonment of Social Security, 18 Nov 1999, http://policy.house.gov/documents/statements/1999/socsec.htm, viewed via http://wayback.archive.org; How the ABA Became a Left-Wing Lobbying Group, 4 Feb 1997, in House Positions on Key Issues: Facts, Analysis, and Background, House Policy Committee, http://policy.house.gov/documents/pdfdocs/keypos.pdf, viewed via http://wayback.archive.org.

20. House Policy Committee, Selected Publications and Activities, 107th Congress, http://policy.house.gov/assets/107yearend.pdf, viewed via http://web.archive.org.

21. Shuster supporters to Michel, 1 Oct 1980, Michel Papers, Leadership Series, Box 2, Folder: 96th Leadership Contest. 96th Congress—Second Session Key Votes, undated, Shuster Papers, Congressional Papers, United States, Box 36A, Folder 18.

22. Susan to Mickey [Edwards] and Vicki [Martyak], 9 Mar 1989, Mickey Edwards Collection, Legislative Series, Box 81, Folder 19; GSJ [Gordon Jones] to Mickey [Edwards] and Vicki [Martyak], 29 Mar 1989, Mickey Edwards Collection, Legislative Series, Box 81, Folder 19.

23. U.S. China Relations: A Policy for Freedom, Oct 1997, Richard Armey Papers, Legislative Series, Box 52, Folder 21.

24. House Positions on Key Issues: Facts, Analysis, and Background, House Pol-

icy Committee, Nov 1998, http://policy.house.gov/documents/pdfdocs/keypos.pdf viewed via http://wayback.archive.org.

25. House Policy Committee: 108th Congress Report, undated [2004], http://upload.wikimedia.org/wikipedia/commons/9/9c/HousePolicyCommittee108th CongressReport.pdf (Accessed 8 Jan 2015).

26. When Cox stepped down in 2005, he was replaced by John Shadegg (R-AZ), who led for only a year before he too stepped down to run for majority leader.

27. The Republican Policy Committee's website in the 111th Congress included many committee publications linking party positions to broader philosophical views. Republican Policy Committee resources, 27 May 2010, http://policy.house.gov/the-committee viewed via http://wayback.archive.org.

28. Interview with Tom Price, *C-SPAN Newsmakers*, C-SPAN, June 15, 2012.

29. Approvingly: Duncan Hunter, quoted in *National Journal* (1989). Critically: "It is not the primary purpose of the Research Committee staff to function as a think tank generating reports and papers on a variety of issues, which is what seems to be happening," Mickey Edwards to Steve [Hofman], 23 Nov 1987, Edwards Papers, Legislative Series, Box 82, Folder 3. Edwards wanted instead for the committee's staff to focus on work that would support active, focused Research Committee task forces.

30. Defense Task Force Synopsis Series #6: The Role and Posture of U.S. Ground Forces, House Republican Research Committee, July 1978, and SALT II Issues and Trends: An Overview, House Republican Research Committee, July 1978, Shuster Papers, Congressional Papers, United States, Box 35A, Folder 1.

31. Research Committee Status Report, 1983, Michel Papers, Leadership Series, Box 6, Folder: 98th Congress: Republican Research Committee.

32. *Ideas for Tomorrow, Choices for Today*, Committee on the First One Hundred Days, Republican Research Committee, Edwards Collection, Legislative Series, Box 81, Folder 31; Updated on *Ideas for Tomorrow*, 8 Jan 1987, Edwards Collection, Legislative Series, Box 81, Folder 32.

33. During the 1986 election season, the committee distributed a 72-page handbook on Reagan and congressional Republican issue stands and the contrasts with Democratic positions (*National Journal* 1986). The committee's staff also disseminated speechwriting materials and information on congressional caucuses to the Republican membership. Edwards Collection, Legislative Series, Box 81, Folder 32.

34. Unsigned Edwards memo to Steve [Hofman], undated, Edwards Collection, Legislative Series, Box 81, Folder 30.

35. Laura Micek to Edwards, 6 Jul 1987, Edwards Collection, Legislative Series, Box 81, Folder 33.

36. Bill Smith to Edwards, 5 Oct 1987, Edwards Collection, Legislative Series, Box 82, Folder 19.

37. Kathy to Steve Hofman, 8 Oct 1987, Edwards Collection, Legislative Series, Box 81, Folder 35; Edwards to Steve Hofman, 8 Oct 1987, Edwards Collection, Legislative Series, Box 81, Folder 35; Hofman to Edwards, 12 Oct 1987, Edwards Collection, Legislative Series, Box 81, Folder 35; Hofman to Edwards, 17 Nov 1987, Edwards Collection, Legislative Series, Box 82, Folder 3.

38. Handbook for Republican Members, 101st Congress, Edwards Collection, Legislative Series, Box 81, Folder 13.

39. Hunter's expansion of the Research Committee's jurisdiction initially led to conflict with the Policy Committee over the appropriate role for the two related party committees. Policy Chair Edwards wrote to Hunter: "I regret that we seem to be having a problem in drawing the line between the activities of the Research Committee, which are properly those of long-range development of Republican alternatives, and those of the Policy Committee, which is charged with dealing with those issues currently being considered by the Congress." Edwards to Hunter, 2 Mar 1989, Edwards Collection, Legislative Series, Box 44, Folder 1.

40. Republican Research Committee, Task Force on Military Personnel Hearing Transcript, 4 Feb 1993, available at: http://dont.stanford.edu/hearings/hearings.htm. Republican Research Committee, Health Care Task Force Hearing, 14 Sep 1993, available at: http://www.c-spanvideo.org/program/RepublicanHeal.

41. John Myers to Bud Shuster, 24 Jul 1980; Invitation to reception for John Myers and The Whips' Fund for a Republican Majority, 27 Aug 1980, Shuster Papers, Congressional Papers, United States, Box 36A, Folder 31.

42. Gingrich to Ben Blaz, 7 Jul 1989, Armey Collection, Legislative Series, Box 64, Folder 1.

43. Memo from Gingrich and Gunderson, 26 May 1989, Armey Collection, Legislative Series, Box 64, Folder 1; Laurie James to Vicky Grant, 7 Jul 1989, Armey Collection, Legislative Series, Box 64, Folder 1; Invitees to Strategy Whip Meetings, undated, Michel Papers, Staff Series, Van Der Meid Files, Box 6, Folder: Campaign Reform: Whip Strategy.

44. Agenda, Strategy Whip Dinner, 11 Jul 1990, Michel Papers, Staff Series, Van Der Meid Files, Box 6, Folder: Campaign Reform: Whip Strategy.

45. A Blueprint for Leadership, Office of the Republican Leader, Michel Papers, Leadership Series, Box 16, Folder: 103rd A Blueprint for Leadership.

46. Theme Team [103rd Congress], Armey Collection, Legislative Series, Box 56, Folder 22.

47. This discussion based on minutes and agendas from DSPC meetings from 1977–1981 found in O'Neill Papers, Series III, Box 61, Folders 4–12, and on DSPC activity summaries in Foley Papers, Box 192, Folder 5669. See also Sinclair (1983, 73–75).

48. Republican Policy Committee forum announcements, 3 Feb 1994, 3 Mar 1994, 14 Jul 1994, Richard Armey Collection, Legislative Series, Box 58, Folder 14.

49. House Policy Committee press release, 26 Mar 2001, http://policy.house.gov/news/releases/2001/SubsandCPABs.PDF viewed via http://wayback.archive.org.

50. House Policy Committee meetings lists, 24 Apr 2003, 8 Oct 2003, 17 Jan 2004, 24 Mar 2004, http://www.policy.house.gov/html/meetings.cfm viewed via http://wayback.archive.org. On Policy Committee subcommittees and their membership, see House Policy Committee: 108th Congress Report, undated [2004], http://upload.wikimedia.org/wikipedia/commons/9/9c/HousePolicyCommittee108thCongressReport.pdf (Accessed 8 Jan 2015).

51. The pattern depicted here in the 107th Congress is also supported by similar evidence from the 108th Congress. House Policy Committee: 108th Congress Report, undated [2004], http://upload.wikimedia.org/wikipedia/commons/9/9c/HousePolicyCommittee108thCongressReport.pdf (Accessed 8 Jan 2015).

52. Irv Sprague to the Speaker, 19 Sep 1977, O'Neill Papers, Series III, Box 70, Folder 2. Irv Sprague, file memo "Anatomy of a Victory," 20 Mar 1978, O'Neill Papers, Series V, Box 20, Folder 2.

53. Records of [William] Pitts Working Group, Michel Papers, Staff Series, White Files, Folder: Pitts Working Group.

54. The label is DeLay's, quoted in Eilperin (1999).

## CHAPTER 6

1. "Whip Count" memo, O'Neill Papers, Series V, Box 2, Folder 1.

2. Sprague to O'Neill, 9 Nov 1978, O'Neill Papers, Series III, Box 70, Folder 10.

3. Ibid.

4. Irv Sprague to the Speaker [with attached whip counts], 19 Sep 1977, O'Neill Papers, Series III, Box 70, Folder 2.

5. 1983 task force lists, Foley Papers, Box 167, Folder 4823.

6. Phase II and Phase III Options Memo, 19 Apr 1983, O'Neill Papers, Series III, Box 20, Folder 1.

7. On Republican procedural opposition: Tom Tauke to Dear Colleague, "Vote to Defeat the Rule Providing for Consideration of HR 3201," Foley Papers, Box 166, Folder 4781. Democrats experienced some internal divisions on the approach to the issue, worked out through leadership compromises early in the summer. "Health Care for the Unemployed" undated memo and agreement drafts in O'Neill Papers, Series III, Box 20, Folder 2.

8. Democratic Leadership to Dear Colleague, 2 Aug 1983; and DSPC resolution, 2 Aug 1983; Foley Papers, Box 166, Folder 4781.

9. Foley memo to the whips, 27 Jul 1983, Foley Papers, Box 201, Folder 6204; Task Force, Health Insurance for the Unemployed, 26 Jul–2 Aug 1983, Foley Papers, Box 167, Folder 4823; Whip count sheets on H.R. 3201, Foley Papers, Box 201, Folder 6204.

10. Whip Counts 1983, Foley Papers, Box 166, Folder 4800; Whip Counts 1984, Foley Papers, Box 166, Folder 4801.

11. Whip Count Analysis, First Budget Resolution, 3/22 and 3/23/83, Foley Papers, Box 166, Folder 4800.

12. "The Work of the Whip Organization," Foley Papers, Box 168, Folder 4846.

13. Ibid.

14. "Whip Ranking System," Foley Papers, Box 168, Folder 4846. Top-ranked whips received special recognition from Coelho (*NJ* 1990).

15. 1993 Daily Schedules, Bonior Papers, Box 144, Folder 1. Bonior's scheduling records from the early 1990s convey a picture of continuity from the late 1980s whip system. Between January and May 1993, for instance, Bonior attended 14 full whip meetings and more than 20 formal whip task force meet-

ings on a range of issues; he also met formally with chief deputy whips, zone whips, and deputy whips. See Price (2004, 195) for a description of the process in the 1990s.

16. Memo to the Whips from David Bonior, 22 Mar 1999, Bonior Papers, Box 35, Folder 31. Census Whip Task Force notes, undated, Bonior Papers, Box 35, Folder 31.

17. Memo to the Whips from David Bonior, 3 Jun 1998, in Regional Whip Handbook, 16 Feb 2000, Bob Wise Papers, Box 3, Folder: Whip 106th.

18. Memo to the Whips from David Bonior, 14 Feb 2000, in Regional Whip Handbook, 16 Feb 2000, Bob Wise Papers, Box 3, Folder: Whip 106th.

19. Y2K Whip Task Force notes, undated, Bonior Papers, Box 35, Folder 84.

20. American Land Sovereignty Whip Task Force notes, undated, Bonior Papers, Box 35, Folder 84.

21. Howard Moon, 15 Jan 1999, in Regional Whip Handbook, 16 Feb 2000, Bob Wise Papers, Box 3, Folder: Whip 106th. Emphasis in original.

22. Regional Whip Handbook, 16 Feb 2000, Bob Wise Papers, Box 3, Folder: Whip 106th.

23. Nancy Pelosi to Bonior, 26 Feb 2002, Bonior Papers, Box 92, Folder 163.

24. Regional Whip Handbook, 16 Feb 2000, Bob Wise Papers, Box 3, Folder: Whip 106th.

25. Howard Moon, 15 Jan 1999, in Regional Whip Handbook, 16 Feb 2000, Bob Wise Papers, Box 3, Folder: Whip 106th.

26. Setting Up Floor Whip Operation, Jerry and Matt to Bonior, 27 Jan 1999, Bonior Papers, Box 4, Folder 37. Underlining in original omitted.

27. "33 Floor Whips," undated (106th Congress), Bonior Papers, Box 4, Folder 37. The floor whip list takes note of inclusion, breaking down the list by women (10), African-Americans (5), Hispanics (2), New Democrats (5), and Blue Dogs (3).

28. Unsigned memo to Bob [Michel], 20 Nov 1974, Michel Papers, Leadership Series, box 1, Folder: 93rd, 1973–74 Whip. Typos in original corrected.

29. Instructions: Whip Poll [undated memo on Michel letterhead], Michel Papers, Leadership Series, Box 2, Folder: Leadership, 95th Congress Whip Instructions.

30. 1975 whip counts contained in Michel Papers, Leadership Series, Box 1, Folder: 94th Congress: 1975–76 Whip Polls.

31. Goodling to Michel and Albert Johnson (R-PA), 18 Feb 1975, Michel Papers, Leadership Series, Box 1, Folder: 94th Congress: 1975–76 Whip Polls. See also Edward Madigan (R-IL) to Michel, 24 Feb 1975.

32. "Oil Import Vote" analysis, 20 Feb 1975; Whip tally, Sustain Pres. Veto [oil tax], 5 Mar 1975, Michel Papers, Leadership Series, Box 1, Folder: 94th Congress: 1975–76 Whip Polls.

33. Details on the farm bill are from *Congress and the Nation* (1977a) and Lyons (1975b).

34. Whip tally sheet, Farm Bill, 21 Apr 1975, Michel Papers, Leadership Series, Box 1, Folder: 94th Congress: 1975–76 Whip Polls.

35. Details on the issue are from Franklin (1975) and *Congress and the Nation* (1977b).

36. Whip tally sheets, Sustain Veto-Surface Mining, 20 May 1975 and Whip tally sheets, Strip Mining-Sustain Veto, 10 Jun 1975, Michel Papers, Leadership Series, Box 1, Folder: 94th Congress: 1975–76 Whip Polls.

37. Whip Polls 1977–1978, Michel Papers, Leadership Series, Box 2, Folder: 95th Congress Whip Polls—Index.

38. Whip Poll—Min Wage, 8 Sep 1977, Michel Papers, Leadership Series, Box 2, Folder: 95th Congress Whip Polls.

39. Accounts of the tax reform battle and related House Republican complaints are in Fessler (1985), *New York Times* (1983), Pressman (1985), and Rosenbaum (1985).

40. The whip office produced computer-generated analyses of all members' voting on whip checks and other key votes in the 100th Congress, and the leadership operated a computer bulletin board system to communicate a range of information, including whip notices. Report for the 100th Congress, 8 Jan 1988 and Leadership Bulletin Board system information, Michel Papers, Staff Series, Kehl Files, Box 12, Folder: Legislative—Republican Party—House (3).

41. Report for the 100th Congress, 8 Jan 1988, Michel Papers, Staff Series, Kehl Files, Box 12, Folder: Legislative—Republican Party—House (3).

42. Gingrich, unfortunately, has not opened his congressional papers publicly to academic researchers.

43. Without detailed whip records from the 1990s, it is not possible to confirm the overall volume of activity, but the numbering of the Right To Know Act report in July of the second session of the 104th Congress (#167) suggests that the majority Republican whip was whipping approximately 80–100 questions per year, a substantial increase over the rate in the late 1980s.

44. Whip Summary Report #167, 8 Jul 1996, Armey Collection, Legislative Series, Box 47, Folder 25.

45. See, e.g., "Questionaire [*sic*] for Republican Leadership and Ranking Member Candidates," undated [1988], Michel Papers, Staff Series, Kehl Files, Box 12, Folder: Legislative, Republican Party-House (1). The survey asks candidates, among other things, whether they have contributed financially to specific vulnerable incumbents, Republican challengers, and special election candidates.

46. The party may also use its fundraising to encourage party loyalty (Barber, Canes-Wrone, and Godbout 2014; Cann 2008b; but see Cantor and Herrnson 1997; Clucas 1997), although evidence on the electoral effects of high party loyalty suggests the party's collective goals may be at odds with members' short-term electoral goals here (Carson, Koger, Lebo, and Young 2010; Jenkins, Crespin, and Carson 2005).

47. The Democratic Steering Committee, in name at least, can be traced back at least to the first New Deal Congress (Herring 1934). Galloway reports the 22-member steering committee was briefly active and "occasionally played an influential role in the early days of the New Deal, as when it induced the party to adopt the bill to guarantee bank deposits in 1934" (1962, 145). The Democratic Steering Committee of the 1960s had been formed after Sam Rayburn's death (Connally 1991, 5); he had long opposed the concept of a policy-oriented steering committee (Ritchie 1997, 13), which had been recommended to the congressional parties by the 1946 Joint Committee on the Organization of the Congress (LaFollette-

Monroney committee) (Stewart 1975). The post-Rayburn Steering Committee did discuss policy issues but met only sporadically prior to the 1973 reorganization. See Notes on 1969–1972 committee meetings, Foley Papers, Box 192, Folder 5672.

48. "Resolution constituting the House Democratic Steering and Policy Committee," O'Neill Papers, Series V, Box 19, Folder 20.

49. "Resolution Designating the Democratic Steering and Policy Committee As the Democratic Committee on Committees," O'Neill Papers, Series V, Box 11, Folder 5.

50. Steering and Policy Committee Resolution, 22 Mar 1983, Foley Papers, Box 193, Folder 5904. Emphasis in original.

51. See Cox and McCubbins (2007, 156–57) for a brief review and critique of early literature that produced inconsistent findings on the effect of party loyalty.

52. O'Neill Papers, Series V, Box 6, Folder 13; Box 7, Folders 1–6; Box 8, Folders 1–3; Box 9, Folders 1–2. Foley Papers, Box 52, Folders 1364–1365.

53. 99th Congress 1st Session Voting Records, O'Neill Papers, Series V, Box 9, Folder 2.

54. Billie [Billie Gay Larson] to the Speaker, 15 Dec 1978; Debt limit voting charts, O'Neill Papers, Series V, Box 12, Folder 1.

55. Democratic Steering and Policy Committee Journal, 101st Congress. Foley Papers, Box 195, Folder 5955.

56. At the start of the 112th Congress, when House Democrats again went into the minority, now-Minority Leader Pelosi faced a serious challenge from conservative Blue Dogs within the caucus. In addition to unsuccessfully challenging Pelosi's bid for her leadership post, the Blue Dogs targeted, among other things, the Democratic leaders' long-standing leadership of the DSPC; Jim Matheson (D-UT) initially proposed making the DSPC chair and vice-chair positions *elected* posts within the caucus. A compromise between the Blue Dogs and Pelosi supporters led to a more minor change—moving the power to name committee chairs from the Speaker to the full DSPC. Subsequently, Pelosi named Blue Dog Henry Cuellar (D-TX) to the vice-chair post and appointed several other Blue Dogs, including Matheson, to the DSPC. See Berman (2010) and Hunter (2011a).

57. Under powerful turn-of-the-century Republican leaders, the top leadership distributed committee seats, with Joe Cannon (R-IL) or James Mann (R-IL) exercising control (Jones 1970, 37; Peters 1997, 99). With their return to the majority in 1919, Republicans initially elected Frederick Gillett (R-MA) as Speaker, but Mann, having lost the speakership, proposed a Committee on Committees that would be structured to consolidate his power within the Conference. Mann's proposal, which defeated a plan for the Committee that would have left greater power with the Speaker, decentralized power in the Conference by giving votes to state Republican delegations according to their size. (The committee itself predated Mann's 1919 maneuver in a somewhat different form. According to Jones [1970, 37], Republicans formed a 17-member Committee on Committees to assist Mann in making assignments in 1917 at the tumultuous start of the previous Congress. This is confirmed in a *New York Times* article Jones cites [*New York Times* 1917]. Masters [1961] dates the committee even earlier, to 1911, after the uprising against Cannon.)

58. Republican Committee on Committees 98th Congress Chronology of Actions Taken, Michel Papers, Leadership Series, Box 5, Folder: 98th Congress:

1983–1984 Committee on Committees; Summary of the Republican Committee Assignment Process, Michel Papers, Leadership Series, Box 5, Folder: 98th Congress: Committee on Committees Notebook 1.

59. Data Notebook, Michel Papers, Leadership Series, Box 8, Folder: 99th Congress: Data Notebook; Committee on Committees Working Book, Michel Papers, Leadership Series, Box 10, Folder: 100th Congress: Committee on Committees Working Book.

60. Preference sheets in Michel Papers, Leadership Series, Box 7, Folder: 99th Congress: Preference Sheet Workbook 1. More examples are in Frisch and Kelly (2006), chapter 5.

61. Balloting records in Michel Papers, Leadership Series, Box 3, Folder: 97th Congress: Committee on Committees.

62. Republicans had considered, but did not adopt, major reforms to the committee process in 1987. Fighting against what Vin Weber (R-MN) called "a winner-take-all process," a coalition of Texans and small-state GOP members collaborated to create their own favored slates for key assignments, upending the usual balance of power for the first time (Hook 1987). This shift in voting alignments, as Frisch and Kelly have shown empirically (2006, chap. 7), reflected the growing discontent among "realigners" in the party from the South and the West. In the wake of this conflict, Bob Michel created a leadership task force with a seven-member subcommittee of the Task Force on Conference Rules on Procedures charged with recommending reforms to the Committee on Committees; Michel appointed Conference Secretary Robert Lagomarsino (R-CA) to chair the panel and the committee selection subcommittee. (Memo to staff from Bob Michel RE: Creation of Special Staff Forces, 19 Jan 1987, Michel Papers, Leadership Series, Box 10, Folder: 100th Congress: Committee on Committees: Working Book 5.) Lagomarsino's group served up a proposal that would have strengthened the top Conference leadership on the committee and moved away from the state-based voting system. Among other changes, the subcommittee proposed abolishing the full Committee on Committees and conferring its name on the Executive Committee, creating an 11-region structure of committee representatives, and placing term limits on most Committee on Committees members. (Cheney and Lagomarsino to Republican Colleagues and attached draft of Committee on Committees proposal, 20 Oct 1988, Edwards Collection, Legislative Series, Box 81, Folder 11.)

63. Republican Committee on Committees, 101st Congress, Michel Papers, Leadership Series, Box 12, Folder: 101st Congress: Committee Data Notebook (5).

64. The Speaker holds five total votes on the Steering Committee but may "designate up to two of his votes to members whom he may appoint to the Steering Committee." Structure Establishing the Republican Steering Committee, 105th Congress, Armey Collection, Legislative Series, Box 55, Folder 4. Gingrich appointed loyalists to cast the two designated votes, but Hastert did not (Hastert 2004, 182).

65. Hitting the Ground Running manual for new Republican members, 6 Nov 1996, Armey Collection, Legislative Series, Box 55, Folder 3.

66. Gingrich to Republican Colleague (with enclosures on Steering Committee), 15 Oct 1998, Armey Collection, Legislative Series, Box 55, Folder 4.

67. By the time the Republicans went into the minority in 2007, the party

required large sums of all members, with over $200,000 required from ranking members on standing committees as well as the cardinals on Appropriations (Zeller and Teitelbaum 2007).

68. Factors other than leadership voting support, including insufficient financial support to the NRCC and responsibility for damaging press for the party, appear to have been relevant for some of the members (Hooper 2013).

### CHAPTER 7

1. See, generally, Eilperin (1999). As Republican Conference Chair in the early 1990s, DeLay had served as leadership liaison to a "Coalitions Advisory Group" within the Conference, a group responsible for building project-specific outside coalitions to support the Republican minority. Armey Collection, Legislative Series, Box 56, Folder 22.

2. Some archives that could shed new light on the subjects covered here will become available in the future. For example, the papers of Trent Lott, who led the Republican Whip system for much of the 1980s, are archived but not yet opened for research.

# References

Aldrich, John H., Mark M. Berger, and David W. Rohde. 2002. "The Historical Variability in Conditional Party Government, 1877–1994." In *Party, Process, and Political Change: New Perspectives on the History of Congress*, edited by David W. Brady and Mathew D. McCubbins. Stanford: Stanford University Press.

Aldrich, John H., Brittany N. Perry, and David W. Rohde. 2013. "Richard Fenno's Theory of Congressional Committees and the Partisan Polarization of the House." In *Congress Reconsidered*, 10th ed., edited by Lawrence C. Dodd and Bruce I. Oppenheimer. Los Angeles: SAGE/CQ Press.

Aldrich, John H., and David W. Rohde. 2000a. "The Consequences of Party Organization in the House: The Role of the Majority and Minority Parties in Conditional Party Government." In *Polarized Politics: Congress and the President in a Partisan Era*, edited by Jon R. Bond and Richard Fleisher. Washington, DC: CQ Press.

Aldrich, John H., and David W. Rohde. 2000b. "The Republican Revolution and the House Appropriations Committee." *Journal of Politics* 62:1–33.

Aldrich, John H., and David W. Rohde. 2001. "The Logic of Conditional Party Government: Revisiting the Electoral Connection." In *Congress Reconsidered*, 7th ed., edited by Lawrence C. Dodd and Bruce I. Oppenheimer. Washington, DC: CQ Press.

Alston, Chuck. 1989. "Party Fights on Election Laws Still Permit Compromises." *CQ Weekly*, September 23.

Alston, Chuck. 1990. "A Wide Gulf Still Separates Parties on Election Laws." *CQ Weekly*, February 17.

Arnold, R. Douglas. 1990. *The Logic of Congressional Action*. New Haven: Yale University Press.

Asmussen, Nicole, and Adam Ramey. 2014. "When Loyalty Is Tested: Do Party Leaders Use Committee Assignments as Rewards." Manuscript. Available at: http://ssrn.com/abstract=2433872.

Austin, Janet. 2012. "2011 Legislative Summary." *CQ Weekly*, January 9.

Barber, Michael, Brandice Canes-Wrone, and Jean-Francois Godbout. 2014. "Party Loyalty and Campaign Contributions." Typescript. Princeton University.

Barry, John M. 1989. *The Ambition and the Power: The Fall of Jim Wright: A True Story of Washington*. New York: Viking.

Beck, Nathaniel, Jonathan N. Katz, and Richard Tucker. 1998. "Taking Time Seriously: Time-Series—Cross-Section Analysis with a Binary Dependent Variable." *American Journal of Political Science* 42:1260–88.

Bellantoni, Christina, and Matt Fuller. 2014. "Unemployment Extension Hearing Scrapped Thanks to Meeting Room Spat." *Roll Call*, May 6. http://blogs.rollcall. com/218/unemployment-extension-hearing-scrapped-democrats-cry-foul/. Accessed 15 May 2014.

Berman, Russell. 2010. "Blue Dogs Accept Compromise on Rules to Curb Pelosi Power." *The Hill*, November 18.

Bernstein, Jonathan, and Casey B.K. Dominguez. 2003. "Candidates and Candidacies in the Expanded Party." *PS: Political Science and Politics* 36:165–69.

Biggs, Jeffrey R., and Thomas S. Foley. 1999. *Honor in the House*. Pullman: Washington State University Press.

Billings, Erin P. 2003a. "Diversity Defines Pelosi's Inner Circle." *Roll Call*, November 13.

Billings, Erin P. 2003b. "Hoyer's No 'Hammer,' But Efforts Get Results." *Roll Call*, June 4.

Billings, Erin P. 2003c. "Pelosi Launches Caucus Meeting Supplement." *Roll Call*, June 9.

Billings, Erin P. 2003d. "Pelosi Revamps the Steering Committee." *Roll Call*, March 13.

Billings, Erin P. 2004a. "Hoyer Adds Six Members to Whip Team." *Roll Call*, February 9.

Billings, Erin P. 2004b. "Rules Change Passes." *Roll Call*, April 1.

Billings, Erin P. 2004c. "Steering to Repay Donors." *Roll Call*, November 29.

Bolton, Alexander. 2003. "House Leaders Tighten Grip, Anger Centrists." *The Hill*, January 15.

Bolton, Alexander. 2004. "Cardinals Up the Ante for Top Job." *The Hill*, July 22.

Box-Steffensmeier, Janet M., Laura W. Arnold, and Christopher J.W. Zorn. 1997. "The Strategic Timing of Position Taking in Congress: A Study of the North American Free Trade Agreement." *American Political Science Review* 91:324–38.

Bradbury, Erin M., Ryan A. Davidson, and C. Lawrence Evans. 2008. "The Senate Whip System: An Exploration." In *Why Not Parties? Party Effects in the United States Senate*, edited by Nathan W. Monroe, Jason M. Roberts, and David W. Rohde. Chicago: University of Chicago Press.

Brady, Jessica. 2012. "Bipartisan Support for IPAB Repeal." *Roll Call*, March 7.

Bresnahan, John. 2001. "GOP Policy Panel May Get Revamped." *Roll Call*, April 12.

Burden, Barry C., and Tammy M. Frisby. 2004. "Preferences, Partisanship, and Whip Activity in the U.S. House of Representatives." *Legislative Studies Quarterly* 29:569–90.

Burger, Timothy J. 1991a. "Foley Taps Kennelly, Derrick, Lewis." *Roll Call*, August 5.

Burger, Timothy J. 1991b. "Foley Will Select 3 Deputy Whips." *Roll Call*, July 18.

Burger, Timothy J. 1994a. "Ax to Fall on Three House Panels: DC, Post Office, Merchant Marine." *Roll Call*, November 17.

Burger, Timothy J. 1994b. "DeLay Won't Get the Budget Bonior Had." *Roll Call*, December 19.

Burger, Timothy J. 1995. "After a Defeat, House Leaders Must Regroup." *Roll Call*, July 17.

Burger, Timothy J. 1996. "Race for House GOP Conference Secretary Could Feature Two Women—If It's Held at All, That Is." *Roll Call*, April 1.

Calmes, Jacqueline, and Rob Gurwitt. 1987. "Profiles in Power: Leaders without Portfolio." *Congressional Quarterly Weekly Report*, January 3.

Camia, Catalina. 1994. "Some Republican Contests May Hinge on Freshmen." *CQ Weekly*, November 19.

Cann, Damon M. 2008a. "Modeling Committee Chair Selection in the U.S. House of Representatives." *Political Analysis* 16:274–89.

Cann, Damon M. 2008b. *Sharing the Wealth: Member Contributions and the Exchange Theory of Party Influence in the U.S. House of Representatives*. Albany: SUNY Press.

Canon, David T. 1989. "The Institutionalization of Leadership in the U.S. Congress." *Legislative Studies Quarterly* 14:415–43.

Cantor, David M., and Paul S. Herrnson. 1997. "Party Campaign Activity and Party Unity in the U.S. House of Representatives." *Legislative Studies Quarterly* 22:393–415.

Caro, Robert A. 2002. *The Years of Lyndon Johnson: Master of the Senate*. New York: Knopf.

Carson, Jamie L., Gregory Koger, Matthew J. Lebo, and Everett Young. 2010. "The Electoral Costs of Party Loyalty in Congress." *American Journal of Political Science* 54:598–616.

Cassata, Donna. 1996. "'Reform Week': Divisions on Display," *CQ Weekly*, July 20.

Clark, Jennifer Hayes. 2012. "Minority Party Strategies and the Evolution of the Motion to Recommit in the House." In *Party and Procedure in the United States Congress*, edited by Jacob R. Straus, 85–100. Lanham, MD: Rowman and Littlefield.

Clucas, Richard A. 1997. "Party Contributions and the Influence of Campaign Committee Chairs on Roll-Call Voting." *Legislative Studies Quarterly* 22:179–94.

Cohen, Richard E. 1978. "The Last Year of the 95th—Reading Congress' Crystal Ball." *National Journal*, January 7.

Cohen, Richard E. 1982a. "The House Loses Its Foremost Student of How to Make the Institution Work." *National Journal*, October 2.

Cohen, Richard E. 1982b. "It's the Democrats' Turn to Squirm on Budget Policy." *National Journal*, February 27.

Cohen, Richard E. 1983. "House Democrats No Longer Can Use the Excuse that They Lack the Votes." *National Journal*, January 22.

Cohen, Richard E. 1984. "Frustrated House Republicans Seek More Aggressive Strategy for 1984 and Beyond." *National Journal*, March 3.

Cohen, Richard E. 1985. "PAC Problems." *National Journal*, June 29.

Cohen, Richard E. 1995. "The Transformers." *National Journal*, March 4.

Cohen, Richard E. 2001. "Hastert's Hidden Hand." *National Journal*, January 20.

Cohen, Richard E. 2002. "The Silent Hammer." *National Journal*, February 2.

Cohen, Richard E. 2004. "Whipping the Whip." *National Journal*, May 1.

Cohen, Richard E. 2005. "Gavel Envy." *National Journal*, June 4.

Coker, David C., and W. Mark Crain. 1994. "Legislative Committees as Loyalty-Generating Institutions." *Public Choice* 81:195–221.

*Congress and the Nation, 1973–1976*. 1977a. "Emergency Farm Bill, 1975 Legislative Chronology." http://library.cqpress.com/catn/catn73-0009169783. Accessed 11 June 2012.

*Congress and the Nation, 1973–1976*. 1977b. "Strip Mining Control, 1975 Legislative Chronology." http://library.cqpress.com/catn/catn73-0009170897. Accessed 11 June 2012.

*Congress and the Nation, 1977–1980*. 1981a. "Energy Policy." http://knowledge.sagepub.com /view/congress-and-the-nation-v/n9.xml. Accessed 30 June 2014.

*Congress and the Nation, 1977–1980*. 1981b. "Full Employment, 1978 Legislative Chronology." http://library.cqpress.com/catn/catn77-0010174545. Accessed 17 Dec 2009.

*Congress and the Nation, 1981–1984*. 1985. "Jobless Health Insurance, 1983 Legislative Chronology." http://library.cqpress.com/catn/catn81-0011175524. Accessed 4 Jan 2010.

*Congress and the Nation, 1989–1992*. 1993. "Campaign Finance, 1989–1990 Legislative Chronology." http://library.cqpress.com/catn/document.php?id=catn89-0000013778. Accessed 10 Jan 2012.

*Congress and the Nation, 1997–2001*. 2002. "U.N. Lands Designation, 1999–2000 Legislative Chronology." http://library.cqpress.com/catn/catn97-97-6348-325250. Accessed 22 May 2012.

*Congressional Quarterly Almanac*. Various editions. Washington, DC: Congressional Quarterly.

*Congressional Quarterly Weekly Report*. 1985. "Today's Whip: Not Just Keeping Pack in Line." November 30.

*Congressional Quarterly Weekly Report*. 1991. "Foley Adds Slots for New Whips." July 20.

*Congressional Staff Directory*. Various editions. Mt. Vernon, VA: Staff Directories, Ltd.

*Congressional Staff Directory*. Various editions. Washington, DC: Congressional Quarterly.

*Congressional Yellow Book*. Various editions. New York: Leadership Directories, Inc.

Conley, Richard S. 2002. "Presidential Influence and Minority Party Liaison on Veto Overrides: New Evidence from the Ford Presidency." *American Politics Research* 30:34–65.

Connelly, William F., Jr. 1988. "The House Republican Policy Committee: Then and Now." Paper presented at the Annual Meetings of the American Political Science Association.

Connelly, William F., Jr. 1991. "Party Policy Committees in Congress." Paper presented at the Annual Meeting of the Western Political Science Association.

Connelly, William F., Jr., and John J. Pitney, Jr. 1994. *Congress' Permanent Minority? Republicans in the U.S. House*. Lanham, MD: Rowman and Littlefield.

Cooper, Ann. 1978. "House Democratic Whips: Counting, Coaxing, Cajoling." *Congressional Quarterly Weekly Report*, May 27.

Cooper, Joseph, and David W. Brady. 1981. "Institutional Context and Leadership Style: The House from Cannon to Rayburn." *American Political Science Review* 75:411–25.

Cormack, Lindsey. 2013. "Sins of Omission: Legislator (Mis)Representation in Constituent Communications." Typescript. New York University.

Cox, Gary W., and Mathew D. McCubbins. 1993. *Legislative Leviathan: Party Government in the House*. Berkeley: University of California Press.

Cox, Gary W., and Mathew D. McCubbins. 2007. *Legislative Leviathan: Party Government in the House*. Second Edition. Cambridge: Cambridge University Press.

*CQ Almanac*. Various editions. Washington, DC: Congressional Quarterly.

*CQ's Politics in America*. Various editions. Washington, DC: Congressional Quarterly.

Crabtree, Susan. 2000. "Decision Day Finally Arrives for High-Stakes Debate." *Roll Call*, May 22.

Crabtree, Susan, and Erin P. Billings. 2002. "Blunt Adds Newcomers to Whip Team." *Roll Call*, December 9.

Crespin, Michael H., Anthony Madonna, Joel Sievert, and Nathaniel Ament-Stone. 2014. "The Establishment of Party Policy Committees in the U.S. Senate: Coordination, not Coercion." Typescript. University of Texas at Dallas.

Currinder, Marian. 2008. *Money in the House: Campaign Funds and Congressional Party Politics*. Boulder: Westview.

Davidson, Roger H., Walter J. Oleszek, Frances E. Lee, and Eric Schickler. 2014. *Congress and Its Members*. 14th ed. Los Angeles: SAGE/CQ Press.

Dennis, Steven T., and Kathleen Hunter. 2011. "Bitter Blue Dogs Ready to Cut Deals." *Roll Call*, January 10.

Dennis, Steven T., and Anna Palmer. 2010. "Pelosi Seems to See No Need for Change." *Roll Call*, December 7.

Desmarais, Bruce A., Raymond J. La Raja, and Michael S. Kowal. 2015. "The Fates of Challengers in U.S. House Elections: The Role of Extended Party Networks in Supporting Candidates and Shaping Electoral Outcomes." *American Journal of Political Science* 59:194–211.

Dodd, Lawrence C. 1979. "The Expanded Roles of the House Democratic Whip System: The 93rd and 94th Congresses." *Congressional Studies* 7:27–56.

Doherty, Carroll J. 1999. "GOP's China Gamble: Back Trade, Attack Policy." *CQ Weekly*, May 29.

Dominguez, Casey B.K. 2005. *Before the Primary: Party Participation in Congressional Nominating Processes*. Ph.D. diss. University of California—Berkeley.

Draper, Robert. 2012. *Do Not Ask What Good We Do: Inside the U.S. House of Representatives*. New York: Free Press.

Drucker, David M. 2013. "Dissecting McCarthy's Whip Operation." *Roll Call*, February 14.

Dynes, Adam, and Andrew Reeves. 2014. "House Caucus Attendance as Private Investment in the Party." Typescript. Yale University.

Edwards, Keith M., and Charles Stewart, III. 2006. "The Value of Committee Assignments in Congress since 1994." Paper presented at the 2006 Annual Meetings of the Southern Political Science Association.

Eilperin, Juliet. 1997a. "GOP Moves, Tentatively, On Ethics Reform Plan." *Roll Call*, September 4.

Eilperin, Juliet. 1997b. "House Ethics Panel Is Reborn, Minus Reform." *Roll Call*, September 11.

Eilperin, Juliet. 1999. "House Whip Wields Fund-Raising Clout." *Washington Post*, October 18.

Eilperin, Juliet, and Jim Vande Hei. 1997. "House GOP Leadership's Fractured Present Pits Gingrich-Armey Alliance against DeLay-Paxon." *Roll Call*, October 9.

Elving, Ronald D. 1989. "Gingrich Lieutenants Balance Political Style and Tactics." *CQ Weekly*, April 8.

Evans, C. Lawrence. 2001. "Committees, Leaders, and Message Politics." In *Congress Reconsidered*, 7th ed., edited by Lawrence C. Dodd and Bruce I. Oppenheimer. Washington, DC: CQ Press.

Evans, C. Lawrence, and Claire E. Grandy. 2009. "The Whip Systems of Congress." In *Congress Reconsidered*, 9th ed., edited by Lawrence C. Dodd and Bruce I. Oppenheimer. Washington, DC: CQ Press.

Evans, C. Lawrence, and Walter J. Oleszek. 1997. *Congress Under Fire: Reform Politics and the Republican Majority*. Boston: Houghton Mifflin.

Evans, C. Lawrence, Douglas D. Roscoe, Timothy M. Deering, and Michael D. O'Neill. 2003. "The House Whip Process and Party Theories of Congress: An Exploration." Paper presented at the Annual Meeting of the American Political Science Association, Philadelphia.

Farrell, John A. 2001. *Tip O'Neill and the Democratic Century*. Boston: Little, Brown.

Fenno, Richard F., Jr. 1978. *Home Style: House Members in Their Districts*. Glenview, IL: Scott, Foresman.

Fenno, Richard F., Jr. 1997. *Learning to Govern: An Institutional View of the 104th Congress*. Washington, DC: Brookings.

Fenno, Richard F., Jr. 2000. *Congress at the Grassroots*. Chapel Hill: University of North Carolina.

Fenno, Richard F., Jr. 2007. *Congressional Travels: Places, Connections, and Authenticity*. New York: Pearson Longman.

Fessler, Pamela. 1985. "House Reverses Self, Passes Major Tax Overhaul." *CQ Weekly*, December 21.

Fleming, James S. 2004. *Window on Congress: A Congressional Biography of Barber B. Conable, Jr.* Rochester: University of Rochester.

Foerstel, Karen. 1993a. "GOP Hits Reform Panel for Delays in Offering Its Plan as Frosh Press Ideas for Changing the Hill." *Roll Call*, October 11.

Foerstel, Karen. 1993b. "GOP Wants Special Orders to Be Given in the Morning." *Roll Call*, April 22.

Foerstel, Karen. 2000. "Choosing GOP Chairmen." *CQ Weekly*, June 17.

Fonder, Melanie. 2001. "GOP Battle Starts for Cox's Seat." *The Hill*, April 11.

Forgette, Richard. 2004. "Party Caucuses and Coordination: Assessing Caucus Activity and Party Effects." *Legislative Studies Quarterly* 29:407–30.

Franklin, Ben A. 1975. "Strip Mine Bill Veto Is Upheld by House on a 3-Vote Margin." *New York Times*, June 11.

Frisch, Scott A., Douglas B. Harris, Sean Q. Kelly, and David C.W. Parker. 2012. *Doing Archival Research in Political Science*. Amherst, NY: Cambria Press.

Frisch, Scott A., and Sean Q. Kelly. 2003. "Don't Have the Data? Make Them Up! Congressional Archives as Untapped Data Sources." *PS: Political Science and Politics* 36:221–24.

Frisch, Scott A., and Sean Q. Kelly. 2006. *Committee Assignment Politics in the U.S. House of Representatives*. Norman: University of Oklahoma Press.

Fuerbringer, Jonathan. 1985. "Pressures and Rewards Face House Members on MX Vote." *New York Times*, March 26.

Galloway, George B. 1962. *History of the House of Representatives*. New York: Crowell.

Gamm, Gerald, and Steven S. Smith. 2002. "Emergence of Senate Party Leadership." In *U.S. Senate Exceptionalism*, edited by Bruce I. Oppenheimer. Columbus: Ohio State University Press.

Garand, James C. 1988. "The Socialization to Partisan Legislative Behavior: An Extension of Sinclair's Task Force Socialization Thesis." *Western Political Quarterly* 41:391–400.

Garand, James C., and Kathleen M. Clayton. 1986. "Socialization to Partisanship in the U.S. House: The Speaker's Task Force." *Legislative Studies Quarterly* 11:409–28.

Glasgow, Garrett. 2002. "The Efficiency of Congressional Campaign Committee Contributions in House Elections." *Party Politics* 8:657–72.

Glassman, Matthew. 2012. "Congressional Leadership: A Resource Perspective." In *Party and Procedure in the United States Congress*. Edited by Jacob R. Straus. Lanham, MD: Rowman and Littlefield.

Glastris, Paul, and Haley Sweetland Edwards. 2014. "The Big Lobotomy." *Washington Monthly*, June/July/August.

Goode, Darren. 2010. "Steering Panel Loaded with John Boehner's Allies." *Politico*, November 29.

Granat, Diane. 1983. "Secret Meetings Restore Vigor: Democratic Caucus Renewed as Forum for Policy Questions." *Congressional Quarterly Weekly Report*, October 15.

Granat, Diane. 1984. "Junior Democrats Gain a Louder Voice: Leadership Panels Will Serve as Forum." *Congressional Quarterly Weekly Report*, December 8.

Granat, Diane. 1985. "House Democrats Expand Leadership." *Congressional Quarterly Weekly Report*, February 9.

Green, Matthew N. 2006. "McCormack Versus Udall: Explaining Intraparty Challenges to the Speaker of the House." *American Politics Research* 34:3–21.

Green, Matthew N. 2007. "Presidents and Personal Goals: The Speaker of the House as a Nonmajoritarian Leader." *Congress and the Presidency* 34:1–22.

Green, Matthew N. 2010. *The Speaker of the House: A Study of Leadership*. New Haven: Yale University Press.

Grimmer, Justin. 2013. "Appropriators Not Position Takers: The Distorting Effects of Electoral Incentives on Congressional Representation." *American Journal of Political Science* 57:624–42.

Grofman, Bernard, William Koetzle, and Anthony J. McGann. 2002. "Congressional Leadership 1965–96: A New Look at the Extremism versus Centrality Debate." *Legislative Studies Quarterly* 27:87–105.

Grossmann, Matt, and Casey B.K. Dominguez. 2009. "Party Coalitions and Interest Group Networks." *American Politics Research* 37:767–800.

Gulati, Girish J. 2004. "Members of Congress and Presentation of Self on the World Wide Web." *Harvard International Journal of Press/Politics* 9:22–40.

Haberkorn, Jennifer. 2012. "House GOP Doctors Talk Health Law." *Politico*, October 10.

Hammond, Susan Webb. 1998. *Congressional Caucuses in National Policy Making.* Baltimore: Johns Hopkins University Press.

Harris, Douglas B. 2006. "Legislative Parties and Leadership Choice: Confrontation or Accommodation in the 1989 Gingrich-Madigan Whip Race." *American Politics Research* 34:189–222.

Harris, Douglas B. 2010. "Partisan Framing in Legislative Debates." In *Winning With Words: The Origins and Impact of Political Framing*, edited by Brian F. Schaffner, 41–59. New York: Routledge.

Harris, Douglas B. 2012. "Behavioral Reality and Institutional Change." In *Doing Archival Research in Political Science*, edited by Scott A. Frisch, Douglas B. Harris, Sean Q. Kelly, and David C.W. Parker. Amherst, NY: Cambria Press.

Harris, Douglas B. 2013. "Let's Play Hardball: Congressional Partisanship in the Television Era." In, *Politics to the Extreme: American Political Institutions in the Twenty First Century*, edited by Scott A. Frisch and Sean Q. Kelly. New York: Palgrave Macmillan.

Hastert, Denny. 2004. *Speaker: Lessons from Forty Years in Coaching and Politics.* Washington, DC: Regnery.

Heberlig, Eric S. 2003. "Congressional Parties, Fundraising, and Committee Ambition." *Political Research Quarterly* 56:151–61.

Heberlig, Eric S., Marc Hetherington, and Bruce A. Larson. 2006. "The Price of Leadership: Campaign Money and the Polarization of Congressional Parties." *Journal of Politics* 68:992–1005.

Heberlig, Eric S., and Bruce A. Larson. 2007. "Party Fundraising, Descriptive Representation, and the Battle for Majority Control: Shifting Leadership Appointment Strategies in the US House: 1990–2002." *Social Science Quarterly* 88:404–21.

Heberlig, Eric S., and Bruce A. Larson. 2012. *Congressional Parties, Institutional Ambition, and the Financing of Majority Control.* Ann Arbor: University of Michigan Press.

Heil, Emily. 2007. "Heard on the Hill." *Roll Call*, March 26.

Herring, E. Pendleton. 1934. "American Government and Politics: First Session of the Seventy-Third Congress." *American Political Science Review* 28:65–83.

Herrnson, Paul S. 1986. "Do Parties Make a Difference? The Role of Party Organizations in Congressional Elections." *Journal of Politics* 48:589–615.

Herrnson, Paul S. 2009. "The Roles of Party Organizations, Party-Connected Committees, and Party Allies in Elections." *Journal of Politics* 71:1207–24.

Herrnson, Paul S., and Kelly D. Patterson. 1995. "Toward a More Programmatic Democratic Party? Agenda-Setting and Coalition-Building in the House of Representatives." *Polity* 27:607–28.

Hibbing, John R. 1991. *Congressional Careers: Contours of Life in the U.S. House of Representatives*. Chapel Hill: University of North Carolina Press.

Hook, Janet. 1986. "House Leadership Elections: Wright Era Begins." *Congressional Quarterly Weekly Report*, December 13.

Hook, Janet. 1987. "Bitterness Lingers from GOP Assignments." *CQ Weekly*, May 16.

Hook, Janet. 1989a. "Gingrich Finds Rhetoric Must Toe Party Line." *CQ Weekly*, July 22.

Hook, Janet. 1989b. "Gingrich's Selection as Whip Reflects GOP Discontent." *CQ Weekly*, March 25.

Hook, Janet. 1990. "Gingrich Weathers a Rough First Term but His Biggest Challenges Lie Ahead." *CQ Weekly*, December 1.

Hooper, Molly K. 2011. "Republican Campaign Chief Furious after Leak." *The Hill*, March 17.

Hooper, Molly K. 2012. "Boehner to Members: Leadership Is Watching Your Voting Patterns." *The Hill*, December 5.

Hooper, Molly K. 2013. "Months after Leadership Punished Them, House Republicans Take Different Paths." *The Hill*, March 13.

Hulse, Carl. 2004. "House Ethics Panel Says DeLay Tried to Trade Favor for a Vote." *New York Times*. October 1, A1.

Hume, Sandy. 1996a. "GOP Assails Newt, Armey on PAC Ban." *The Hill*, May 29.

Hume, Sandy. 1996b. "PAC Ban Decision Nears." *The Hill*, June 5.

Hunter, Kathleen. 2011a. "Blue Dogs' Complaints Challenged." *Roll Call*, February 9.

Hunter, Kathleen. 2011b. "Pelosi Finds Her Footing as Democrats' Attack Dog." *Roll Call*, March 1.

Isenstadt, Alex. 2011. "Key Committees Are Golden Ticket." *Politico*, January 19.

Jacobson, Louis. 2001. "Speak Bluntly and Carry a Soft Stick." *National Journal*, June 16.

Jacoby, Mary. 1993. "GOP Tries to Preempt Discharge Abuses." *Roll Call*, October 7.

Jenkins, Jeffery A., Michael H. Crespin, and Jamie L. Carson. 2005. "Parties as Procedural Coalitions in Congress: An Examination of Differing Career Tracks." *Legislative Studies Quarterly* 30:365–89.

Jenkins, Jeffery A., and Charles Stewart, III. 2008. "Speakership Elections since 1860: The Rise of the Organizational Caucus." Paper presented at the 2008 History of Congress Conference, Washington, DC.

Jenkins, Jeffrey A., and Charles Stewart, III. 2013. *Fighting for the Speakership: The House and the Rise of Party Government*. Princeton: Princeton University Press.

Jones, Charles O. 1964. *Party and Policy Making: The House Republican Policy Committee*. New Brunswick, NJ: Rutgers University Press.

Jones, Charles O. 1970. *The Minority Party in Congress*. Boston: Little, Brown.

Kahn, Gabriel. 1994a. "Democrats May Create Policy Panel." *Roll Call*, November 28.

Kahn, Gabriel. 1994b. "Democrats: 'This Is Outrageous.' GOP Plan for Panel Ratios, Cuts Sends Shock Wave to Minority." *Roll Call*, December 5.

Kahn, Gabriel. 1995. "Bonior Overhauls His Whip Operation." *Roll Call*, January 16.

Kane, Paul. 2013. "Farm Bill Illustrates the Perils of a Whip's Vote-Counting Job." *Washington Post*, June 21.

Kanthak, Kristin. 2004. "Exclusive Committee Assignments and Party Pressure in the U.S. House of Representatives." *Public Choice* 121:391–412.

Kaplan, Jonathan E. 2005. "House GOP Leaders Could Face Complex Committee Shuffle." *The Hill*, July 20.

Keller, Amy. 1997. "Despite Defeat in Senate, House's Campaign Reformers Vow to Continue to Press for Vote." *Roll Call*, October 16.

Kelly, Sean Q. 1995. "Democratic Leadership in the Modern Senate: The Emerging Roles of the Democratic Policy Committee." *Congress and the Presidency* 22:113–39.

Kimitch, Rebecca. 2007. "CQ Guide to the Committees: Democrats Opt to Spread the Power." *CQ Weekly*, April 16.

King, David C., and Richard J. Zeckhouser. 2003. "Congressional Vote Options." *Legislative Studies Quarterly* 28:387–411.

Kliff, Sarah. 2012. "Lawmakers Debate Contraceptive Mandate." *Washington Post*, February 17.

Koger, Gregory, Seth Masket, and Hans Noel. 2009. "Partisan Webs: Information Exchange and Party Networks." *British Journal of Political Science* 39:633–53.

Koger, Gregory, Seth Masket, and Hans Noel. 2010. "Cooperative Party Factions in American Politics." *American Politics Research* 38:33–53.

Kolodny, Robin. 1998. *Pursuing Majorities: Congressional Campaign Committees in American Politics.* Norman: University of Oklahoma Press.

Kolodny, Robin, and Diana Dwyre. 1998. "Party-Orchestrated Activities for Legislative Party Goals: Campaigns for Majorities in the US House of Representatives in the 1990s." *Party Politics* 4:275–95.

Kosterliz, Julie. 1989. "Watch Out for Waxman." *National Journal*, March 11.

Krehbiel, Keith. 1998. *Pivotal Politics: A Theory of U.S. Lawmaking.* Chicago: University of Chicago Press.

Kucinich, Jackie. 2010. "Request to Disband GOP Policy Committee Divides Leaders." *Roll Call*, July 2.

Kucinich, Jackie, and Anna Palmer. 2010. "Chairmen Face Changes, Challenges." *Roll Call*, December 8.

Kuntz, Phil. 1991. "Individualists Finding It Hard to Resist Loyalty Lures." *Congressional Quarterly Weekly Report*, December 28.

Lardner, George, Jr., and Spencer Rich. 1983. "House Approves Health Insurance for Unemployed." *Washington Post*, August 4.

Larson, Bruce A. 2004. "Incumbent Contributions to the Congressional Campaign Committees, 1990–2000." *Political Research Quarterly* 57:155–61.

Lawrence, Christine C. 1988a. "House-Passed Drug Bill Has Clear GOP Imprint." *CQ Weekly*, September 24.

Lawrence, Christine C. 1988b. "Parties' Proposals Begin to Emerge: Drug Issue Ignites Partisan Bickering in House." *CQ Weekly*, May 28.

Lawrence, Christine C. 1988c. "Partisan Lines Drawn for Debate on Drug Bill." *CQ Weekly*, September 3.

Lebo, Matthew J., Adam J. McGlynn, and Gregory Koger. 2007. "Strategic Party

Government: Party Influence in Congress, 1789–2000." *American Journal of Political Science* 51:464–81.

Lee, Frances E. 2009. *Beyond Ideology: Politics, Principles, and Partisanship in the U.S. Senate*. Chicago: University of Chicago Press.

Lee, Frances E. 2011. "Making Laws and Making Points: Senate Governance in an Era of Uncertain Majorities." *The Forum* 9(4).

Lipinski, Daniel. 2004. *Congressional Communication: Content and Consequences*. Ann Arbor: University of Michigan Press.

Little, Thomas H., and Samuel C. Patterson. 1993. "The Organizational Life of the Congressional Parties." *American Review of Politics* 14:39–70.

Loomis, Burdett A. 1984. "Congressional Careers and Party Leadership in the Contemporary House of Representatives." *American Journal of Political Science* 28:180–202.

Lyons, Richard D. 1975a. "House Drops Bid to Defeat Ford Veto." *New York Times*, March 12.

Lyons, Richard D. 1975b. "Veto of Farm Bill Upheld in House on 245–182 Vote." *New York Times*, May 14.

Malecha, Gary Lee, and Daniel J. Reagan. 2012. *The Public Congress: Congressional Deliberation in a New Media Age*. New York: Routledge.

Maltzman, Forrest. 1997. *Competing Principals: Committees, Parties, and the Organization of Congress*. Ann Arbor: University of Michigan Press.

Mann, Thomas E., and Norman J. Ornstein. 2012. *It's Even Worse Than It Looks*. New York: Basic Books.

Martinez, Gebe, and Jackie Koszczuk. 1999. "Tom DeLay: 'The Hammer' That Drives the House GOP." *CQ Weekly*, June 5.

Masket, Seth E. 2009. *No Middle Ground: How Informal Party Organizations Control Nominations and Polarize Legislatures*. Ann Arbor: University of Michigan Press.

Masters, Nicholas A. 1961. "Committee Assignments in the House of Representatives." *American Political Science Review* 55:345–57.

Mayhew, David R. 1974. *Congress: The Electoral Connection*. New Haven: Yale University Press.

McCutcheon, Chuck. 1999. "With Cox Report's Release, Struggle for Consensus Begins." *CQ Weekly*, May 29.

Meinke, Scott R. 2008. "Who Whips? Party Government and the House Extended Whip Networks." *American Politics Research* 61:445–57.

Meinke, Scott R. 2013. "Loyalty from the Leaders' Perspective: Measuring House Party Voting from Leadership Records." Paper presented at the Annual Meeting of the Midwest Political Science Association, Chicago.

Milbank, Dana. 2012. "An Expert Witness on the GOP's Gender Gap." *Washington Post*, February 26.

Millman, Jason. 2011. "Dems Tee Up Arguments against GOP Repeal Vote." *The Hill*, January 18.

Mills, Mike. 1988. "Close Race to Lead Republican Conference." *CQ Weekly*, December 10.

Mitchell, Alison. 1999. "Congress Chasing Campaign Donors Early and Often." *New York Times*, June 14.

Mitchell, Alison, and Marc Lacey. 1999. "DeLay Inc.—A Special Report: A Law-maker Amasses Power, and Uses It." *New York Times*, October 16.

Moscardelli, Vincent G. 2010. "Harry Reid and Health Care Reform in the Sen-ate: Transactional Leadership in a Transformational Moment?" *The Forum* 8(1): Article 2.

Moscardelli, Vincent G., and Moshe Haspel. 2007. "Campaign Finance Reform as Institutional Choice: Party Difference in the Vote to Ban Soft Money." *American Politics Research* 35:79–102.

*National Journal*. 1977. "The Forces of Republicanism." October 29.

*National Journal*. 1978. "Washington Update." December 16.

*National Journal*. 1980. "The New House Leaders: Bipartisan Compromisers." December 13.

*National Journal*. 1981. "Weevil Power." October 3.

*National Journal*. 1986. "The Case for a Republican Congress." October 18.

*National Journal*. 1989. "New Breed of House GOP Leaders." June 3.

*National Journal*. 1990. "Wise: Doing Grunt Work." January 27.

*National Journal*. 1995. "House Leadership Biographies." June 17.

*National Journal*. 2003. "The Hill People: House Leadership." June 21.

*New York Times*. 1917. "Republicans See Speakership Fade." April 1.

*New York Times*. 1983. "White House Aides Draw GOP Barbs." August 5.

Newhauser, Daniel. 2012. "Republicans Eye Ryan's Spot on Budget Panel." *Roll Call*, September 13.

Newhauser, Daniel. 2014. "Would-Be Whips Woo Conservatives, Reassure Mod-erates." *Roll Call Blogs*, 17 June. http://blogs.rollcall.com/218/whip-race-ros kam-scalise-stutzman/. Accessed 17 Jun 2014.

Newhauser, Daniel, and Jonathan Strong. 2012. "'Obstinate' Factor Continues to Roil GOP." *Roll Call*, December 12.

Nitschke, Lori. 1999. "Minimum Wage Bill's Prospects Uncertain as Opinions Form over Timetable, Tax Provisions." *CQ Weekly*, October 16.

Niven, David, and Jeremy Zilber. 2001. "Do Women and Men in Congress Culti-vate Different Images? Evidence from Congressional Web Sites." *Political Com-munication* 18:395–405.

Oleszek, Walter J. 1985. *Majority and Minority Whips of the Senate: History and Devel-opment of the Party Whip System in the U.S. Senate*. 98th Cong., 2nd Sess., S. Doc. 98–45. Washington, DC: Government Printing Office.

Oleszek, Walter J. 2011. *Congressional Procedures and the Policy Process*. 8th ed. Wash-ington, DC: CQ Press.

Palmer, Anna, and Kathleen Hunter. 2011. "A Deficit Reckoning, Or Not?" *Roll Call*, April 13.

Patty, John W. 2008. "Equilibrium Party Government." *American Journal of Political Science* 52:636–55.

Pershing, Ben. 2003. "Bass off Whip Roster Again." *Roll Call*, July 7.

Pershing, Ben. 2004. "GOP Puts Smith under Scrutiny." *Roll Call*, June 15.

Pershing, Ben. 2005. "'Team Players' Boosted in GOP." *Roll Call*, January 10.

Peters, Ronald M., Jr. 1997. *The American Speakership: The Office in Historical Per-spective*. 2nd ed. Baltimore: Johns Hopkins University Press.

Peters, Ronald M., Jr., and Cindy Simon Rosenthal. 2010. *Speaker Nancy Pelosi and the New American Politics*. New York: Oxford University Press.

Petersen, R. Eric. 2009. "Senate Policy Committees." CRS Report for Congress RL32015.

Petersen, R. Eric, Parker H. Reynolds, and Amber Hope Wilhelm. 2010. "House of Representatives and Senate Staff Levels in Member, Committee, Leadership, and Other Offices, 1977–2010." CRS Report for Congress R41366, 10 Aug 2010.

Phillips, Kevin. 1991. *The Politics of the Rich and Poor: Wealth and the American Electorate in the Reagan Aftermath*. New York: HarperCollins.

Poole, Keith T., and Howard Rosenthal. 2007. *Ideology and Congress*. New Brunswick, NJ: Transaction.

Pressman, Steven. 1985. "House Republicans Outflank White House as Frustrations with the Tax Bill Boil Over." *CQ Weekly*, December 14.

Price, David E. 1992. *The Congressional Experience: A View from the Hill*. Boulder: Westview.

Price, David E. 2004. *The Congressional Experience*. 3rd ed. Cambridge, MA: Westview/Perseus.

Rae, Nicol C. 1998. *Conservative Reformers: The Republican Freshmen and the Lessons of the 104th Congress*. Armonk, NY: M.E. Sharpe.

Remini, Robert V. 2006. *The House: The History of the House of Representatives*. New York: Smithsonian Books.

*Report of the Clerk of the House*. Various editions. Washington, DC: United States Government Printing Office.

Riehle, Thomas. 1984. "People: Washington's Movers and Shakers." *National Journal*, December 15.

Ringe, Nils, and Jennifer Nicoll Victor, with Christopher J. Carman. 2013. *Bridging the Information Gap: Legislative Members Organizations as Social Networks in the United States and the European Union*. Ann Arbor: University of Michigan Press.

Ripley, Randall B. 1964. "The Party Whip Organizations in the United States House of Representatives." *American Political Science Review* 58:561–76.

Ritchie, Donald A. 1997. *A History of the United States Senate Republican Policy Committee 1947–1997*. 105th Congress, 1st Session, Senate Document 105–5. Washington, DC: U.S. Government Printing Office.

Roberts, Steven V. 1982. "Keeping the Troops in Line by Letting Them Stray." *New York Times*, February 9.

Rohde, David W. 1991. *Parties and Leaders in the Postreform House*. Chicago: University of Chicago Press.

*Roll Call*. 2006. "Policy Committee Candidates: In Their Own Words." January 25.

Rosenbaum, David E. 1975. "Freshmen Democrats Air Complaints about House Leaders in 3 Meetings." *New York Times*, June 19.

Rosenbaum, David E. 1985. "Years of Republican Frustration Underlay House Revolt on Taxes." *New York Times*, December 15.

Schickler, Eric. 2001. *Disjointed Pluralism: Institutional Innovation and the Development of the U.S. Congress*. Princeton: Princeton University Press.

Schlesinger, Robert. 1997. "China MFN Foes Warn against 'Bait and Switch' Strategy." *The Hill*, June 18.

Schneider, Judy. 2003. "Senate Leadership Structure: Overview of Party Organization." CRS Report for Congress RS20933.

Schneider, Judy. 2007. "One Minute Speeches: Current House Practices." CRS Report for Congress RL30135.

Schroeder, Peter. 2012. "GOP Ousts Lawmakers from Plum Posts." *The Hill*, December. 3.

Secter, Bob. 1987. "Power in the House." *Los Angeles Times*, January 11.

*Seinfeld*. 1995. "The Scofflaw." Transcript at http://www.seinology.com/scripts/script-99.shtml. Accessed 9 Jul 2012.

Sherman, Jake, and Simmi Aujla. 2010. "Fill This Out: Forms for GOP Chairmen." *Politico*, December 6.

Simendinger, Alexis. 2000. "Turning Up the Heat." *National Journal*, March 11.

Sinclair, Barbara. 1983. *Majority Leadership in the U.S. House*. Baltimore: Johns Hopkins University Press.

Sinclair, Barbara. 1995. *Legislators, Leaders, and Lawmaking: The U.S. House of Representatives in the Postreform Era*. Baltimore: Johns Hopkins University Press.

Sinclair, Barbara. 2006. *Party Wars: Polarization and the Politics of National Policy Making*. Norman: University of Oklahoma Press.

Smith, Steven S. 2007. *Party Influence in Congress*. Cambridge: Cambridge University Press.

Smith, Steven S., and Gerald Gamm. 2009. "The Dynamics of Party Government in Congress." In *Congress Reconsidered*, 9th ed., edited by Lawrence C. Dodd and Bruce I. Oppenheimer. Washington, DC: CQ Press.

Smith, Steven S., and Bruce A. Ray. 1983. "The Impact of Congressional Reform: House Democratic Committee Assignments." *Congress and the Presidency* 10:219–40.

Society of American Archivists. 1992. *The Documentation of Congress: Report of the Congressional Archivists Roundtable, Task force on Congressional Documentation*. Senate Publication 102–20.

Speed, Ronald K. 1964. *The Republican Policy Committee of the House of Representatives*. N.p.: privately printed.

Stanton, John. 2011. "Freshmen Are Central in GOP Budget Strategy." *Roll Call*, January 31.

Stanton, John, and Anna Palmer. 2011. "McCarthy: Whipping without a Hammer." *Roll Call*, March 21.

*Statement of Disbursements of the House*. Various editions. Washington, DC: United States Government Printing Office.

Stetler, Brian. 2012. "Limbaugh Advertisers Flee Show Amid Storm." *New York Times*, March 5.

Stewart, Charles, III. 2012. "Congressional Committees in a Partisan Era: The End of Institutionalization as We Know It?" In *New Directions in Congressional Politics*, edited by Jamie L. Carson. New York: Routledge.

Stewart, John G. 1975. "Central Policy Organs in Congress." *Proceedings of the Academy of Political Science* 32:20–33.

Strahan, Randall. 2007. *Leading Representatives: The Agency of Leaders in the Politics of the U.S. House*. Baltimore: Johns Hopkins University Press.

Strahan, Randall W. 2011. "Party Leadership." In *The Oxford Handbook of the American Congress*, edited by Eric Schickler and Francis E. Lee. New York: Oxford University Press.

Strahan, Randall, and Daniel J. Palazzolo. 2004. "The Gingrich Effect." *Political Science Quarterly* 119:89–114.

Strong, Jonathan. 2012a. "GOP Steering Committee Shuffles Conservatives." *Roll Call*, December 3.

Strong, Jonathan. 2012b. "Purged Conservatives Are Taking Aim at Leadership." *Roll Call*, December 4.

Swift, Elaine K., Robert G. Brookshire, David T. Canon, Evelyn C. Fink, John R. Hibbing, Brian D. Humes, Michael J. Malbin, and Kenneth C. Martis. 2000. Database of Congressional Historical Statistics. [Computer file] (Study #3371). Ann Arbor, MI: Inter-university Consortium for Political and Social Research [producer and distributor].

Theriault, Sean M. 2008. *Party Polarization in Congress*. Cambridge: Cambridge University Press.

Victor, Jennifer, Stephen Haptonstahl, and Nils Ringe. 2014. "Can Caucuses Alleviate Partisan Polarization in the U.S. Congress?" Paper presented at the 2014 meetings of the American Political Science Association.

Voteview. 2013. "Democrat and Republican Party Voting Splits Congresses 35–112." http://voteview.com/partycount.htm. Accessed 6 Aug 2013.

Waldman, Sidney. 1980. "Majority Leadership in the House of Representatives." *Political Science Quarterly* 95:373–93.

Wallison, Ethan. 2003. "Hoyer Taps Lewis." *Roll Call*, January 8.

Whittington, Lauren. 2007. "McCotter Leaves Message Project." *Roll Call*, November 14.

Wildavsky, Ben. 1997. "Pitching the Goods." *National Journal*, August 2.

Willis, Derek. 2002. "House GOP Leadership Places 'Cardinals' on Precarious Perch." *CQ Weekly*, November 16.

Woodward, Bob. 1994. *The Agenda: Inside the Clinton White House*. New York: Simon and Schuster.

Wyler, Grace. 2013. "House Majority Whip Tells Us How Republicans Are Making a Comeback." *Business Insider*, April 2.

Yachnin, Jennifer. 2006. "No 'Sharp Elbows' for Whip Clyburn." *Roll Call*, December 11.

Yachnin, Jennifer, and Tory Newmyer. 2007. "The Inner Circle: A Few Key Members, Family Guide Pelosi." *Roll Call*, January 22.

Yiannakis, Diana Evans. 1982. "House Members' Communications Styles: Newsletters and Press Releases." *Journal of Politics* 44:1049–71.

Zeller, Shawn, and Michael Teitelbaum. 2007. "GOP Fundraising on the Quota System." *CQ Weekly*, January 15.

Zorn, Christopher J. W. 2001. "Generalized Estimating Equation Models for Correlated Data: A Review with Applications." *American Journal of Political Science* 45:470–90.

# Index

Abrams, Elliot, 130
Affordable Care Act, 7, 118 (*table*)
Albert, Carl, 92–93, 138, 191–92n22
Alexander, Bill, 119, 196n7
Amash, Justin, 164, 165
appointive whip system, 87, 138, 140,
    143, 145, 166, 171, 187n5. *See also*
    zone whip system
Armey, Dick, 36, 107, 126

Baird, Brian, 79
Barriere, John, 92, 191–92n22
Bass, Charlie, 163
Bass, Karen, 80–81
Blue Dog Democrats, 203n56
Blunt, Roy, 60–61, 62, 112, 132–33,
    154–55
Boehlert, Sherwood, 160
Boehner, John, 17, 165
Boggs, Hale, 90, 91, 191n10
Bolling, Richard, 92, 95, 117
Bonior, David, 36
    coordination function and, 97,
        192n33, 193n35
    Democratic whip organization and,
        44–46, 79, 97, 119–20, 145, 146,
        158, 187n11, 192n33, 193n35,
        200–201n15
    external communication function and,
        119–20

persuasion process and, 145, 146, 158
Brademas, John, 92, 117
Brodhead, William, 88, 186–87n2
Brzezinski, Zbigniew, 130
Burton, Dan, 160
Butterfield, G. K., 81

campaign finance reform, Republicans
    and, 5–6, 15, 103, 107, 108, 129,
    153, 163
Cannon, Joe, 203n57
Carter, Jimmy, administration of, 42, 93,
    94, 120, 125, 130, 139, 148, 152
Chandler, Rod, 160
Cheney, Dick, 99–100, 120–21, 130–31,
    193n43, 194n53
Clawson, Del, 98
Clinton, Bill, administration of, 39, 106,
    117, 122, 123, 127, 130–31, 145,
    146, 174
Clyburn, James, 81, 148
Coelho, Tony
    coordination function and, 96–97
    Democratic whip system under, 44–
        45, 96–97, 133, 143, 144, 145,
        172, 200n14
    and external communication function,
        133
    and partisanship, 143, 200n14
    collective electoral and policy goals

collective electoral and policy goals
(*continued*)
coordination function and, 10, 25, 26,
88–89, 112, 169
Democratic Caucus and, 27, 166, 170
external communication function and,
15–16, 17, 25, 26–27, 100
participatory organizations and, 17–
18, 24–28, 31
persuasion process and, 25, 27, 136–
37, 166, 170
committee assignments
partisanship and, 156–59, 166
party loyalty and, 75–76, 75 (*table*), 95,
96, 157–58
persuasion process and, 155–65, 166
seniority and, 75 (*table*), 76, 76 (*table*)
Committee on Committees, Republican,
12, 55–56, 58, 159–60, 161, 162,
194n60, 203n57, 204n62. *See also*
Republican Steering Committee
committee transfers. *See* committee
assignments
communication. *See* external communication in party leadership organizations
Conable, Barber, 186n5
conditional party government theory
(CPG), 15, 18, 20–23, 28–29, 185n3
congressional campaign committees.
*See* Democratic Congressional
Campaign Committee (DCCC);
National Republican Congressional
Committee (NRCC)
Conservative Opportunity Society
(COS), 55, 102, 120–21
coordination in party leadership organizations
and changing government conditions,
30–31, 30 (*table*), 33–34, 89
collective electoral and policy goals
and, 10, 25, 26, 88–89, 112, 169
communication function and, 26, 89,
90, 94, 97, 98, 107, 113, 114, 115,
116, 120, 169
declining role of, 16, 29, 116, 122,
134, 177
Democratic leadership and, 13, 33–
34, 46, 89–97, 112–13, 192n33,
193n35

Democratic Policy Council and,
192n32
Democratic Steering and Policy Committee and, 10, 12, 15, 41–42,
91–96, 97, 98, 111 (*fig.*), 112, 117,
132, 156–57, 169, 170, 171, 173,
176, 177, 202–3n47
Democratic whip organization and,
12, 89–91, 96–97, 119, 171, 173
Humphrey-Hawkins legislation and,
4–5, 10, 15
organization staff and, 109–10, 110
(*fig.*), 111 (*figs.*), 112
persuasion process and, 89, 90, 112,
136, 148, 151–52, 169
Republican leadership and, 13, 101–3,
106–8, 194–95n60
Republican Policy Committee and,
10, 15, 61, 98–103, 104–5 (*table*),
106–7, 112–13,
120, 121–22, 125, 159, 169, 170, 171,
172, 176, 177, 194–95n60
Republican Research Committee
and, 61, 100, 103, 106, 172, 177,
194–95n60
Republican whip organization and, 8,
12, 99, 101–2, 106, 107–8, 111
(*fig.*), 173
and role of participatory party organizations, 9–10, 11, 25–26, 28–29,
30–31, 30 (*table*), 89,
169–170, 177–78, 186n8
Cox, Christopher, 107, 122, 123–24,
130–31, 198n26
Crowley, Joseph, 82–83
Cuellar, Henry, 190n49, 203n56

DCCC. *See* Democratic Congressional
Campaign Committee (DCCC)
DeGette, Diana, 81
DeLay, Tom
coordination function and, 88, 101,
107–8, 111–12
and election as majority whip, 70, 172
as "The Hammer," 132
and leadership use of expanded party
networks, 132–33, 154, 172,
205n1
and partisan persuasion, 135

Republican whip organization and, 60, 88, 107–8, 111–12, 132–33, 154, 172, 173
Democratic Congressional Campaign Committee (DCCC), 1, 12–13
Democratic Policy Committee, House. *See* Democratic Steering and Policy Committee (DSPC)
Democratic Policy Committee, Senate, 176, 192n22
Democratic Policy Council, 192n32
Democratic Steering and Policy Committee (DSPC)
and collective electoral and policy goals, 93, 169, 171
committee assignment role of, 12, 42, 44–45, 51, 82, 95, 156, 157–59, 171
communication function and, 3–4, 6–7, 12, 19, 46, 94, 98, 108, 110, 112, 117–18, 118 (*table*), 128, 129–30, 133, 134, 141–42, 169
coordination function and, 3, 10, 12, 15, 41–42, 91–96, 97, 98, 109, 111 (*fig.*), 112, 117, 132, 156–57, 169, 170, 171, 173, 177, 192n33, 202–3n47
Democratic Caucus and, 7, 92–93, 191–92n22
Democratic whip organization and, 141–42
and extended party leadership expansion, 2, 38–39, 41–42, 44, 46, 47
under Foley, 96, 109–10, 158
Gephardt restructuring of, 46–47, 47 (*fig.*), 117, 159
Humphrey-Hawkins legislation and, 3–5
and inclusion strategy, 42, 46, 48
membership of, 47, 47 (*fig.*), 51, 52 (*table*), 53, 53 (*table*)
under O'Neill, 41–42, 92–94, 95, 98, 109, 130, 157, 186–87n2, 187n4, 192n25
organization staff and, 109–10, 111 (*fig.*), 195n67
and party loyalty, 45, 51, 157–59, 171
and party polarization, 112, 113, 156, 173

under Pelosi, 6–7, 47, 51, 53, 81, 82, 97, 118, 159, 203n56
and persuasion process, 141–42, 156–59, 166, 169, 171
and public hearings, 6–7, 10, 117–18, 118 (*table*), 128, 134, 169, 185n23, 196n6
in Reagan era, 94–95, 117
seniority and, 51, 52 (*table*), 53, 53 (*table*)
solicitations for appointments to, 186–87n2, 4, 12, 188n21
and task forces, 91–92, 117, 138, 170
under Wright, 92, 94, 95–96, 109–10, 158, 172
Democratic Steering Committee, 202–3n47. *See also* Democratic Steering and Policy Committee (DSPC)
Democratic whip organization
communication function and, 42, 43–44, 46, 96–97, 119–20
coordination function and, 12, 89–91, 96–97, 119, 171, 173
Democratic Caucus and, 1, 12, 90–91, 97, 119–20, 137, 148, 166, 170
effectiveness of, 143–46, 144 (*table*)
expansion of, 43–44, 44 (*fig.*)
partisanship and, 119, 138–48, 166, 200n4
party loyalty and, 147–48, 147 (*table*),
persuasion process and, 135–36, 138–48, 139 (*table*), 144 (*table*), 146, 147 (*table*), 158, 165, 166, 200n14
procedural development in, 146–48
task forces and, 138–39, 140, 141, 143, 144, 145, 146, 148, 166, 168, 170, 200–201n15
Tip O'Neill and, 42–43, 49, 90–91, 138, 139, 140, 144, 148
Derrick, Butler, 46
Diaz-Balart, Lincoln, 190n49
Dingell, John, 119
DSPC. *See* Democratic Steering and Policy Committee

Eckstein, Otto, 130
Edwards, Mickey, 36, 100–101, 102, 121, 123, 126–27, 172, 194n56, 198n29, 199n39

electoral competition
  and collective party goals, 26, 29, 30–
    31, 33–34, 100, 114, 115–16, 118,
    134, 154, 155–56, 171, 177
  and communication function, 16, 26,
    29, 30–31, 33–34, 100, 114, 115–
    16, 118, 134, 154, 177
  Democratic Steering and Policy Com-
    mittee and, 171, 173
  after 1994 midterm elections, 171
  and participatory party organizations,
    14, 16, 29, 30–32, 30 (*table*), 155–
    56, 171, 175, 177
  and party leadership power, 29–30,
    32, 173
  and party polarization, 14, 173
  and persuasion process, 29, 30–31,
    155–56, 177
  strengthening of, 14, 16, 134, 171, 173
Executive Committee on Committees,
    Republican. *See* Committee on
    Committees, Republican; Republi-
    can Steering Committee
expanded party networks
  electoral goals and, 27, 115, 116,
    168–69
  external communication and, 4, 6–7,
    26–27, 115–16, 129–33, 131
    (*table*), 132, 134
extended party leadership structure
  and constituencies, 77–84, 85 (*fig.*), 87
  in Democratic Caucus, 41–49, 44
    (*fig.*), 46 (*table*), 47 (*fig.*), 50 (*table*),
    51, 52 (*table*), 53, 53 (*table*), 86–87
  expansion of, 38–41, 39 (*fig.*)
  House member careers and, 69–77,
    71 (*table*), 72 (*fig.*), 73 (*table*), 75
    (*table*), 76 (*table*), 77 (*table*), 87
  in Republican Conference, 53–58, 56
    (*fig.*), 57 (*table*), 59 (*figs.*), 60–62,
    60 (*table*), 63 (*table*), 64–65, 65
    (*fig.*), 66 (*table*), 67–69, 67 (*table*),
    68 (*table*), 69 (*table*)
  *See also* Democratic Steering and
    Policy Committee (DSPC);
    Democratic whip organization;
    Republican Policy Committee;
    Republican Research Committee;
    Republican whip organization

external communication in party leader-
    ship organizations
  campaign finance reform legislation
    and, 5–6
  changing government conditions and,
    30, 30 (*table*), 31, 32–33, 33–34
  collective electoral and policy goals
    and, 15–16, 17, 25, 26–27, 29, 30–
    31, 33–34, 100, 114, 115–16, 118,
    134, 154, 177
  constituencies and, 78–88, 85 (*fig.*), 86
    (*table*), 114
  coordination function and, 26, 89, 90,
    94, 97, 98, 107, 113, 114
  Democratic Steering and Policy Com-
    mittee and, 3–4, 6–7, 10, 12, 19,
    46, 94, 98, 108, 110, 112, 117–18,
    118 (*table*), 128, 129–30, 133, 134,
    141–42, 169, 174, 185n23, 196n6
  Democratic whip organization and,
    42, 43–44, 46, 96–97, 119–20,
    196n7
  electoral competition and, 16, 29, 30–
    31, 114, 134, 177
  and expanded party network, 4, 6–7,
    26–27, 115–16, 129–33, 131
    (*table*), 132, 134
  Gingrich-led Strategy Whip team
    and, 128–29
  and Humphrey-Hawkins legislation,
    3–5, 10
  individual leadership goals and, 129
  lobbyists and, 132–33
  organization staff and, 109, 110,
    196n7
  participatory party organizations and,
    11, 14, 15, 25
  partisanship and, 121, 133
  and party image, 114–15, 116
  persuasion process and, 29, 31, 115,
    132, 141–42
  public hearings and, 6–7, 10, 117–18,
    118 (*table*), 126–28, 134, 169,
    185n23, 196n6
  Republican Policy Committee and,
    4–6, 10, 12, 98, 99–100, 106–7,
    112, 120–25, 130–32, 131 (*table*),
    133, 134, 169
  Republican Research Committee and,

125–28, 127 (*table*), 133, 134, 169, 198n29
after 2010 midterm elections, 6–9
whip system and, 12, 19, 33, 99, 106, 107–8, 119–20, 128–29, 196n7

Foley, Tom, 33, 35–36, 43, 46, 96, 109–10, 140, 142, 143, 158
Ford, Gerald, administration of, 99, 149–52, 174, 191–92n22
Fluke, Sandra, 7, 118

Gates, Bob, 130
Gephardt, Richard A., 46–47, 48, 79, 117, 122, 159
Gilchrest, Wayne, 84
Gillett, Frederick, 203n57
Gingrich, Newt
    coordination function and, 101–2, 194–95n60
    individual policy goals of, 33, 172
    minority whip election of, 101, 194n53
    Republican organizational restructuring by, 38, 55, 58, 60, 101–2, 106, 107, 128, 153, 161, 162–63, 164, 172, 194–95n60
    Republican Steering Committee and, 162–63, 164, 172, 204n64
    Republican whip organization and, 38, 55, 60, 101–2, 106, 107, 128–29, 134, 153, 172
Goodling, William, 149
Gray, William H., 187n11
Gunderson, Steve, 102, 128

Hastert, Dennis, 70, 163, 164, 204n64
Hatch Act, 120
Hawkins, Augustus, 2–3
Health Care for the Unemployed Act, 141–43
Heller, Walter, 130
"home style," constituencies and House members, 78, 79–80, 83, 85
Hoyer, Steny, 97, 148
Huelskamp, Tim, 164, 165
Humphrey, Hubert, 2–3
Humphrey-Hawkins legislation, 3–5, 10, 15, 109, 138, 184n14

Hunter, Duncan, 127, 198n29, 199n39
Hyde, Henry, 130

inclusion strategy, party leadership
    collective party goals and, 47–48
    Democrats and, 41–43, 45–46, 48–49, 51, 144, 149
    Democratic Steering and Policy Committee and, 19, 41, 42, 44, 46–48, 47 (*table*), 48
    Democratic whip organization and, 19, 41–44, 45–48, 46 (*table*), 49, 51, 60, 144–45, 147–48, 149, 201n27
    party loyalty and, 41, 44
Issa, Darrell, 7

Johnson, Lyndon, 135
Jones, Walter, 164
Jordan, Hamilton, 130

Keyserling, Leon, 130
Kildee, Dan, 187n7
Kirkland, Lane, 4
Kostmayer, Peter, 93
K-Street Project, 132–33

Lagomarsino, Robert, 204n62
Lankford, James, 125
lobbyists, whip system and, 132–33, 154, 172
Long, Gillis, 94–95
Lott, Trent, 55, 60, 101, 152–53, 205n2

Madigan, Edward, 101–2
Mann, James, 203n57
Mansfield, Mike, 191–92n22
Margolies-Mezvinsky, Marjorie, 135
Martin, James, 126, 151–52
Matheson, Jim, 203n56
McCarthy, Kevin, 8, 9, 10, 108, 155, 165, 185n25
McCotter, Thaddeus, 124
McIntosh, David, 78
Meany, George, 4, 130
Michel, Bob, 5, 36, 54, 99, 101, 132, 148–49, 153, 161, 204n62
midterm elections, 1994: 6–7, 10, 100, 121, 171, 194n60

Mondale, Walter, 94, 130
Moore, Henson, 54, 188n24
Murtha, John, 158
Myers, John, 128

Napier, John, 160–61
National Republican Congressional
    Committee (NRCC), 1, 12–13, 164,
    205n68
"92 Group," 55, 102
North American Free Trade Agreement
    (NAFTA) legislation, 33, 132
NRCC. *See* National Republican Con-
    gressional Committee (NRCC)

O'Neill, Thomas P. "Tip," 35
    Democratic Steering and Policy
        Committee under, 41–42, 92–94,
        95, 98, 109, 130, 157, 186–87n2,
        187n4, 192n25
    Democratic whip organization and,
        41–43, 49, 90–91, 138, 139, 140,
        144, 148, 149
    and election as Speaker, 41, 138
    and inclusion strategy, 41–42, 49, 144,
        149

Pallone, Frank, 81
participation in party leadership organi-
    zations
    changing party conditions and, 28–31,
        30 (*table*), 31 (*table*), 170–71
    constituencies and, 78–80, 83, 85,
        168–69, 175
    and decline in policy and strategy
        development, 177–78
    individual leader goals v. collective
        party objectives and, 10, 11,
        13–15, 16–17, 18, 22–28, 29, 31,
        32–33, 34, 39–40, 53, 58, 74–75,
        77–78, 88, 96, 112, 114–15, 125,
        129, 133–34, 140, 167, 168–70,
        172–73, 178, 186n5
    roles of, 25–28
party government conditions, 14, 24,
    28–31, 30 (*table*), 31 (*table*), 44, 47–
    48, 50–51, 62, 89, 122, 170–71. *See
    also* conditional party government
    theory (CPG)

party loyalty
    committee assignments and, 45, 51,
        75–76, 75 (*table*), 76 (*table*), 95,
        96, 157–59, 158 (*table*), 171
    Democratic whip organization and,
        144, 147, 147 (*table*)
    fundraising and, 51, 154, 163,
        202nn45, 46
    persuasion process and, 135–36, 155–
        59, 161, 163, 164–65, 166
    Republican Executive Committee on
        Committees and, 68 (*table*)
    Republican Policy Committee and, 66
        (*table*), 67 (*table*), 102, 103
    Republican Steering Committee and,
        69 (*table*)
    Republican whip organization and, 63,
        64, 146
    whip effectiveness and, 144, 144 (*table*)
party voting loyalty. *See* party loyalty
Pastor, Ed, 70
Pelosi, Nancy, 6–7, 47, 51, 53, 81, 82, 97,
    118, 159, 203n56
Penny, Tim, 143
Perle, Richard, 130
persuasion process in party leadership
    organizations
    and changing party conditions, 30–31,
        30 (*table*), 33–34
    collective electoral and policy goals
        and, 25, 136–37
    and committee assignments, 155–65,
        166
    communication function and, 29, 31,
        115, 132
    coordination function and, 89, 90,
        112, 136, 148, 151–52, 169
    Democratic leadership and, 27, 90,
        145, 146, 158, 166, 170
    Democratic Steering and Policy Com-
        mittee and, 141–42, 142 (*table*),
        156–59, 166, 169, 171
    Democratic whip organization and,
        136, 138–48, 139 (*table*), 141–42,
        142 (*table*), 144 (*table*), 145, 146,
        147 (*table*), 158, 166
    electoral competition and, 29, 30–31,
        155–56, 177
    organization staff and, 109

party loyalty and, 135–36, 155–59, 161, 163, 164–65, 166
  Republican Executive Committee on Committees and, 159–60
  Republican Steering Committee and, 16, 161–63, 164–65, 166
  Republican whip organization and, 136, 148–55, 151 (*table*)
  role of participatory party organizations in, 11, 14, 25
Phillips, Kevin, 129
Platts, Todd, 163
Price, David, 23–24, 145, 148
Price, Tom, 124–25
Pryce, Deborah, 83–84, 163
public hearings
  Democratic Steering and Policy Committee and, 6–7, 10, 117–18, 118 (*table*), 128, 134, 169, 185n23, 196n6
  Republican Policy Committee and, 169
  Republican Research Committee and, 126–28, 169
  *See also* external communication in party leadership organizations
Putnam, Adam, 124

Rayburn, Sam, 202–3n47
Reagan, Ronald, administration of, 42, 54, 94–95, 117, 126, 153, 198n33
Regula, Ralph, 70
Republican Policy Committee
  campaign finance reform and, 5–6
  communication function and, 4–6, 10, 12, 98, 99–100, 106–7, 112, 122–25, 172
  Congressional Policy Advisory Board of, 130–31
  coordination function and, 10, 15, 61, 98–103, 120, 121–22, 125, 159, 169, 170, 171, 173
  external communication and, 12, 120–25, 129, 130–32, 131 (*table*), 133, 134, 159, 169, 171, 174, 197n14, 198n27
  leadership of, 100–101, 102, 120–25, 130–31, 172, 193n43, 199n39

partisanship and, 121, 122–25, 133, 159–61, 172, 197n14
  party loyalty and, 66 (*table*), 67 (*table*), 102, 103
Republican Research Committee
  communication function and, 125, 126–27, 127 (*table*), 128, 134, 169, 174, 198n29, 198n33, 199n39
  coordination function and, 61, 100, 103, 106, 172, 177, 194–95n60
  elimination of, 12, 38, 58, 171, 194–95n60
  Mickey Edwards as chair of, 126–27, 172, 198n29
  1988 drug bill and, 103, 106
  task force activity of, 54–55, 58, 103, 106, 125, 126–28, 127 (*table*), 195n60
Republican Steering Committee
  committee assignments and, 12, 69 (*table*), 137, 159, 161–65, 166
  Gingrich restructuring of, 162, 171, 172
  growth of, 58, 59 (*fig.*)
  Hastert speakership and, 163, 204n64
  and party loyalty, 68–69, 69 (*table*), 166, 171, 204n64
  and persuasion process, 16, 161–63, 164–65, 166
  role of, 1, 12, 58, 163
Republican Study Committee (RSC), 55, 124
Republican whip organization
  coordination function and, 8, 12, 99, 101–2, 106, 107–8, 111 (*fig.*), 173
  Humphrey-Hawkins legislation and, 4–5, 184n14
  leadership and membership of, 12
  Newt Gingrich changes to, 38, 55, 60, 101–2, 106, 107, 128–29, 134, 153, 172
  organization staff and, 110, 111 (*fig.*), 112
  party loyalty and, 63, 64, 146
  party polarization and, 154–55
  persuasion process and, 148–55, 151 (*table*)
  Tom Delay expansion of, 107–8, 111–12, 154, 173

research methodology and analysis, 13, 15, 34–37, 73–74, 84–86, 176, 179–81, 190n47
Reuss, Henry, 94
Rice, Condoleezza, 130–31
Rivlin, Alice, 130
Rose, Charlie, 3
Roskam, Peter, 185n25
Rostenkowski, Dan, 96
Rumsfeld, Donald, 130–31
Ryan, Paul, 8–9, 165
Ryan, Tim, 82

Scammon, Richard, 130
Schlesinger, James, 130
Schroeder, Pat, 70
Schumer, Chuck, 187n12
Schweikert, David, 164
Senate Democratic Policy Committee, 92, 192n22
Senate Republican Policy Committee, 176
Shadegg, John, 198n26
Shuster, Bud, 36, 98, 123
Simmons, Rob, 163
Small Business Liability Reform Act, 145
Smith, Chris, 163–64
Smith, Spencer, 195n66
Sprague, Irv, 138
Stearns, Cliff, 70–71
steering committees. *See* Democratic Steering and Policy Committee (DSPC); Republican Steering Committee
Sundquist, Don, 126
Swinehart, Leonard, 161

task forces
    communication function and, 43–44, 187n10
    coordination function and, 107
    Democratic Steering and Policy Committee and, 91–92, 117, 138, 170

Democratic whip organization and, 119, 138–39, 140, 141, 143, 144, 145, 146, 148, 166, 168, 170, 200–201n15
Republican Research Committee and, 54–55, 103, 106, 125, 126–27, 127 (*table*), 195n60
Tea Party, 8, 124, 155, 164

Udall, Morris, 151

Vander Jagt, Guy, 5
voting loyalty. *See* party loyalty

Walden, Greg, 83
Walker, Robert, 102
Walsh, James, 70
Weber, Vin, 204n62
Wednesday Group, 55
whip system. *See* appointive whip system; Democratic whip organization; Republican whip organization; zone whip system
Wilkinson, Paul, 24, 131–32
Wilson, Joe, 80
Wise, Bob, 36
Wright, Jim, 36
    Democratic Steering and Policy Committee and, 92, 94, 95–96, 109–10, 158, 172
    Gingrich strategy against, 101
    and party loyalty in committee transfers, 95, 96, 158
    whip system and, 43, 49, 51, 96, 143, 144

Y2K liability bill, 146

zone whip system, 42, 43, 49, 90, 138, 140, 144, 148, 187n5, 191n10. *See also* appointive whip system

Printed and bound by CPI Group (UK) Ltd, Croydon, CR0 4YY

13/04/2025